CHAMBERS

Dictionary of

Foreign Words
and
Phrases

CHAMBERS

Dictionary of Foreign Words *and* Phrases

Edited by
Rosalind Fergusson

CHAMBERS

CHAMBERS
An imprint of Larousse plc
43-45 Annandale Street
Edinburgh EH7 4AZ

A CIP catalogue record for this book
is available from the British Library

ISBN 0-550-18302-7 (Paperback)
ISBN 0-550-18306-X (Hardback)

Typeset by Hewer Text Composition Services, Edinburgh

Printed in Great Britain by Clays Ltd, St Ives plc

Contents

Preface

The notion of foreign words and phrases being part of everyday English needs some explanation. We are all aware that many external influences have been at work in shaping the language we know as modern English. Essentially, it is derived from two major sources, Anglo-Saxon (or Old English) and a romance element (ie one derived ultimately from Late Latin) that came into being at the time of the Norman Conquest of the eleventh century. In addition, English was influenced at an early date by the Norse language of the Scandinavian invaders, and there are a number of words like *egg*, *skull*, and *window* that have this origin. Words like these, and thousands of romance words like *table*, *face*, and *serve* (all chosen here for not being obviously Latinate), as well as more recent borrowings retained in their original forms like *café*, *brusque*, *anorak*, and *kiosk*, form part of the core of English. They are said to be naturalized, ie they behave as English words and normally follow English rules of orthography, pronunciation, and inflection.

Some of the noteworthy naturalized words of more recent origin are included here. Most of the items included, however, are non-naturalized words and phrases that conventionally appear in italics in print and are thought of as loans rather than as belonging to the vocabulary of English. Normally, a loan occurs because there is no word in English that is quite suitable. For example, it would be hard to identify satisfactory synonyms of *blasé* or *cachet* or *quid pro quo*. Of course, such a procedure is susceptible to fashions, and literary English, in particular, has been prone to the use of French loanwords that have later fallen out of use, as an affectation rather than from practical necessity.

In the twentieth century, new influences are discernible. For example, political conflict in the Middle East has given rise to a whole glossary of culture-resonant terms of which the most notable are *fatwa*, *intifada*, and *jihad*. Political change in eastern Europe has produced *perestroika* and *glasnost*, the second of which is rapidly developing a more general sense independent of its cultural origin. The growth of international communications and the holiday industry have made us more aware of the cuisines of other countries, with remarkable consequences for the language, as will be seen from many terms included here from languages as diverse as Russian, Japanese, Spanish, and Arabic, in addition to the rich gastronomic language of

French. This use of French virtually has the status of a lingua franca; similarly, we can point to the continued use of Italian as the language of music, and of German as the language of philosophy.

It should be emphasized that words and phrases are only included if they are used *in English contexts*. That is the only workable rationale, and it explains why the number of headwords is fewer than in some books that have a similar title but are padded out with entries of no relevance outside the culture of their source language. Such ill-considered inclusiveness can tell us nothing about English, which is (paradoxically, it may seem) the main purpose of this book.

In each entry, the immediate source language is given, preceded by a flag symbol ⚑. In many cases, earlier sources are given, with any further historical or linguistic information that adds to an understanding of the term. At the end of the book there is an index of languages to enable users to investigate the role of any particular language in contributing to the English vocabulary.

We believe users will find the dictionary informative, enriching, and entertaining.

A

à bas
FRENCH
down with ...!

> followed by the name of a person, institution, etc

abat-jour
FRENCH for 'lampshade'
1 a skylight
2 a screen or shutter

abattoir
FRENCH
a slaughterhouse

> introduced by Napoleon in 1810

abattu
FRENCH
cast down or dejected
feminine ***abattue***

abat-voix
FRENCH
a sounding board, a structure over a pulpit, etc, for carrying a speaker's voice towards the audience

abbé
FRENCH for 'abbot'
a title for a priest or any other French cleric

> also applied to a professor, private tutor, or master of a household, although such a person has no assigned ecclesiastical duties

Aberglaube
GERMAN
superstition

ab extra
LATIN
from the outside

à bientôt
FRENCH
see you soon

> a form of farewell

ab initio
LATIN
from the beginning
abbrev **ab init.**

ab intra
LATIN
from the inside

ab officio et beneficio
LATIN, literally 'from office and benefice'
(said of a member of the clergy) suspended from office

à bon droit
FRENCH
1 legitimately
2 with good reason

abonnement
FRENCH
1 a subscription (to a newspaper, magazine, etc)
2 a season-ticket (for a theatre, cinema, the use of ski slopes, etc)

ab origine
LATIN
from the origin, from the beginning

ab ovo
LATIN, literally 'from the egg'
from the beginning

à bras ouverts
FRENCH
with open arms

abrégé
FRENCH
an abridgement or summary

abseil
GERMAN
1 to let oneself down a rock face or vertical drop using a double rope secured from above and wound round one's body
2 the technique of abseiling

absente reo
LATIN
in the absence of the accused
abbrev **abs re**

absit
LATIN, literally 'let him, her, or it be absent'
permission given to a student to be absent

absit invidia
LATIN, literally 'may there be no ill-will'
no offence

absit omen
LATIN, literally 'may there be no (ill) omen'
(said of a word just used) touch wood

> intended to dispel any possibility that by mentioning some unpleasant event, one could be predicting it or causing it to happen again

ab uno disce omnes
LATIN, literally 'from one learn all'
from one example you may know or judge the rest

ab urbe condita
LATIN
from the founding of the city (of Rome) in 753BC

> used in the ancient Roman world to indicate a point in time from which dates were calculated

abbrev **AUC**

abusus non tollit usum
LATIN, literally 'abuse does not take away use'
(law) the abuse of something, eg a right, does not render it invalid

AC
see APPELLATION (D'ORIGINE) CONTRÔLÉE

ac or ***a.c.***
see ANTE CIBUM

a cappella or ***alla cappella***
ITALIAN, literally 'in the church style'
(music)
1 (said of choral music) sung without an accompaniment or with an accompaniment in unison with the singers
2 alla breve

accablé
FRENCH
depressed or overwhelmed

accelerando
ITALIAN
(music) with increasing speed
abbrev **accel.**

acciaccatura
ITALIAN
(music) a short appoggiatura

accouchement
FRENCH
childbirth or the period of confinement

accoucheur
FRENCH
a person who assists women in childbirth, a midwife
feminine ***accoucheuse***

à chacun son goût
see CHACUN À SON GOÛT

acharné
FRENCH
(said especially of battles) furious or desperate

Achates
see FIDUS ACHATES

Acherontis pabulum
LATIN
(said of a bad person) food for Acheron

in Greek mythology, Acheron was one of the rivers of Hades over which Charon ferried the souls of the dead

à cheval
FRENCH, literally 'on horseback'
(said of a bet) laid on two adjacent numbers or cards

Achtung
GERMAN
attention!

à compte
FRENCH
on account; in part payment

à contrecoeur or ***à contre coeur***
FRENCH
reluctantly

à corps perdu
FRENCH
desperately, with might and main

à coup sûr
FRENCH
certainly, definitely

à couvert
FRENCH
under cover, protected

acta sanctorum
LATIN
deeds of the saints

acte gratuit
FRENCH
an impulsive act lacking motive

borrowed from the writings of André Gide, who was concerned with the conflict between self-fulfilment and what we are compelled to do by duty and convention

actualités
FRENCH
a newsreel or current affairs programme

actus reus
LATIN, literally 'guilty act'
(law) the act which is necessary for the crime to be constituted
plural ***actus rei***

acushla
from IRISH *a chuisle*
darling

a common term of endearment

AD
see ANNO DOMINI

adagio
ITALIAN, literally 'at ease'
(music)
1 slowly
2 slow
3 a slow movement
4 a piece in adagio time
plural ***adagios***

ad aperturam libri
LATIN
as the book opens

ad arbitrium
LATIN
at pleasure

ad astra
LATIN
to the stars

ADC
see AIDE-DE-CAMP

ad Calendas Graecas
LATIN
at the Greek calends, ie never, as the Greeks had no calends

> the calends were the first day of each month in the ancient Roman calendar

ad captandum (vulgus)
LATIN
with the intention of pleasing or appealing to the emotions of the crowd

ad clerum
LATIN
to the clergy

ad crumenam
see ARGUMENTUM AD CRUMENAM

addendum
LATIN, literally 'that which is to be added'
an appendix
plural ***addenda***

adelantado
SPANISH
1 a grandee
2 a provincial governor
plural ***adelantados***

à demi
FRENCH
by halves or half

à dessein
FRENCH
on purpose

ad eundem (gradum)
LATIN, literally 'to the same (degree)'
the admission of a graduate of one university to the same level or status in another without examination

à deux
FRENCH
1 of, for, or between two, two-handed
2 (said of a dinner, etc) for two people
3 (said of two people) in private together, without the presence of a third person

à deux mains
FRENCH
1 with both hands
2 for two hands

ad finem
LATIN
at, to, or towards the end
abbrev **ad fin.**

ad hanc vocem
LATIN
at this word
abbrev **ahv, a.h.v.**

adharma
SANSKRIT
unrighteousness

> the opposite of DHARMA

ad hoc
LATIN
for this special purpose

> used of a makeshift body, committee, measures, etc, often with the derogatory connotation of having been hastily cobbled together

ad hominem
see ARGUMENTUM AD HOMINEM

ad hunc locum
LATIN
at this place
abbrev **ahl, a.h.l.**

adieu
FRENCH, literally 'to God'
1 goodbye
2 a farewell
plural ***adieus*** or ***adieux***

ad ignorantiam
see ARGUMENTUM AD IGNORANTIAM

ad infinitum
LATIN
to infinity, endlessly
abbrev **ad inf.**

ad initium
LATIN
at or to the beginning
abbrev **ad init.**

ad inquirendum
LATIN, literally 'for making inquiry'
the name of a writ

ad interim
LATIN
for or in the meantime
abbrev **ad int.**

ad invidiam
see ARGUMENTUM AD INVIDIAM

adiós
SPANISH, literally 'to God'
goodbye

ad judicium
see ARGUMENTUM AD JUDICIUM

ad libitum
LATIN
1 at will, at pleasure
2 extempore, impromptu
abbrev **ad lib.**

> the abbreviation has been naturalized (in the form 'ad-lib') as an adverb (meaning spontaneously or freely), an adjective (impromptu or extemporized), a verb (to extemporize or speak without preparation, especially to fill up time), and a noun (an improvised speech or a spontaneous, often humorous, remark)

ad litem
LATIN
(said of a guardian, etc) appointed to represent someone in a lawsuit who is unable or unfit to take part in the proceedings

ad locum
LATIN
at the place
abbrev **ad loc.**

ad majorem Dei gloriam
LATIN
to the greater glory of God

> the motto of the Society of Jesus (the Jesuits)

abbrev **AMDG**

ad manum
LATIN
at or to hand, ready

ad misericordiam
see ARGUMENTUM AD MISERICORDIAM

ad modum
LATIN
after the manner (of)

ad nauseam
LATIN, literally 'to the point of nausea'
to a sickening or excessive extent

➪ used to express the idea of something continuing for so long or being repeated so often that it becomes tedious

ad patres
LATIN
(gathered) to his or her fathers, dead

ad referendum
LATIN
to be further considered

ad rem
LATIN
to the point; to the purpose
see also ARGUMENTUM AD REM

à droite
FRENCH
1 to the right
2 on the right

adsum
LATIN
I am present; here!

➪ used in response to a roll-call, etc

ad summum
LATIN
to the highest point

ad unguem
LATIN, literally 'to the (finger)nail'
to a nicety

ad unum omnes
LATIN
all to a man

ad valorem
LATIN
(said of taxes) in proportion to value, as opposed to weight, content, or quantity of the goods taxed
abbrev **ad val.**

ad verbum
LATIN, literally 'to a word'
word for word

ad verecundiam
see ARGUMENTUM AD VERECUNDIAM

adversus
LATIN
against
abbrev **adv.**

ad vitam aut culpam
LATIN, literally 'for life or till fault'
(said of appointments) for life unless misconduct necessitates dismissal

ad vivum
LATIN
to the life, lifelike

advocatus diaboli
LATIN, literally 'devil's advocate'
1 an advocate at the papal court whose duty it is to propose objections against a canonization
2 a person who states the case against a proposal, course of action, etc, usually for the sake of argument

aegis
from GREEK *aigis* meaning 'shield'
protection; patronage

aegrotat
LATIN, literally 'he or she is sick'
1 in universities, a certificate allowing a candidate to pass an examination although they have missed all or part of it through illness
2 a degree or other certificate granted in such circumstances

aequo animo
LATIN
with an equable mind

aes alienum
LATIN, literally 'another's copper or brass'
debt

aes triplex
LATIN, literally 'triple brass'
a strong defence

aetatis
LATIN
aged ...

> followed by the number of years

abbrev **ae., aet.**

aetatis suae
LATIN
of his or her age

affaire
FRENCH
1 a liaison or intrigue
2 (usually with name of chief person involved) an episode or incident arousing speculation and scandal

affaire d'amour
FRENCH
a love affair

affaire de coeur
FRENCH, literally 'affair of the heart'
a love affair

affaire d'honneur
FRENCH, literally 'affair of honour'
a duel

affettuoso
ITALIAN
(music)
1 tender
2 tenderly

affiche
FRENCH
notice, placard

affidavit
LATIN, literally 'he or she has pledged'
a written declaration made upon oath before a person authorized to administer oaths

afflatus
LATIN
creative inspiration, especially of divine origin

aficionado
SPANISH
1 an enthusiast, an ardent follower or fan
2 a devotee of bullfighting
plural ***aficionados***
feminine ***aficionada***

à fond
FRENCH, literally 'at bottom'
thoroughly
compare AU FOND

a fortiori
LATIN, literally 'from the stronger'
for similar but more convincing reasons

> used to indicate the greater validity of a proposition when a weaker proposition has been proved

aga or ***agha***
TURKISH
a Turkish commander or chief officer

agaçant
FRENCH
provoking or alluring
feminine ***agaçante***

agacerie
FRENCH
allurement, coquetry

Aga Khan
TURKISH
the title of the head of the Ismaili Muslims

agathodaimon
GREEK
one's good genius

à gauche
FRENCH
1 to the left
2 on the left

agent provocateur
FRENCH
a person employed to provoke suspected persons to commit unlawful acts so that they can be arrested

aggiornamento
ITALIAN
modernization

the term used by the Second Vatican Council in 1962 to describe the proposals to reform the church

agitato
ITALIAN
(music)
1 agitated
2 agitatedly

agitprop, Agitprop or ***agit-prop***
from RUSSIAN *agitpropbyuro* meaning 'office of agitation and propaganda'
1 pro-communist agitation and propaganda
2 any narrow political propaganda

Agnus Dei or ***agnus dei***
LATIN, literally 'Lamb of God'
1 a part of the Roman Catholic mass beginning with these words
2 a musical setting of this
3 a figure of a lamb emblematic of Christ, bearing the banner of the cross

à gogo or ***à go-go***
FRENCH
1 in abundance, galore
2 to one's heart's content

agora
GREEK
in ancient Greece, an assembly, place of assembly, or market-place

the term *agoraphobia*, meaning 'a pathological fear of open spaces or public places', is a derivative of this

à grands frais
FRENCH
at great expense

agrégation
FRENCH
a competitive university examination for teaching posts

agrégé
FRENCH
a successful candidate in the agrégation
feminine ***agrégée***

agréments or ***agrémens***
FRENCH
1 amenities
2 courtesies, charms, or blandishments
3 *(music)* embellishments, such as grace notes and trills
4 approval given by a government to the appointment of another country's ambassador

aguardiente
SPANISH, from *agua ardiente*, literally 'burning water'
1 a brandy made in Spain and Portugal
2 any spirituous liquor

à haute voix
FRENCH
aloud

ahimsa
SANSKRIT
1 the doctrine of the sacredness of animal life
2 non-violence

ahl or ***a.h.l.***
see AD HUNC LOCUM

AHS
see ANNO HUMANAE SALUTIS

à huis clos
FRENCH
behind closed doors; in camera

ahv or ***a.h.v.***
see AD HANC VOCEM

aide
FRENCH for 'assistant'
1 a confidential assistant to a person of senior rank, eg an ambassador or president
2 an aide-de-camp

aide-de-camp
FRENCH, literally 'assistant on the field'
an officer who attends a general, governor, etc, and acts as a personal assistant
plural ***aides-de-camp***
abbrev **ADC**

aide-mémoire
FRENCH
1 an aid to the memory; a reminder or memorandum
2 a written summary of a diplomatic document
plural ***aides-mémoire***

aidos
GREEK
shame, modesty

aigre-doux
FRENCH
bitter-sweet, sourish
feminine ***aigre-douce***

aigrette
FRENCH for 'egret (feather)'
1 an ornamental feather, plume, or tuft
2 a spray of jewels
3 *(cookery)* a savoury cooked in deep fat

aiguille
FRENCH for 'needle'
1 a rock or peak shaped like a needle
2 an instrument for boring holes

aikido
JAPANESE
a Japanese martial art using locks and pressure against joints

aileron
FRENCH, literally 'little wing'
a flap on an aeroplane wingtip for lateral balancing

aîné
FRENCH
elder or senior
feminine ***aînée***
compare CADET

aïoli or ***aioli***
PROVENÇAL
a garlic-flavoured mayonnaise

à jamais
FRENCH
for ever

akvavit
see AQUAVIT

à la
FRENCH
1 in the manner of
2 *(cookery)* prepared with or in the manner of (a person or place)

> as the phrase is a contraction of *à la mode de*, the definite article remains feminine, even before a masculine name, as in *à la James Joyce*

à l'abandon
FRENCH for 'neglected, uncared for'
carelessly, recklessly

à la belle étoile
FRENCH
under the stars; in the open air

à la bonne femme
see BONNE FEMME

à la bonne heure
FRENCH, literally 'at the right time'
1 well done!
2 that's fine!

à l'abri
FRENCH
under shelter

à la campagne
FRENCH
in the country

à la carte
FRENCH, literally 'according to the bill of fare'
1 with each dish charged individually at the price shown on the menu
2 *(figurative)* with the freedom to pick and choose

à la dérobée
FRENCH
by stealth

à la guerre comme à la guerre
FRENCH, literally 'in war as in war'
one must take things as they come, one must take the rough with the smooth

à la hauteur de
FRENCH
1 on a level with; abreast of
2 able to understand or deal with

à la lanterne
FRENCH, literally 'to the lamp'
away with them and hang them

> during the French Revolution many people were hanged from the chains supporting the street lamps

à la main
FRENCH
1 in hand or ready
2 by hand

à la maître d'hôtel
FRENCH
(cookery) served plain with a parsley garnish
see also MAÎTRE D'HÔTEL

à la mode
FRENCH
1 according to the fashion, fashionable
2 *(cookery)* (said of beef) braised and stewed with vegetables

à la page
FRENCH
up to date

a latere
LATIN, literally 'from the side'

(said of a legate sent by the pope) confidential

Albanensis
LATIN
of St Albans
abbrev **Alban.**

albergo
ITALIAN
an inn, a hotel
plural ***alberghi***

albricias
SPANISH
a reward to the bearer of good news

alcaicería
SPANISH
a bazaar

alcaide or ***alcayde***
SPANISH
1 governor of a fortress
2 a jailer

alcalde
SPANISH
1 a mayor
2 *(formerly)* a judge or magistrate

alcarraza
SPANISH
a porous vessel for cooling water

alcázar
SPANISH
any of the various palaces or fortresses built in Spain by the Moors

al contrario
SPANISH
on the contrary

aldea
SPANISH
a village or hamlet

al dente
ITALIAN, literally 'to the tooth'
(cookery) (said of pasta) still firm after cooking, not overcooked

alea jacta est
see JACTA EST ALEA

alectryon
GREEK
a cock

à l'envi
FRENCH
in emulation

à l'époque
FRENCH
at the time

alférez
SPANISH
a standard-bearer

alforja
SPANISH
a saddlebag

alfresco or ***al fresco***
ITALIAN
1 in the fresh or open air
2 *(painting)* on fresh or moist plaster

alias
LATIN, literally 'at another time, otherwise'
1 otherwise known as
2 an assumed name
plural ***aliases***

alibi
LATIN, literally 'elsewhere'
1 the plea in a criminal charge of having been elsewhere at the time the crime was committed
2 the fact of being elsewhere
3 *(informal)* an excuse for failure

à l'improviste
FRENCH
suddenly; unexpectedly; unawares

alla breve
ITALIAN, literally 'according to the breve'
(music) in quick common time; with 2 or 4 minims to the bar

alla cappella
see A CAPPELLA

Allahu akbar
ARABIC
God is great

alla marcia
ITALIAN
(music) in the manner of a march

alla prima
ITALIAN
a technique of painting in which only one layer of pigment is applied to the surface to complete the canvas

allargando
ITALIAN, literally 'broadening'
(music) slowing

alla stoccata
ITALIAN
thrusting with a pointed weapon

alla vostra salute
ITALIAN
to your health

allée
FRENCH
an avenue, walk, or garden path

allegretto
ITALIAN
(music)
1 moderately brisk
2 an allegretto piece or movement
plural ***allegrettos***

allegro
ITALIAN
(music)
1 brisk; lively and rather fast
2 an allegro piece or movement
plural ***allegros***

allemande
FRENCH, feminine of *allemand* meaning 'German'
1 *(music)* a smooth-running movement of moderate tempo, coming after the prelude in a classical suite
2 a German dance
3 a figure in country or square dancing

allez-vous-en
FRENCH
away with you!

allonge
FRENCH
a piece of paper attached to a bill of exchange for further endorsement

allons
FRENCH
1 let's go
2 come on
3 come

allumeuse
FRENCH
a woman who arouses a man's sexual desire but refuses to satisfy it; a flirt or tease

alma
ITALIAN
soul, essence

alma mater
LATIN, literally 'benign mother'
applied by alumni to their university, school, or college

aloha
HAWAIIAN for 'love, kindness'

1 greetings
2 farewell

à l'outrance
see À OUTRANCE

alpargata
SPANISH
a light sandal with rope or hemp sole

Alpenhorn, alpenhorn or ***alphorn***
GERMAN
a long powerful horn made of wood and bark, used chiefly by Alpine cowherds

Alpenstock or ***alpenstock***
GERMAN
a mountain traveller's long spiked staff

al più
ITALIAN
at most

alta moda
ITALIAN
high fashion, the art of designing and making exclusive, fashionable clothes

alter ego
LATIN, literally 'other self'
1 one's second self
2 a trusted, intimate friend
3 a second side to one's personality, which others rarely see
plural ***alter egos***

alternat
FRENCH
the diplomatic practice of determining precedence among powers of equal rank by lot or of otherwise avoiding the difficulty

alternis vicibus
LATIN
alternately

alterum tantum
LATIN
as much more; twice as much

altiplano
SPANISH
a plateau, especially one in the Andes

alto
ITALIAN for 'high'
(music)
1 a high falsetto male voice
2 the highest male voice, the counter-tenor
3 the lowest female voice, the contralto
4 a person with a counter-tenor or contralto voice
5 a part or piece of music written for a voice or instrument of this pitch
plural ***altos***

alto-rilievo
see HAUT-RELIEF

altum silentium
LATIN
profound silence

alumnus
LATIN, literally 'foster-son, pupil'
a former pupil or student
plural ***alumni***
feminine ***alumna,*** *plural* ***alumnae***

a.m., am or ***AM***
see ANTE MERIDIEM

amah
from PORTUGUESE *ama* meaning 'nurse'
(in oriental countries) a native maidservant or child's nurse

à main armée
FRENCH, literally 'with armed hand'
by force of arms, with mailed fist

a majori (ad minus)
LATIN
from the greater (to the less)

amanuensis
LATIN
a literary assistant, especially one who writes to dictation or copies from manuscript
plural ***amanuenses***

amaretto
ITALIAN
an Italian liqueur flavoured with almonds
plural ***amarettos***

ambiance or ***ambience***
FRENCH
1 atmosphere
2 surrounding influence; environment

AMDG
see AD MAJOREM DEI GLORIAM

âme damnée
FRENCH, literally 'damned soul'
someone who is completely and blindly devoted to another person

âme de boue
FRENCH, literally 'soul of mud'
a low-minded person

amende
FRENCH
a fine or penalty

amende honorable
FRENCH
a frank admission of wrong, satisfying the honour of the injured person; a public apology

a mensa et toro or ***a mensa et thoro***
LATIN, literally 'from bed and board'
(law) (relief granted to a married couple) from connubial relations or the obligation to cohabit

> used in cases of judicial separation

âme perdue
FRENCH, literally 'lost soul'
a desperate character

à merveille
FRENCH
wonderfully, perfectly

ami
FRENCH
a friend
see also AMIE

amicus curiae
LATIN, literally 'friend of the law-court'
1 (formerly, in Scots law) a disinterested adviser, not a party to the case
2 a person or group not directly involved in a case who may be represented by request or permission of the court

> sometimes wrongly used of a friend in high places

plural ***amici curiae***

ami de cour
FRENCH, literally 'court friend'
an untrustworthy friend

ami du peuple
FRENCH
friend of the people

> applied to the French revolutionist Jean Paul Marat

amie
FRENCH
1 a female friend
2 a mistress

amigo
SPANISH
a friend
plural ***amigos***

a minori (ad majus)
LATIN
from the less (to the greater)

à moitié
FRENCH
half; by halves

à mon avis
FRENCH
in my opinion

amontillado
SPANISH
a light medium-dry sherry originally from Montilla
plural ***amontillados***

amoretto or ***amorino***
ITALIAN
a cupid
plural ***amoretti*** or ***amorini***

amoroso
ITALIAN
1 *(music)* tender
2 *(music)* tenderly
3 a lover
4 a ladies' man
plural ***amoroso***
feminine ***amorosa***

amor patriae
LATIN
love of one's country; patriotism

amor vincit omnia
see OMNIA VINCIT AMOR

amour
FRENCH for 'love'
a love affair, especially a secret or illicit one

amour courtois
FRENCH
courtly love

> the medieval social and literary tradition of chivalric love and etiquette first developed by the troubadours of S France

amour de voyage
FRENCH
a shipboard romance or other temporary love affair

amourette
FRENCH
a trivial love affair

amour-propre
FRENCH
self-esteem

> sometimes used of excessive self-esteem, as shown by readiness to take offence

amphora
LATIN
a two-handled jar used by the Greeks and Romans for holding liquids
plural ***amphorae***

amrit
PUNJABI
1 a sacred sweetened water used in the Sikh baptismal ceremony
2 the ceremony itself

amrita
from SANSKRIT *amrta* meaning 'immortal'
the drink of the Hindu gods

amritattva
SANSKRIT
immortality

amuse-gueule
FRENCH

a small snack such as a bite-sized pizza, a small quiche, etc, that is served with drinks, usually before a meal

ananke
GREEK
necessity

anathema
GREEK, literally 'a thing dedicated or accursed'
1 a solemn ecclesiastical curse involving excommunication
2 a curse or execration
3 a person or thing cursed
4 an object of abhorrence
plural ***anathemas***

a natura rei
LATIN
from the nature of the case

ancienne noblesse
FRENCH
the old nobility; the nobility of the ancien régime

ancien régime
FRENCH
the old order, especially the social and political system of France before the outbreak of the French Revolution

andante
ITALIAN, literally 'going'
(music)
1 moderately slow
2 a movement or piece in andante time

andantino
ITALIAN
(music)
1 somewhat slower than andante
2 an andantino movement or piece

confusingly, *andantino* can also mean 'somewhat quicker than andante'

plural ***andantinos***

andouillette
FRENCH
a small chitterling sausage

angelus
LATIN
1 a short devotional exercise in honour of the Incarnation, repeated three times daily
2 the bell rung in Roman Catholic countries at morning, noon, and sunset, to invite the faithful to recite the angelus

from the introductory words, *angelus domini nuntiavit Mariae*

angina (pectoris)
LATIN, literally 'strangling (of the breast)'
a heart disease marked by paroxysms of intense pain, radiating from the breastbone mainly towards the left shoulder and arm

Angst or ***angst***
GERMAN
anxiety, especially a general feeling of anxiety produced by awareness of the uncertainties and paradoxes inherent in the state of being human

anguis in herba
LATIN
a snake in the grass; a lurking danger
see also LATET ANGUIS IN HERBA

anima
LATIN
1 the soul, the innermost part of the personality
2 in Jungian psychology, the female component of the male personality
compare ANIMUS

animal bipes
LATIN
a two-footed animal, man

animal rationale
LATIN
a reasoning animal

anima mundi
LATIN
the soul of the world

animo et fide
LATIN
by courage and faith

animus
LATIN for 'spirit, soul'
1 intention
2 motive or purpose
3 hostility
4 in Jungian psychology, the male component of the female personality
compare ANIMA

animus furandi
LATIN
(law) the intention of stealing

ankh
EGYPTIAN for 'life'
a T-shaped cross with a loop above the horizontal bar, the symbol of life

ankus
HINDUSTANI
an elephant goad

anno
LATIN
in the year

anno Christi
LATIN
in the year of Christ

anno Domini
LATIN
1 in the year of the Lord
2 *(informal)* advancing old age
abbrev **AD**

> used in numbering the years since Christ is thought to have been born. The abbreviation is traditionally placed before the year number, eg AD95

anno humanae salutis
LATIN
in the year of human salvation
abbrev **AHS**

anno mundi
LATIN
in the year of the world

> used in reckoning dates from the supposed time of creation

anno regni
LATIN
in the year of the reign ...

> followed by a number

abbrev **AR**

anno salutis
LATIN
in the year of salvation
abbrev **AS**

annos vixit
LATIN
he or she lived ... years
abbrev **av, a.v.**

anno urbis conditae
LATIN
in the year of the founding of the city (ie Rome, in 753BC)
abbrev **AUC**

annus horribilis
LATIN
year of horrors

> coined by analogy with ANNUS MIRABILIS, and applied by

Queen Elizabeth II to 1992, a year of ill fortune for the royal family

annus mirabilis
LATIN
year of wonders, applied to years of remarkable or catastrophic event

especially applied to 1666, the year of the plague and fire of London

anomie or *anomy*
FRENCH, from GREEK meaning 'lawlessness'
(in society or in an individual) a condition of hopelessness caused or characterized by breakdown of rules of conduct and loss of belief and sense of purpose

anorexia nervosa
LATIN, from GREEK
(psychology or *medicine)* a condition characterized by loss of appetite and aversion to food due to emotional disturbance, normally leading to marked emaciation, etc, and sometimes death

Anschauung
GERMAN for 'perception, intuition, view'
1 *(psychology* or *philosophy)* direct perception through the senses; intuition
2 an attitude or point of view

Anschluss
GERMAN
union, especially the political union of Germany and Austria in 1938

ante bellum
LATIN
before the war

the phrase may refer to any war

ante cibum
LATIN
before food

used in medical prescriptions

abbrev **ac, a.c.**

ante lucem
LATIN, literally 'before light'
before dawn

ante meridiem
LATIN
before noon, ie in the morning
abbrev **a.m., am, AM**

the abbreviation is the usual form

ante mortem
LATIN
before death

ante prandium
LATIN
before a meal

used in medical prescriptions

abbrev **ap, a.p.**

antipasto
ITALIAN
an hors d'oeuvre, an appetizer
plural ***antipasti***

antipodes
GREEK, literally 'with feet opposite, feet to feet'
a point or place diametrically opposite to another on the surface of the globe, especially Australia and New Zealand in relation to Britain or Europe

anziani
ITALIAN for 'elders'
councillors, senators

AOC
see APPELLATION (D'ORIGINE) CONTRÔLÉE

ao dai
VIETNAMESE
a traditional Vietnamese long high-necked tunic for women, slit to the waist at the sides and worn over trousers

à outrance or ***à l'outrance***
FRENCH
1 to the utmost
2 to the death
3 to the bitter end

apage (Satanas)
GREEK
away, depart (Satan)!

apagoge
GREEK, literally 'leading away'
reduction to absurdity, indirect proof by showing the falsehood of the opposite

apartheid
AFRIKAANS
segregation and separate development of races, especially as formerly practised in S Africa

also used figuratively, eg of segregation of the sexes

à pas de géant
FRENCH
with a giant's stride

aperçu
FRENCH, literally 'perceived'
1 a summary, a brief exposition or outline
2 a glimpse
3 an immediate intuitive insight

apéritif or ***aperitif***
FRENCH
a drink taken as an appetizer

à perte de vue
FRENCH
(reaching) out of sight; as far as the eye can see

à peu près
FRENCH
nearly

Apfelstrudel
GERMAN
a sweet pastry containing apples, spices, etc

a piacere
ITALIAN
at pleasure

aplomb
FRENCH
self-possession, coolness

à point
FRENCH
1 to a nicety
2 (said of food) done to a turn; just right

apologia
GREEK
a formal written statement in defence of a belief or cause

à portée
FRENCH
within reach or range

a posteriori
LATIN
(said of reasoning) from experience, from effect to cause; inductive; empirical
compare A PRIORI

appalto
ITALIAN
a contract or monopoly
plural ***appalti***

apparat
RUSSIAN for 'apparatus'
the political machine of a communist party

apparatchik
RUSSIAN
1 a member of a communist bureaucracy or party machine
2 a communist agent
3 a party official in any political party
plural ***apparatchiks*** or ***apparatchiki***

apparatus criticus
LATIN
materials for the critical study of a document, especially palaeographical and critical notes intended to help study a text printed from manuscript, but also any footnotes, appendices, etc, that accompany a scholarly edition of a text

appartement
FRENCH for 'flat'
a suite of rooms in a house for an individual or a family

appel au peuple
FRENCH, literally 'call to the people'
a vote of all the electors, taken to decide a matter of public importance; a referendum

appellation (d'origine) contrôlée
FRENCH
(in the labelling of French wines) a guarantee that the wine conforms to certain specified conditions of origin, strength, etc
abbrev **AC, AOC**

appliqué
FRENCH, literally 'applied'
(in needlework, metalwork, etc) decorative work applied to, or laid on, another material, eg a fabric shape stitched to a larger piece of fabric

appoggiatura
ITALIAN
(music)
1 a grace-note written in smaller size, taking its time at the expense of the following note
2 a similar note with a stroke through the tail, played very quickly, ie an acciaccatura

après coup
FRENCH
too late, after the event, as an afterthought

après-goût
FRENCH
an aftertaste

après nous le déluge
FRENCH, literally 'after us the deluge'
once we are dead, let the heavens open

> attributed to Madame de Pompadour, mistress of Louis XV, with reference to the French Revolution. The variant *après moi le déluge* is also attributed to Louis XV himself

après-ski or ***apres-ski***
FRENCH
1 the evening period of recreation after the day's skiing
2 (said of clothes, etc) suitable for this period of recreation

a prima vista
ITALIAN
at first sight

a priori
LATIN
(said of reasoning) from what is prior logically or chronologically, eg from cause to effect, from a general principle to its

consequences, etc; deductive
compare A POSTERIORI

apropos
from FRENCH *à propos*
1 to the purpose
2 appropriately
3 (followed by 'of') in reference to
4 by the way, incidentally

à propos de bottes
FRENCH, literally 'talking of boots'
without real relevance; by the way

introducing something unconnected with what has gone before

à propos de rien
FRENCH
apropos of nothing, while I think of it

AQPS
see AUTRE QUE PUR SANG

aqua
LATIN
water

aqua caelestis
LATIN, literally 'water from heaven'
1 rain water
2 rectified spirits
3 cordial

aqua fontana
LATIN
spring water

aqua fortis or ***aquafortis***
LATIN, literally 'strong water'
1 concentrated nitric acid
2 etching with nitric acid

aqua mirabilis
LATIN, literally 'wonderful water'
a preparation distilled from cloves, nutmeg, ginger, and spirit of wine

aqua pura
LATIN
pure water

aqua regia
LATIN, literally 'royal water'
a mixture of nitric and hydrochloric acids, used to dissolve gold and platinum

aquarelle
FRENCH
1 watercolour painting
2 a kind of painting with ink and very thin transparent watercolours, used to represent flowers, etc

à quatre
FRENCH
of, for, or between four; four together

à quatre mains
FRENCH
for four hands, ie two performers

a quattr' occhi
ITALIAN, literally 'between four eyes'
(said of two people) face to face, tête-à-tête

aquavit or ***akvavit***
from DANISH, SWEDISH, and NORWEGIAN *akvavit*
a Scandinavian spirit made from potatoes or grain, flavoured with caraway seeds

aqua vitae
LATIN, literally 'water of life'
alcohol; brandy, whisky, etc

à quoi bon?
FRENCH
what's the good of it?, what's the use?

AR
see ANNO REGNI

arabesque
FRENCH
1 *(ballet)* a posture in which one leg is stretched out backwards parallel with the ground and the body is bent forward from the hips
2 a type of decoration in painting, metalwork, etc, with intricate intertwining designs
3 a short ornate piece of music

arame
JAPANESE
a type of edible seaweed, which looks like black bootlaces

à ravir
FRENCH
ravishingly

arbiter elegantiarum
LATIN, literally 'judge of elegance'
a judge or authority on matters of taste

arbitrium
LATIN
power of decision, absolute authority

arboretum
LATIN
a botanical garden used to display trees and shrubs for scientific, educational, and recreational purposes
plural ***arboreta***

arcanum
LATIN
1 a secret or mystery
2 a secret remedy or elixir
plural ***arcana***

arcanum imperii
LATIN
a state secret
plural ***arcana imperii***

> the plural form is more frequent

arc de triomphe
FRENCH
triumphal arch

> the Arc de Triomphe at the end of the Champs Elysées in Paris was designed by Jean Chalgrin (1739–1811) to commemorate Napoleon's victories

plural ***arcs de triomphe***

arc-en-ciel
FRENCH
a rainbow
plural ***arcs-en-ciel***

arco
ITALIAN for 'bow'
(music) with the bow

> a direction marking the end of a pizzicato passage. The full form is *coll' arco*

ardentia verba
LATIN
words that burn, glowing language

à rebours
FRENCH
against the grain; contrarily

arête
FRENCH for 'fish-bone, spine'
1 a sharp ridge
2 a rocky edge on a mountain

argent comptant
FRENCH
ready money

argot
FRENCH
slang used and understood only by a

particular group of people, originally that of thieves and vagabonds; cant

argumenti causa
LATIN
for the sake of argument

argumentum
LATIN
(rhetoric or logic) argument, proof

argumentum ad baculum
see ARGUMENTUM BACULINUM

argumentum ad crumenam
LATIN, literally 'argument addressed to the purse'
an appeal to the personal financial interests or desires of the listener

argumentum ad hominem
LATIN, literally 'argument addressed to the man'
1 an appeal to the known feelings, prejudices, or preferences of the hearer or reader
2 an argument relying on personal abuse, or an attack on the opponent's character, rather than his or her viewpoint

argumentum ad ignorantiam
LATIN
an argument founded on the ignorance of an opponent

argumentum ad invidiam
LATIN
an appeal to prejudices

argumentum ad judicium
LATIN
an appeal to common sense or judgement

argumentum ad misericordiam
LATIN
an appeal to pity

argumentum ad rem
LATIN
an argument to the purpose, directed at the real issue
see also AD REM

argumentum ad verecundiam
LATIN
an appeal to awe or reverence (towards a prestigious or authoritative name or figure)

argumentum baculinum or ***argumentum ad baculum***
LATIN
the argument of the stick or rod, ie of force

argumentum per impossibile
LATIN
proof from the absurdity of a contradictory supposition

aria
ITALIAN
(music) an air or melody, especially an accompanied vocal solo in a cantata, oratorio, or opera

arietta
ITALIAN
(music) a little aria or air

arioso
ITALIAN
(music) in the melodious manner of an aria, or between aria and recitative

ariston metron
GREEK
1 the middle, or moderate, course is the best
2 the golden mean

a rivederci
see ARRIVEDERCI

armes parlantes
FRENCH, literally 'talking arms'
used of arms that indicate the name of the family that bears them, such as a press and a tun for Preston

armoire
FRENCH
a large, decorative wardrobe or cupboard

armure
FRENCH
a type of fabric with a pebbled surface

arpeggio
ITALIAN, literally 'I play the harp'
(music)
1 a chord whose notes are played or sung one at a time in rapid succession
2 the notes of a chord played or sung in such a way
plural ***arpeggios***

arpillera
SPANISH for 'sackcloth'
a pictorial Peruvian wall decoration consisting of colourful threads and scraps stitched onto a sackcloth backing

arrectis auribus
LATIN
with ears pricked up

arriéré
FRENCH
backward, old-fashioned

arrière-ban
FRENCH
1 (in medieval France) a summons to the king's vassals to do military service
2 the vassals so assembled for military service

arrière-garde
FRENCH
rearguard

arrière-goût
FRENCH
an aftertaste, especially an unpleasant one

arrière-pensée
FRENCH
1 a mental reservation
2 a subsidiary or concealed aim, an ulterior motive

arriero
SPANISH
a muleteer
plural ***arrieros***

arrivé
FRENCH, literally 'arrived'
successful, having made one's way in the world
feminine ***arrivée***

arrivederci or ***a rivederci***
ITALIAN, literally 'until we meet again'
goodbye

arriviste
FRENCH
1 a person who is bent on self-advancement
2 a parvenu, an upstart

arrondissement
FRENCH
in France, a subdivision of a department, or a municipal subdivision of some large cities, especially Paris

arroyo
SPANISH
1 a rocky ravine
2 the dried-up bed of a stream, etc

chiefly used in the US

plural ***arroyos***

ars est celare artem
LATIN
true art is to conceal art

ars gratia artis
LATIN
art for art's sake

ars longa, vita brevis
LATIN
art is long, life is short

from a Greek phrase generally translated as 'the life so short, the craft so long to learn'

art brut
FRENCH, literally 'raw art'
the primitive, unrefined, or naive art of non-professional or untrained artists, such as children, mental patients, prisoners, etc

artel
RUSSIAN
a Russian workers' co-operative

artiste
FRENCH
a public performer or entertainer

art nouveau
FRENCH, literally 'new art'
a style of art and decoration popular in Europe and the US at the end of the 19th century, characterized by naturalistic plant and flower motifs, and patterns of sinuous, curling lines

AS
see ANNO SALUTIS

a salti
ITALIAN, literally 'in jumps'
by fits and starts

asana
SANSKRIT
any of the positions taught in yoga

ashram
from SANSKRIT *āśrama*
(Hinduism)
1 a hermitage for a holy man
2 a place of retreat for a religious community
3 such a community

the ashram of Mahatma Gandhi is a well-known example

assai
ITALIAN
(music) very

assegai or ***assagai***
FRENCH OR PORTUGUESE, from ARABIC *azzaghāyah*
a slender spear of hard wood tipped with iron, either for hurling or for thrusting with, used in S Africa

assemblé
FRENCH
(ballet) a leap with extended leg followed by a landing with both legs together

assez bien
FRENCH
pretty well

atabal
SPANISH, from ARABIC *at-tabl*
a Moorish kettledrum

atabeg or ***atabek***
TURKISH
a Turkish ruler or high official

ataman
RUSSIAN
a Cossack headman or general, a hetman
plural ***atamans***

à tâtons
FRENCH
gropingly, tentatively

atelier

FRENCH

a workshop, especially an artist's studio

a tempo

ITALIAN

(music) in time, ie revert to the previous or original tempo

atlatl

NAHUATL for 'spear-thrower'

a throwing-stick used by American Indians and Eskimos

atman

SANSKRIT

(Hinduism) the divine within the self, the essential self, the soul

à tort et à travers

FRENCH, literally 'wrongly and across'

at random, haphazardly

à toute force

FRENCH

by all means, absolutely

à tout hasard

FRENCH

on the off chance, just in case

à tout prix

FRENCH

at any price

à tout propos

FRENCH

on every occasion

à travers

FRENCH

across, through

à trois

FRENCH

1 of, for, or between three

2 (said of a dinner, etc) for three people

3 (said of three people) without further company

see also MÉNAGE À TROIS

attaché

FRENCH, literally 'attached'

a junior official in an embassy

> an *attaché case* is a small rigid leather case suitable for carrying official documents

attentat

FRENCH

an attempt at a crime of violence, especially an attempted assassination

> usually refers to an unsuccessful attempt with a political motive

aubade

FRENCH

a poem or short piece of music to announce the dawn

auberge

FRENCH

an inn

AUC

see AB URBE CONDITA, ANNO URBIS CONDITAE

au contraire

FRENCH

on the contrary

au courant

FRENCH, literally 'in the current or stream'

1 well-informed

2 up-to-date with the facts or situation

audax et cautus

LATIN

bold and cautious

au désespoir
FRENCH
in despair

audi alteram partem
LATIN
(law) hear the other side; both sides of a case must be heard before a decision can be reached

audita querela
LATIN, literally 'the suit having been heard'
(law) the name of a writ giving leave to appeal

au fait
FRENCH
1 well-acquainted with a matter; well-informed
2 conversant, proficient, expert

Aufgabe
GERMAN
(psychology) a task set as an experiment, etc

Aufklärung
GERMAN for 'enlightenment'
the Age of Enlightenment, the Age of Reason

> a philosophical movement of the 18th century based on rational thought and questioning traditional political and social conventions

Auflage
GERMAN
edition
abbrev **Aufl.**

au fond
FRENCH, literally 'at the bottom'
fundamentally
compare À FOND

au fromage
FRENCH
(cookery) with cheese

auf Wiedersehen
GERMAN, literally 'until we meet again'
goodbye

au grand galop
FRENCH, literally 'at full gallop'
full tilt

au grand sérieux
FRENCH
in all seriousness
see also AU SÉRIEUX

au gratin
FRENCH
(cookery) cooked with a topping of breadcrumbs and/or grated cheese
see also GRATIN, GRATINÉ

au jour le jour
FRENCH, literally 'from day to day'
from hand to mouth

aula
LATIN
a hall, especially one in a collegiate university

au mieux
FRENCH, literally 'at the best'
on the best of terms

au naturel
FRENCH, literally 'in the natural state'
1 *(cookery)* cooked plainly; uncooked; without dressing
2 nude, naked

> in French, *thon au naturel* is tuna in brine

au pair
FRENCH

a young person from abroad, usually female, who lives with a family and helps with housework, looking after children, etc, in return for board and lodging, especially to learn the language

➪ originally meaning 'by mutual service without payment'

au pied de la lettre
FRENCH, literally 'to the foot of the letter'
exactly, literally

au pis aller
FRENCH
1 at the worst
2 as a last resort

au poivre
FRENCH
(cookery) with pepper

au premier
FRENCH
on the first floor

aura popularis
LATIN, literally 'the popular breeze'
the breeze of popular favour

aurea mediocritas
LATIN
the golden mean, the happy medium

au reste
FRENCH
1 as for the rest
2 besides

au revoir
FRENCH, literally 'until we meet again'
goodbye

aurora
LATIN
1 the dawn
2 the appearance of diffuse bands or curtains of red, green, or yellow lights in the night sky, most often observed from the Arctic and Antarctic regions
plural ***auroras*** or ***aurorae***

aurora australis or ***Aurora Australis***
LATIN
the southern aurora or southern lights, seen in the southern hemisphere

aurora borealis, Aurora Borealis or ***aurora septentrionalis***
LATIN
the northern aurora or northern lights, seen in the northern hemisphere

aurum potabile
LATIN, literally 'potable gold'
a former medicine or cordial containing a small quantity of gold

au second
FRENCH
on the second floor

au secours
FRENCH
help!

au sérieux
FRENCH
seriously
see also AU GRAND SÉRIEUX

Ausgleich
GERMAN
1 a settlement
2 an arrangement
3 the agreement between Austria and Hungary in 1867

Ausländer
GERMAN
a foreigner

Auslese
GERMAN, literally ‘choice, selection’
a high-quality wine made from selected late-picked bunches of grapes

Aussichtspunkt
GERMAN
a selected position for admiring scenery, a vantage point
plural ***Aussichtspunkte***

Aussiedler
GERMAN, literally ‘out-settler’
an immigrant

aut Caesar aut nihil
LATIN, literally ‘either Caesar or nothing’
1 all or nothing
2 complete success or utter failure

> the variant *aut Caesar aut nullus* literally means ‘either Caesar or nobody’

auteur
FRENCH for ‘author’
a film director whose work shows a unique personal stamp, especially one thought of as the creator of a particular genre

Autobahn or ***autobahn***
GERMAN
a motorway

autocritique
FRENCH
self-criticism, especially as undertaken by devout Marxists

auto-da-fé
PORTUGUESE, literally ‘act of faith’
1 the public declaration of the judgement passed on heretics in Spain and Portugal by the Inquisition
2 the infliction of the punishment that immediately followed, especially the public burning of the victims

> the Spanish form is *auto-de-fe*

plural ***autos-da-fé*** or ***autos-de-fe***

auto-de-fe
see AUTO-DA-FÉ

autopista
SPANISH
a motorway

autoroute
FRENCH
a motorway

autostrada
ITALIAN
a motorway

autrefois acquit
FRENCH, literally ‘previously acquitted’
(law) a defence plea arguing that a defendant cannot be charged a second time with an offence of which they have been acquitted

autrefois convict
FRENCH, literally ‘previously convicted’
(law) a defence plea arguing that a defendant cannot be charged a second time with a (capital) offence of which they have been found guilty

autre que pur sang
FRENCH, literally ‘other than pure blood’
(horse-racing) non-thoroughbred
abbrev **AQPS**

autre temps, autre moeurs
FRENCH, literally ‘other times, other manners’
other days, other ways

aut vincere aut mori
LATIN
to conquer or die

au voleur
FRENCH
stop thief!

aux armes
FRENCH
to arms!

av or ***a.v.***
see ANNOS VIXIT

avant-coureur, avant-courrier or ***avant-courier***
FRENCH
1 forerunner
2 a scout; a person who runs or is sent ahead

avant-garde
FRENCH for 'vanguard'
1 those writers, painters, musicians, etc, whose ideas and techniques are the most modern or advanced
2 (said of a work of art, idea, etc) using or supporting the most modern and advanced ideas in literature, art, music, etc

avant-goût
FRENCH
a foretaste

avanti
ITALIAN
forward!

avant-propos
FRENCH
preliminary matter; preface

avatar
SANSKRIT
1 the appearance of a Hindu god in human or animal form
2 *(figurative)* a visible manifestation of an abstract concept

ave
LATIN, literally 'be well!'
hail!

ave atque vale
LATIN
hail and farewell

avec plaisir
FRENCH
with pleasure

ave Maria
LATIN
the Hail Mary, a recitation of the address or prayer to the Virgin Mary

avenir
FRENCH
future

a verbis ad verbera
LATIN
from words to blows

avgolemono
GREEK
a soup or sauce made from chicken stock, lemon juice, and egg yolks

avion
FRENCH
an aeroplane
see also PAR AVION

avis au lecteur
FRENCH
notice to the reader

avise la fin
FRENCH
consider the end

avoirdupois
from OLD FRENCH *aveir de peis*, literally 'goods of weight'
1 a system of weights in which the pound (lb) equals 16 ounces (oz)
2 *(informal* and *facetious)* weight,

especially heaviness or stoutness

➪ used in English since the 14th century

à volonté
FRENCH
at pleasure

a vostra salute
ITALIAN
to your health!

a vostro beneplacito
ITALIAN
at your pleasure, at your will

à votre santé
FRENCH
to your health!

a vuestra salud
SPANISH
to your health!

axioma medium
LATIN
a generalization from experience

ayah
from HINDI *āyā*, from PORTUGUESE *aia* meaning 'nurse, governess'
an Indian or S African nursemaid or female attendant

ayatollah
PERSIAN, from ARABIC, literally 'sign of God'
1 a Shiite religious leader in Iran
2 (loosely) an ideological leader or policy maker

ayuntamiento
SPANISH
a municipal council
plural ***ayuntamientos***

azione (sacra)
ITALIAN
(music) a composition, like an oratorio in form, but performed as a drama

azulejo
SPANISH
a painted and glazed pottery tile
plural ***azulejos***

B

baas
AFRIKAANS, from DUTCH
a master, an overseer, an employer

used as a term of address, especially by a black or coloured S African addressing a white. The Dutch word is the origin of the noun 'boss'

baba au rhum
FRENCH
a small cake leavened with yeast, with or without fruit and soaked in a rum syrup

from POLISH *baba* meaning 'old woman'. the anglicized form *rum baba* is more frequent in english

babu or ***baboo***
HINDI
1 a title for Hindus in some parts of India corresponding to 'Mr'
2 (formerly) an Indian clerk who could write English

babushka
RUSSIAN for 'grandmother'
1 a headscarf tied under the chin, worn by Russian peasant women
2 a grandmother, an elderly woman

baccarat or ***baccara***
FRENCH
a card game played by betters and a banker

Backfisch
GERMAN, literally 'fish for baking'
a girl in her teens

badinage
FRENCH
light playful talk; banter

bagarre
FRENCH
a scuffle, a brawl, a rumpus

bagatelle
FRENCH
1 a knick-knack, a trinket, something of little value, a trifle
2 a short light piece of music
3 a board game with balls and a cue or spring, the object being to put the balls into numbered holes or sections

bagnio
from ITALIAN *bagno* meaning 'bath'
1 an oriental prison for slaves
2 a brothel
plural ***bagnios***

baguette
FRENCH for 'stick'
1 a long narrow loaf of white bread
2 a precious stone cut in the shape of a long rectangle

bahut
FRENCH
an ornamented chest or cabinet, especially one with a rounded top

baignoire
FRENCH for 'bathtub'
a theatre box on a level with the stalls

bain-marie
FRENCH, literally 'bath of Mary'

(cookery) a vessel of hot or boiling water into which another vessel is placed to cook slowly or keep hot

> perhaps from Mary or Miriam, the sister of Moses, who reputedly wrote a book on alchemy. The Latin equivalent is *balneum Mariae*

plural ***bains-marie***

baklava or ***baclava***
TURKISH
a rich Middle-Eastern dessert consisting of layers of filo pastry filled with nuts and honey

baksheesh or ***backsheesh***
PERSIAN *bakhshīsh*
a gratuity or tip

baladin
FRENCH
a theatrical dancer
feminine ***baladine***

balalaika
RUSSIAN
a Russian musical instrument, like a guitar, with a triangular body and usually three strings

bal costumé
FRENCH
a fancy-dress ball

ballon d'essai
FRENCH, literally 'trial balloon'
a feeler or preliminary sounding of public opinion

bal masqué
FRENCH
a masked ball

balneum Mariae
see BAIN-MARIE

bal paré
FRENCH
a dress ball

bambino
ITALIAN
1 a child
2 a picture of the infant Jesus, exhibited at Christmas in churches in Italy
plural ***bambinos*** or ***bambini***

banc
FRENCH
(law) the judges' bench

Band
GERMAN
a volume of a book or journal
plural ***Bände***

bandeau
FRENCH
1 a headband
2 a band inside a hat
3 a bandage for the eyes
plural ***bandeaux***

banderilla
SPANISH
a dart with a streamer attached that skilled bullfighters stick into the neck and shoulders of the bull

banderillero
SPANISH
a bullfighter who uses banderillas
plural ***banderilleros***

banlieue
FRENCH
the suburbs or outskirts

banquette
FRENCH
a built-in wall-sofa used instead of individual seats, eg in a restaurant

banzai
JAPANESE for 'ten thousand years, forever'
1 a Japanese battle-cry or salute to the emperor
2 an exclamation of joy

bapu
HINDI
spiritual father

baragouin
FRENCH
jargon, gibberish, double Dutch

> from BRETON *bara gwenn* meaning 'white bread', said to have originated in the breton soldiers' astonishment at white bread

barca
ITALIAN
a boat or barge

bar mitzvah, Bar Mitzvah, bar mizvah or ***bar mitsvah***
HEBREW, literally 'son of the law'
1 in the Jewish religion, a boy reaching the age of religious responsibility (usually 13 years)
2 the festivities held to celebrate this event

barre
FRENCH
a horizontal rail fixed to the wall at waist level, which ballet-dancers use to balance themselves while exercising

barrette
FRENCH
a bar-shaped hair slide

bas-bleu
FRENCH
a bluestocking

> from the blue worsted stockings worn by members of an 18th-century literary society

bascule
FRENCH for 'seesaw'
an apparatus which acts on the principle of the lever, whereby one end rises when pressure is put on the other end

Bashi-Bazouk
TURKISH, literally 'wild head'
a Turkish irregular soldier

bashlik
from RUSSIAN *bashlyk*
a kind of hood with long side flaps, worn by Russians in cold weather

basho
JAPANESE
(in sumo wrestling) a tournament
plural ***basho***

basque
FRENCH
1 a type of close-fitting bodice worn by women
2 a short-skirted jacket

bas-relief
FRENCH for 'low relief'
a sculpture in which the figures project slightly from the background on which they are formed

> the Italian equivalent is *basso-rilievo*

basso profondo or ***basso profundo***
ITALIAN
1 an extremely deep bass voice
2 a singer with such a voice

basso-rilievo
see BAS-RELIEF

basta
ITALIAN
enough!

bateau
FRENCH
a light river-boat
plural ***bateaux***

bateau-mouche
FRENCH, literally 'fly-boat'
a passenger boat on the Seine
plural ***bateaux-mouches***

bath mitzvah, Bath Mitzvah, bath mizvah or ***bath mitsvah***
HEBREW, literally 'daughter of the law'
1 in the Jewish religion, a girl reaching the age of religious responsibility (usually 12 years)
2 the festivities held to celebrate this event

> other variants have *bas* or *bat* in place of *bath*

batik
MALAY, from JAVANESE meaning 'painted'
1 a method of producing designs on cloth by covering with wax those parts that are to be protected from the dye
2 fabric patterned by this method

> of Indonesian origin

batiste
FRENCH for 'cambric'
a fine fabric of linen, cotton, or wool

> from *Baptiste*, the reputed original maker, or from its use in wiping the heads of children after baptism

baton
from FRENCH *bâton*
1 a staff of office
2 a policeman's truncheon
3 a short stick passed on from one runner to the next in a relay-race
4 a thin stick used by the conductor of an orchestra
5 a staff with a knob at one end, carried, tossed, and twirled by a drum major, etc, at the head of a marching band

battement
FRENCH for 'beating'
(ballet) one of a variety of movements in which one leg is extended to the front, side, or back

batterie de cuisine
FRENCH
pots and pans; cooking utensils

battue
FRENCH
1 a method of shooting in which the game is driven from cover by beaters to a place where the shooters are waiting
2 indiscriminate slaughter, especially of unresisting crowds

Bauhaus
GERMAN, literally 'building-house'
1 a German school of art and architecture (1919–33) having as its aim the integration of art and technology in design
2 (said of architecture) influenced by this school

bayadère
FRENCH
1 a Hindu dancing-girl
2 a horizontally-striped woven fabric

bazaar
from PERSIAN *bāzār*
1 an Eastern market-place
2 a fair, often selling goods in aid of charity
3 a shop where a variety of goods is sold

beatae memoriae
LATIN
of blessed memory

> sometimes used ironically

abbrev **BM**

beati pacifici
LATIN
blessed are the peacemakers

beatus ille
LATIN, literally 'happy he'
happy the man

beau
FRENCH for 'fine, beautiful'
1 a man who pays a lot of attention to his clothes and appearance; a fop or dandy
2 a lover
plural ***beaux***

beau geste
FRENCH, literally 'fine gesture'
a noble or gracious gesture or act

beau idéal or ***beau ideal***
FRENCH, literally 'ideal beauty'
the highest conceivable type of beauty or excellence

beau monde
FRENCH, literally 'fine world'
the world of fashion and high society

beauté du diable
FRENCH, literally 'beauty of the devil'
1 irresistible or overpowering beauty
2 the charm and sparkle of youth

beaux arts
FRENCH
1 the fine arts
2 influenced by the style of the École des Beaux-Arts in Paris

beaux yeux
FRENCH, literally 'beautiful eyes'
1 good looks
2 a pretty woman

bécasse
FRENCH
a woodcock

bêche-de-mer
FRENCH, from PORTUGUESE *bicho do mar*
a sea-slug or trepang

beg
see BEY

begum
from URDU *begam*
1 a Muslim princess or lady of rank
2 a polite way of addressing any Muslim woman

bel air
FRENCH
fine deportment

bel canto
ITALIAN, literally 'beautiful singing'
a style of operatic singing characterized by beauty of tone rather than dramatic strength

bel esprit
FRENCH
a wit or genius
plural ***beaux esprits***

bel étage
FRENCH
the best storey, usually the first floor

bella figura
ITALIAN
good impression or appearance

belle
FRENCH
1 a beautiful woman or girl
2 the most attractive woman of a place or occasion, especially in the phrase *the belle of the ball*

belle amie
FRENCH
a female friend or mistress

belle assemblée
FRENCH
a fashionable gathering

belle époque or ***Belle Époque***
from FRENCH *la belle époque*, literally 'the fine period'
the time of security and gracious living for the well-to-do, ended by World War I

belle laide
see JOLIE LAIDE

belle passion
FRENCH
the tender passion, love

belle peinture
FRENCH, literally 'fine painting'
naturalistic painting as distinct from Impressionism

belles-lettres
FRENCH, literally 'fine letters'
works of literature, especially ones valued for their aesthetic content

belle vue
FRENCH
a fine view

bellum internecinum
LATIN
a war of extermination

bel sangue
ITALIAN
gentle blood

bene decessit
LATIN, literally 'he has left well'
a leaving certificate given to a schoolboy, curate, etc

bene esse
LATIN
wellbeing, comfort, luxury, prosperity

bénéficiaire
FRENCH
1 a sports player who receives or is about to receive a benefit
2 one who benefits or profits by something

bene merentibus
LATIN
to the well-deserving

bene vale
LATIN
farewell
abbrev **BV**

bene vobis
LATIN
health to you!

ben trovato
ITALIAN, literally 'well found'
apt but untrue; well invented
see also SE NON È VERO, È (MOLTO) BEN TROVATO

ben venuto
ITALIAN
welcome!

berceau
FRENCH
1 a cradle
2 a shaded or foliage-covered walk
plural ***berceaux***

berceuse
FRENCH
1 a lullaby or cradle song
2 a musical composition in similar rhythm

beret
from FRENCH *béret*
a flat, round, woollen or felt cap, like those worn by Basque peasants

bergère
FRENCH for 'shepherdess'
a type of easy chair or sofa with a cane back and arms, of a style fashionable in the 18th century

Bergfall or ***bergfall***
GERMAN, literally 'mountain fall'
a fall of mountain rock

Bergschrund or ***bergschrund***
GERMAN, literally 'mountain cleft'
a crevasse formed where a glacier or snowfield moves away from a mountain wall

bertillonage
FRENCH
the system of identifying criminals by detailed measurements, fingerprints, etc

devised by Alphonse *Bertillon* (1853–1914)

Berufsverbot
GERMAN
in Germany, the policy of excluding political extremists from public service

besoin
FRENCH
need, want, desire

beso las manos
SPANISH
I kiss your hands

a form of salutation

Besserwisser
GERMAN
someone who always knows better than anyone else, or thinks they do

often facetious

bête
FRENCH for 'beast'
1 a brute
2 a stupid person

bête noire
FRENCH, literally 'black beast'
a bugbear; a person or thing that one especially dislikes, dreads, or fears
plural ***bêtes noires***

bêtise
FRENCH
a foolish or tactless remark or action

béton
FRENCH
concrete

beurre
FRENCH
butter

beurre manié
FRENCH, literally 'handled butter'
(cookery) a butter and flour mixture for thickening sauces or soups

bevue
from FRENCH *bévue*
a blunder

bey or ***beg***
TURKISH for 'lord'
1 in the Ottoman Empire, the title given to the governor of a province
2 in modern Turkey, the usual term of address to adult males, corresponding to 'Mr'

bhajee, bhagee or ***bhaji***
HINDI for 'vegetable'
(in Indian cookery) an appetizer consisting of vegetables deep-fried in batter

bhakti
SANSKRIT for 'portion'

1 (in Hinduism) devotion to a god, as a path to salvation

2 a form of yoga

bhang

HINDI

a preparation of the leaves and seeds of Indian hemp, which is chewed, smoked, or eaten for its narcotic and intoxicating effects

bhangra

HINDI

a type of Asian pop music that combines elements of traditional Punjabi music with Western pop

bhindi

HINDI

okra as used in Indian cookery

bibelot

FRENCH

a small curio or knick-knack

bidet

FRENCH

a small low rectangular basin for washing the genital and anal areas

bidon

FRENCH

a container for liquids, such as a wooden cup, water bottle, tin-can, or oil-drum

bidonville

FRENCH

a shanty town with dwellings made from oil-drums

bien-aimé

FRENCH

beloved

bien élevé

FRENCH

well brought up, well-mannered

bien entendu

FRENCH

of course; it goes without saying

bien-être

FRENCH

a sense of wellbeing

bien pensant

FRENCH

1 right-thinking

2 orthodox

bienséance

FRENCH

propriety, good breeding

bijou

FRENCH

1 a trinket, a jewel

2 a 'gem' of architecture, etc

3 (applied especially to houses) small and elegant; luxurious

plural ***bijoux***

bijouterie

FRENCH

jewellery, especially trinkets

Bildungsroman or ***Erziehungsroman***

GERMAN

a novel that has as its main theme the early emotional or spiritual development or education of its hero

> the classic example is Flaubert's *L'Éducation Sentimentale* (1869)

billet-doux

FRENCH, literally 'sweet note'

a love-letter

plural ***billets-doux***

bint

ARABIC for 'daughter'

1 a girl or woman

2 a girlfriend

> informal, usually derogatory

bis
LATIN
1 twice
2 *(music)* a direction indicating that a section is to be repeated

bis dat qui cito dat
LATIN
he gives twice who gives promptly

bise
FRENCH
a cold N or NE wind prevalent at certain seasons in and near Switzerland

bismillah
ARABIC
in the name of Allah!

> a common Muslim exclamation

bisque
FRENCH
a rich shellfish soup, made with wine and cream

bistro
FRENCH
a small bar or restaurant

> possibly from RUSSIAN *bystro* meaning 'quickly'

plural ***bistros***

bitte
GERMAN
1 please
2 don't mention it
3 I beg your pardon

bizarre
FRENCH
odd; fantastic; extravagant

blague
FRENCH for 'joke'
humbug, pretentious nonsense

blagueur
FRENCH for 'joker'
a practical joker or person who talks pretentious nonsense

blanchisseuse
FRENCH
a laundress

blancmange
from FRENCH *blancmanger*, literally 'white food'
a flavoured milk dessert thickened with cornflour or gelatine and set in a mould

blanquette
FRENCH
a ragout of light meat, especially chicken or veal, in a white sauce

blasé
FRENCH
indifferent to something because of familiarity; lacking enthusiasm; bored
feminine ***blasée***

blini
RUSSIAN for 'pancakes'
a small buckwheat pancake, especially as eaten with caviar and sour cream
plural ***blini*** or ***blinis***

blitz
from GERMAN *Blitzkrieg* meaning 'lightning war'
1 a violent and sustained attack from the air, especially one involving bombing
2 any sudden, overwhelming attack
3 *(informal)* an intensive campaign
4 *(informal)* a burst of intense activity in order to achieve something
5 (in American football) a defensive charge on the quarterback

> the full form *blitzkrieg* is also used in English for senses 1 and 2

bloc
FRENCH for 'block'
a unification of parties, countries, etc, to achieve a common purpose

blond
FRENCH
1 (said of hair, etc) light-coloured
2 (said of a person) having light-coloured hair and usually a fair complexion
3 such a person
feminine ***blonde***

> the feminine form is the more frequent in sense 1, and is sometimes used in place of the masculine for senses 2 and 3

blouson
FRENCH
a loose jacket or blouse gathered into a waistband

bluette
FRENCH
1 a spark, flash
2 a short playful piece of music

Blut und Eisen or ***Eisen und Blut***
GERMAN, literally 'blood and iron'
relentless force, especially military force used to achieve a specific purpose

> first used by Bismarck in the Prussian House of Deputies in 1886, but he had already used the form *Eisen und Blut* in 1862

Blutwurst or ***blutwurst***
GERMAN
blood-pudding

BM
see BEATAE MEMORIAE

bocca
ITALIAN
mouth

bodega
SPANISH
1 a wine shop
2 a warehouse or cellar for storing and maturing wine

boeuf bourguignon
FRENCH, literally 'Burgundy beef'
a beef casserole cooked in red wine

boîte de nuit
FRENCH
a nightclub

bolas
SPANISH for 'balls'
a S American missile, consisting of two or more balls or stones strung together, swung round the head and hurled so as to entangle an animal

bolero
SPANISH
1 a lively Spanish dance
2 a tune to which it may be danced
3 a jacket or waistcoat neither reaching the waist nor meeting in front
plural ***boleros***

bombe
FRENCH
a dessert, usually ice cream frozen in a round or melon-shaped mould

bombé
FRENCH for 'bulging, convex'
(said of furniture) having a rounded, convex front

bon accueil
FRENCH
1 good reception
2 due honour

bona fide
LATIN, literally 'in good faith'
1 genuine
2 done or carried out in good faith

bona fides
LATIN
1 good faith
2 genuineness
3 proofs of trustworthiness

bonamano
see BUONAMANO

bon ami
FRENCH
1 good friend
2 lover
feminine ***bonne amie***

bona mobilia
LATIN
(law) movable goods

bonanza
SPANISH, literally 'good weather (at sea), prosperity'
1 a rich mine or vein of precious ore
2 a large amount of silver
3 any source of wealth or stroke of luck

bona peritura
LATIN
(law) perishable goods

bon appétit
FRENCH, literally 'good appetite'
enjoy your meal!

> said politely to those who are about to start eating

bona vacantia
LATIN
(law) unclaimed goods

bonbon
FRENCH, literally 'good-good'
a confection, a sweet

bonbonnière
FRENCH
a fancy box for holding sweets

bon goût
FRENCH
good taste

bon gré, mal gré
FRENCH
willing or unwilling, willy-nilly

bonhomie
FRENCH
easy good-naturedness; overflowing friendliness

bonjour
FRENCH
1 good day
2 good morning

bon marché
FRENCH
1 a bargain
2 cheapness
3 cheap
4 cheaply

bon mot
FRENCH, literally 'good word'
a clever remark, a witticism
plural ***bons mots***

bonne
FRENCH
a maid or nursemaid

bonne amie
see BON AMI

bonne à tout faire
FRENCH
a maid of all work

bonne bouche
FRENCH, literally 'good mouth'
a tasty morsel

> not used in this sense in French, where the meaning is 'pleasant taste'

plural ***bonnes bouches***

bonne chance
FRENCH
good luck

bonne compagnie
FRENCH
good society

bonne femme or ***à la bonne femme***
FRENCH
(cookery) cooked simply and garnished with fresh vegetables and herbs

bonne foi
FRENCH
good faith

bonne mine
FRENCH
good appearance, pleasant looks

bonsai
JAPANESE, literally 'tray cultivation'
1 an ornamental dwarf tree growing in a pot, produced by special methods of cultivation
2 the art of growing such trees
plural ***bonsai***

bonsoir
FRENCH
good evening

bon ton
FRENCH
1 the world of fashion
2 good breeding

bon vivant
FRENCH, literally 'good living'
1 a jovial companion
2 a person who lives well, especially one who enjoys fine food and drink
plural ***bons vivants***

bon viveur
FRENCH
a bon vivant, especially a man-about-town

not used in French

bon voyage
FRENCH
have a good journey!

bordello
ITALIAN
a brothel
plural ***bordellos***

bordereau
FRENCH
a memorandum or detailed statement
plural ***bordereaux***

Borgen macht Sorgen
GERMAN
borrowing makes sorrowing

borné
FRENCH
limited, narrow-minded
feminine ***bornée***

borsch, borscht or ***bortsch***
from RUSSIAN *borshch*
a Russian and Polish beetroot soup

bossa nova
PORTUGUESE, literally 'new trend'
1 a dance similar to the samba, originating in Brazil
2 the music for such a dance

bottega
ITALIAN
1 a wine shop
2 an artist's workshop or studio

bouché
FRENCH
1 stoppered
2 corked while still fermenting

bouchée
FRENCH for 'mouthful'
a small pastry

bouclé
FRENCH, meaning 'curled, looped'
1 a yarn consisting of numerous small loops to give a bulky effect
2 a fabric made of such a yarn

bouderie
FRENCH
pouting, sulking

boudoir
FRENCH, literally 'a room for sulking in'
a woman's bedroom or private sitting room

bouffant
FRENCH
1 (said of a hairstyle) with extra height and width, usually through backcombing
2 (said of a sleeve, skirt, etc) puffed out

bouillabaisse
FRENCH, from PROVENÇAL *bouiabaisso*, literally 'boil down'
a rich spicy stew or soup made of fish and vegetables

bouillon
FRENCH
(cookery) clear broth or stock

boules
FRENCH
a form of bowls played on rough surfaces

boulevard
FRENCH
1 a broad road, walk, or promenade bordered with trees
2 a broad main road

> from MIDDLE DUTCH *bolwerc* meaning 'bulwark', so-called because boulevards were originally often built on the ruins of old ramparts

bouleversement
FRENCH
1 an overturning
2 overthrow, ruin

bouquet
FRENCH
1 a bunch of flowers
2 the perfume given off by wine
3 a compliment or expression of praise

bouquet garni
FRENCH, literally 'garnished bouquet'
(cookery) a bunch or sachet of herbs used for flavouring soups, stews, etc, and removed before the dish is served

bourgeois
FRENCH for 'middle-class (person)'
1 a member of the middle class, especially one with capitalist, materialistic, or conventional values
2 middle-class
3 conventional, conservative
4 capitalist, materialistic
feminine **bourgeoise**

bourgeoisie
FRENCH
the middle class of citizens, especially seen as capitalistic, materialistic, etc

bourse
FRENCH for 'purse'
1 an exchange where merchants meet for business
2 any European stock exchange (especially the *Bourse*, the stock exchange in Paris)

boutade
FRENCH
a sudden outburst or fit of temper

boutique
FRENCH
a small shop, or a department in a shop, selling fashionable clothes, etc

bouts rimés
FRENCH, literally 'rhymed ends'
rhyming words given out by someone as the line-endings of a verse, for others to fill up the lines

boyar
from RUSSIAN *boyarin*
a member of the old Russian aristocracy next in rank to the ruling princes, before the reforms of Peter the Great

boyg
NORWEGIAN *bøig*
1 an ogre
2 an obstacle or problem difficult to get to grips with

bozzetto
ITALIAN
a small model or sketch of a projected sculpture
plural ***bozzetti***

brachium civile
LATIN
the civil arm

brachium seculare
LATIN
the secular arm

brasero
SPANISH
1 a brazier
2 a place for burning criminals or heretics
plural ***braseros***

brasserie
FRENCH for 'brewery'
a bar serving food; a simple restaurant

brassière or ***brassiere***
FRENCH
the full form of the word 'bra'

> not currently used in this sense in France

bravura
ITALIAN for 'bravery, spirit'
1 *(music)* a piece of music with difficult and rapid passages
2 spirit and dash in execution
3 a brilliant or daring display

brevet d'invention
FRENCH
a patent

breveté
FRENCH
patented

brevi manu
LATIN, literally 'with a short hand'
offhand

bric-à-brac or ***bricabrac***
FRENCH
old curiosities, knick-knacks, or other treasured odds and ends

brindisi
ITALIAN
1 a toast
2 a drinking-song

brio
ITALIAN
liveliness, vivacity, spirit

brioche
FRENCH
a type of light, soft loaf or roll rich with butter and eggs

➩ the 'cake' of Marie Antoinette's 'Let them eat cake!'

briquette or ***briquet***
FRENCH, literally 'little brick'
1 a small brick made of compressed coal-dust, charcoal, etc, used for fuel
2 a small brick-shaped slab

brise-bise
FRENCH, literally 'wind-break'
a net curtain on the lower half of a window

brise-soleil
FRENCH, literally 'sun-break'
a louvred screen to keep sunlight from walls and windows of buildings

brochette
FRENCH
a skewer or small spit for holding pieces of meat, etc, while roasting or grilling

brochure
FRENCH
a pamphlet or booklet, especially one containing brief or introductory information or publicity material

broderie anglaise
FRENCH, literally 'English embroidery'
openwork embroidery, usually on white cotton or linen

Brotstudien
GERMAN, literally 'bread studies'
studies by which one earns one's living

brouhaha
FRENCH
a loud confused noise; hubbub; uproar

➩ of imitative origin

bruit
FRENCH for 'noise'
1 a rumour or report
2 to rumour or report

brûlé
FRENCH, literally 'burnt'
(cookery) with a coating of caramelized sugar
feminine ***brûlée***

brunette
FRENCH
1 a woman or girl with brown or dark hair
2 (said of hair) dark brown

➩ the masculine form *brunet* is not in general usage

brusque
FRENCH
blunt and abrupt in manner or speech

brut
FRENCH
(said of wines) unsweetened, dry

brutum fulmen
LATIN, literally 'random thunderbolt'
an empty threat
plural ***bruta fulmina***

budo
JAPANESE, literally 'the way of the warrior'
the system or philosophy of the martial art
plural ***budos***

buenas noches
SPANISH
goodnight

buenas tardes
SPANISH
good afternoon

buenos dias
SPANISH
1 good day
2 good morning

buffet
FRENCH
1 a refreshment counter or bar
2 a meal set out on a table, etc, from which the guests serve themselves

buffo
ITALIAN
a comic actor in an opera
plural ***buffi***
feminine ***buffa***, *plural* ***buffe***

bulgur or ***bulghur***
TURKISH
a form of cooked, broken wheat

Bund
GERMAN
a league or confederacy

Bundesbank
GERMAN
the state bank of Germany

Bundesrat
GERMAN
1 the upper house of the parliaments of Germany and Austria
2 the executive council of the federal republic of Switzerland

Bundestag
GERMAN
the lower house of the parliament of Germany

Bundeswehr
GERMAN
the German armed forces

established by the Treaty of Paris (1954–5) under Supreme Allied Command

bunnia or ***bunia***
HINDI
a Hindu merchant

bunraku
JAPANESE
a Japanese form of puppet theatre in which the puppets, usually about one metre high, are each manipulated by three men who remain visible throughout the performance

bunyip
ABORIGINAL
1 a fabulous monster of Australian Aboriginal legend
2 an impostor

buonamano or ***bonamano***
ITALIAN
a tip
plural ***buonamani*** or ***bonamani***

buona sera
ITALIAN
good evening

buon giorno
ITALIAN
good day

buran
RUSSIAN
a violent blizzard blowing from the NE in Siberia and Central Asia

bureau
FRENCH
1 a writing-desk, especially one with pigeonholes, small drawers, etc, concealed behind a sloping front which can be let down to form a writing surface
2 a room or office where a writing-desk is used
3 a department or office, especially one providing services for the public
plural ***bureaux*** or ***bureaus***

bureau de change
FRENCH
an office where currency can be exchanged

burrito
MEXICAN SPANISH, literally 'a young donkey'
a Mexican dish consisting of a flour tortilla, filled with meat, beans, chilli, etc, and folded
plural ***burritos***

burro
SPANISH
a donkey
plural ***burros***

Bursch
GERMAN
a student in a German university
plural ***Burschen***

Burschenschaft
GERMAN
a students' association

bushido
JAPANESE, literally 'warrior doctrine'
the ethical code of the samurai

bustier
FRENCH
a type of tight-fitting usually strapless bodice worn by women

BV
see BENE VALE

bwana
SWAHILI
master; sir

C

c or ***ca***
see CIRCA

cabaret
FRENCH
1 an entertainment at a nightclub or restaurant, with performances by singers, dancers, comedians, etc
2 a nightclub or restaurant where such entertainment is provided

cabochon
FRENCH
a precious stone polished but uncut, or cut without facets
see also EN CABOCHON

cabriole
FRENCH
1 *(ballet)* a leap with one leg outstretched and the other struck against it
2 (said of a furniture leg) ornamentally curved to resemble an animal's leg

cabriolet
FRENCH
1 a light horse-drawn carriage with two wheels and a folding hood
2 formerly, a motor car like a coupé, with folding top

cacciatore
ITALIAN for 'hunter'
(cookery) (said of meat, especially chicken or veal) cooked with tomatoes, mushrooms, onions, and herbs

cache
FRENCH
1 a hiding-place for treasure, provisions, ammunition, etc
2 a hoard

cachepot
FRENCH, literally 'hide-pot'
an ornamental container that conceals the flowerpot of a potted plant

cache-sexe
FRENCH, literally 'hide-sex'
a piece of fabric, etc, covering only the genitals; a G-string

cachet
FRENCH
1 a private seal, especially one affixed to a letter or document
2 *(figurative)* any distinctive stamp or distinguishing characteristic, especially something showing or conferring prestige

cachou
FRENCH
a lozenge sucked or chewed to sweeten the breath

cacoethes
LATIN, from GREEK for 'itch'
1 a bad habit
2 an uncontrollable urge or desire

cacoethes loquendi
LATIN, literally 'an itch for speaking'
a mania for talking, especially for giving speeches

cacoethes scribendi
LATIN, literally 'an itch for writing'
a mania for writing or getting things into print

cadeau
FRENCH
a gift or present
plural ***cadeaux***

cadenza
ITALIAN
(music) an elaborate, sometimes improvised, virtuoso passage performed by a solo instrument or voice, usually towards the end of a concerto movement, aria, etc

cadet
FRENCH
younger or junior
feminine ***cadette***
compare AÎNÉ

cadit quaestio
LATIN, literally 'the question drops'
that is the end of the discussion, there is nothing more to discuss

cadre
FRENCH
an inner group of key personnel in any organization, such as the nucleus of a military unit

caetera desunt
see CETERA DESUNT

caeteris paribus
see CETERIS PARIBUS

cafard
FRENCH for 'cockroach'
depression, the blues

café au lait
FRENCH
1 coffee with milk
2 the light brown colour of this

café-chantant
FRENCH, literally 'singing café'
a café providing musical entertainment

café noir
FRENCH
black coffee (ie without milk)

cafetière
FRENCH
a coffee-pot with a plunger that separates the grounds from the liquid

caftan or ***kaftan***
from TURKISH *qaftān*
1 a long-sleeved Persian or Turkish garment, reaching to the ankles and often tied with a sash
2 a loose-fitting dress of similar design, chiefly worn by Western women

cagoule or ***kagoule***
FRENCH for 'monk's hood, cowl'
a lightweight waterproof hooded garment, often knee-length

in France the word is often used of the balaclava-type mask worn by a robber

cahier
FRENCH
1 a notebook
2 a report, especially of the proceedings of a meeting

caille
FRENCH
(cookery) quail

calamari
ITALIAN, plural of *calamaro* meaning 'squid'
(in Mediterranean cookery) squid

calculus
LATIN for 'little stone'
1 the branch of mathematics concerned with the differentiation and integration of functions
2 a stone-like concretion that forms

in certain parts of the body, such as the kidney or gall bladder

> the Latin word originally referred to one of the pebbles used in counting or calculating

plural ***calculuses*** (sense 1) or ***calculi*** (sense 2)

calembour
FRENCH
a pun

calpa
see KALPA

calpac or ***calpack***
see KALPAK

calzone
ITALIAN
a folded-over pizza
plural ***calzoni*** or ***calzones***

camaraderie
FRENCH
a feeling of friendship and mutual support within a group of people

camarilla
SPANISH, literally 'little room'
a group of people who secretly plot or conspire, especially against legitimate ministers at court; a cabal or coterie

camelot
FRENCH
1 a hawker or pedlar
2 a news-vendor

camera lucida
LATIN, literally 'light chamber'
a device by which the image of an object under a microscope is reflected on a piece of paper so that it may be viewed and drawn simultaneously

camera obscura
LATIN, literally 'dark chamber'
a dark room in which an image of outside objects is projected on a screen

camino real
SPANISH, literally 'royal road'
a main road

camouflage
FRENCH
a means of disguise or concealment using the colour, texture, etc, of natural surroundings

camoufleur
FRENCH
a person or animal skilled in the art of camouflage

campanile
ITALIAN
a bell-tower, especially a tall one detached from a church
plural ***campaniles*** or ***campanili***

campo santo
ITALIAN, literally 'sacred field'
a cemetery

campus
LATIN for 'field'
1 university or college grounds
2 a university or college, especially one in which all the buildings are on a single site
3 the academic world
plural ***campuses***

cañada
SPANISH
a small narrow canyon, especially in the US

canaille
FRENCH
the mob, the rabble, the masses

canapé
▮ FRENCH
1 a small piece of bread, toast, pastry, etc, with a savoury filling or spread, usually served with drinks
2 a sofa

canard
▮ FRENCH for 'duck'
a false rumour, a hoax

cancan
▮ FRENCH for 'chatter, scandal'
a lively dance of French origin, with high kicking and raising of skirts, usually performed on stage by chorus girls

cancionero
▮ SPANISH
a collection of songs or poems
plural ***cancioneros***

ça ne fait rien or ***cela ne fait rien***
▮ FRENCH
it doesn't matter

cannelloni
▮ ITALIAN
hollow tubes of pasta filled with cheese, meat, etc

cantabile
▮ ITALIAN, literally 'suitable for singing'
(music) flowing and melodious

Cantabrigiensis
▮ LATIN
of Cambridge
abbrev **Cantab.**

cantatrice
▮ ITALIAN and FRENCH
a female singer

cante jondo or ***cante hondo***
▮ SPANISH, literally 'intense song'
an emotional and melancholy song sung especially by Andalusian gypsies

cantilena
▮ LATIN
1 a ballad or light song
2 a vocal or instrumental melody

cantina
▮ SPANISH and ITALIAN
1 a bar
2 a wine shop

canto
▮ ITALIAN for 'song'
1 a division of a long poem
2 the part in a piece of music that carries the melody
3 the highest part in a piece of choral music
plural ***cantos***

canto fermo
▮ ITALIAN
a melody, especially plainsong, to which other parts in counterpoint may be added

➪ the Latin equivalent is *cantus firmus*

Cantuaria
▮ LATIN
Canterbury (as the archiepiscopal see of the primate of the Church of England)
abbrev **Cantuar.**

cantus
▮ LATIN for 'song'
1 a melody or chant, especially in medieval ecclesiastical music
2 the highest part in a piece of choral music
plural ***cantus***

cantus firmus
see CANTO FERMO

canzone

ITALIAN

1 a song resembling a madrigal, but less elaborate

2 an instrumental piece of similar character

3 a Provençal or Italian form of lyric poetry

plural ***canzoni***

caoutchouc

FRENCH

raw rubber; the latex of rubber trees

capias

LATIN, literally 'you should seize'

(law) a writ authorizing the arrest of the person named in it

capo d'opera

ITALIAN

a masterpiece

capotasto or ***capo***

from ITALIAN *capo tasto* meaning 'head stop'

a movable device fastened over the fingerboard of a guitar, etc, to alter the pitch of all the strings simultaneously

plural ***capotastos*** or ***capos***

capote

FRENCH

a long cloak or coat, usually with a hood

cappuccino

ITALIAN for 'Capuchin'

1 black coffee with a little milk

2 white coffee made frothy with pressurized steam and often topped with powdered or grated chocolate

> perhaps from the colour of a Capuchin's gown

plural ***cappuccinos***

capriccio

ITALIAN

(music) a free composition that does not follow the rules of any particular form

plural ***capriccios*** or ***capricci***

caprice

FRENCH

1 a sudden change of mind, etc, for no obvious reason

2 a sudden idea or desire; a whim

3 *(music)* a capriccio

caput

LATIN

head

plural ***capita***

see also PER CAPITA

caput mortuum

LATIN, literally 'dead head'

1 the residue of distillation or chemical analysis

2 any worthless residue

carabiner

see KARABINER

carabiniere

ITALIAN

a member of the Italian national police force

plural ***carabinieri***

carafe

FRENCH

1 a water-bottle or wine-flask for the table

2 the amount contained in a carafe

caramba

SPANISH

an exclamation of admiration, annoyance, or surprise

carême or ***Carême***

FRENCH

Lent

caret
LATIN, literally 'there is missing'
(in proofreading, etc) a mark to show where to insert something omitted

carillon
FRENCH
1 a set of bells for playing tunes
2 a melody played on them

carioca
PORTUGUESE
1 a Brazilian dance resembling the tango
2 the tune for such a dance

caritas
LATIN
(Christian) charity

carnet
FRENCH for 'notebook'
1 a customs permit or similar document
2 a book of tickets, vouchers, or coupons

carnifex
LATIN
an executioner

carpe diem
LATIN, literally 'seize the day'
enjoy the present; make the most of today

carte
FRENCH
1 a card
2 a menu
3 a ticket
see also À LA CARTE

carte blanche
FRENCH, literally 'blank card'
unlimited authority or freedom of action

carte des vins
FRENCH
wine list

carte de visite
FRENCH
1 visiting card
2 a small photographic portrait pasted on a card

carte d'identité
FRENCH
identity card

carte du jour
FRENCH
the menu of the day

carte du pays
FRENCH, literally 'map of the country'
the lie of the land

carton-pierre
FRENCH
a kind of papier mâché, imitating stone

casa
ITALIAN and SPANISH
a house

ça saute aux yeux or ***cela saute aux yeux***
FRENCH, literally 'that leaps to the eyes'
it is obvious or self-evident

casbah
see KASBAH

cascara (sagrada)
from SPANISH *cáscara sagrada* meaning 'sacred bark'
the bark of the cascara buckthorn shrub used as a tonic and laxative

casino
ITALIAN, literally 'little house'
an establishment for gambling,

usually with roulette, card games, etc
plural ***casinos***

cassette
FRENCH, literally 'little case'
1 a plastic case containing a reel of audio or video tape, which can be loaded into a suitable machine for recording or playback
2 a lightproof case containing a roll of film for loading into a camera, projector, etc

cassis
FRENCH
a blackcurrant syrup or liqueur

cassone
ITALIAN
a large chest, elaborately carved and painted

cassoulet
FRENCH
a stew consisting of haricot beans, onions, herbs, and various kinds of meat

castrato
ITALIAN
a male singer castrated before puberty to preserve his soprano or alto voice

this practice probably originated in the 16th century at the Vatican to compensate for the lack of female voices in the choirs

plural ***castrati***

casus belli
LATIN
something that causes, involves, or justifies war

casus conscientiae
LATIN
a case of conscience

casus foederis
LATIN
a case that clearly comes within the provisions of a treaty

catachresis
from GREEK *katachrēsis* meaning 'misuse'
misapplication or incorrect usage of a word

catalogue raisonné
FRENCH
a classified descriptive catalogue

cauchemar
FRENCH
a nightmare

caudillo
SPANISH
(in Spanish-speaking countries) a military or political leader
plural ***caudillos***

causa
LATIN
cause

causa causans
LATIN
(law) the immediate cause; the cause in action

causa sine qua non
LATIN
(law) an indispensable cause or condition that allows the causa causans to be operative
see also SINE QUA NON

cause célèbre
FRENCH
1 a legal case or trial that attracts considerable public attention
2 a notorious controversy or highly controversial person
plural ***causes célèbres***

causerie
FRENCH
1 a chat or gossip
2 a short informal article, especially about literature or art, in a newspaper or magazine

c.a.v.
see CURIA ADVISARI VULT

cavaliere servente
ITALIAN
1 a married woman's lover
2 a ladies' man

ça va sans dire or ***cela va sans dire***
FRENCH
that goes without saying; of course

cave
LATIN
beware!

> chiefly used in schoolboy slang

caveat
LATIN, literally 'let him or her beware'
1 a notice or warning
2 a formal request that no action be taken in a particular matter without warning the person lodging the caveat

caveat actor
LATIN
let the doer beware

caveat emptor
LATIN
let the buyer beware; the purchaser bears the responsibility or risk

cave canem
LATIN
beware of the dog

cavendo tutus
LATIN
safe by taking care

ceilidh
GAELIC for 'a visit'
in Scotland and Ireland, an informal evening of song, storytelling, and dancing

> also used in England, of an evening of folk dancing and music

ceinture
FRENCH
a belt

cela ne fait rien
see ÇA NE FAIT RIEN

cela saute aux yeux
see ÇA SAUTE AUX YEUX

cela va sans dire
see ÇA VA SANS DIRE

cendré
FRENCH
ash-blond

ce n'est que le premier pas qui coûte
see IL N'Y A QUE LE PREMIER PAS QUI COÛTE

censor morum
LATIN
censor of morals

census
LATIN for 'register'
an official count of inhabitants, with statistics relating to sex, age, occupation, etc

cento
LATIN for 'patchwork'
1 a composition made up of bits and pieces from various authors

2 a string of commonplace phrases and quotations
plural ***centos*** or ***centones***

cerveza
SPANISH
beer

certum est quia impossibile est
LATIN
it is certain because it is impossible

c'est-à-dire
FRENCH
that is to say

c'est la guerre
FRENCH, literally 'that's war'
that's the way it happens

c'est la vie
FRENCH
that's life

c'est le commencement de la fin
FRENCH
it is the beginning of the end

c'est magnifique, mais ce n'est pas la guerre
FRENCH
it is magnificent, but it is not war

> said at Balaklava by a French general watching the charge of the Light Brigade

c'est pire qu'un crime, c'est une faute
FRENCH
it is worse than a crime, it is a blunder

> attributed to various persons, including Boulay de la Meurthe, on the execution of the Duc d'Enghien in 1804. A variant has *plus*, meaning 'more', in place of *pire*

cestui que trust
OLD FRENCH
a person entitled to the benefit of a trust

cestui que use
OLD FRENCH
a person for whose benefit property is granted in trust to another

cetera desunt or ***caetera desunt***
LATIN
the rest is missing

> referring to the remainder of a manuscript, etc

ceteris paribus or ***caeteris paribus***
LATIN
other things being equal
abbrev **cet. par.**

cf
see CONFER

cha or ***char***
from CHINESE *ch'a*
tea

chacun à son goût or ***à chacun son goût***
FRENCH
everyone to their own taste

chacun à son métier
FRENCH
everyone to their own trade

chadar, chaddar, chuddah or ***chuddar***
from PERSIAN *chaddar* meaning 'a square cloth'
1 the large veil worn by Muslim and Hindu women, covering head and body
2 a cloth spread over a Muslim tomb

chagrin
FRENCH
a feeling of annoyance, disappointment, or embarrassment

chaîné
FRENCH
(ballet) a series of small fast turns, often with the arms extended, used to cross a floor or stage

chaise-longue
FRENCH, literally 'long chair'
a couch with a back at one end only and a short armrest, designed for lying on

chakra
from SANSKRIT *cakra* meaning 'wheel'
1 a disc-shaped knife used as a missile
2 a disc representing the sun, as in portrayals of Hindu gods
3 (in yoga) a centre of spiritual power in the body

chalaza
GREEK for 'hail, lump'
in a bird's egg, one of two spiral chords of albumen that hold the yolk sac in position
plural ***chalazas*** or ***chalazae***

chalet
FRENCH
1 a style of house typical of the Swiss Alps, usually built of wood, with a heavy, sloping, wide-eaved roof
2 a small house built for use by holidaymakers, etc

chambré
FRENCH
(said of wine) at room temperature

most red wines are traditionally served *chambré*

champlevé
from FRENCH *champ levé* meaning 'raised field'
a type of enamel work in which engraved channels on a metal base are filled with vitreous powders before firing

Champs Elysées
FRENCH for 'Elysian Fields'
a famous avenue in Paris

chandelle
FRENCH for 'candle'
a sharp upward turn of an aircraft using momentum to achieve the maximum rate of climb

chanoyu
JAPANESE, literally 'hot water for tea'
a Japanese tea ceremony

chanson
FRENCH
a song

chanson de geste
FRENCH, literally 'song of deeds'
a type of French epic poem popular in the Middle Ages, usually celebrating the exploits of knights

chantage
FRENCH
blackmail, the extortion of money by threatening to make scandalous facts public

chanteuse
FRENCH
a female nightclub singer

chaparajos or ***chaparejos***
MEXICAN SPANISH
a cowboy's leather riding leggings
abbrev **chaps**

chaparral
SPANISH
a thicket of dense tangled brushwood

chapati or ***chapatti***
HINDI
(in Indian cookery) a thin flat piece of unleavened bread

chapeau
FRENCH
a hat
plural ***chapeaux***

chapeaux bas
FRENCH
hats off!

chapelle ardente
FRENCH, literally 'burning chapel'
a chapel or room in which a corpse lies in state before burial, surrounded by lighted candles

chaperon or ***chaperone***
FRENCH
1 an older woman accompanying a younger unmarried one on social occasions, for the sake of respectability
2 someone who supervises a group of children or young people, eg on school outings, etc

> the French word originally meant 'hood': *le Petit Chaperon Rouge* is Little Red Riding Hood

chappal
HINDI
a type of open sandal worn in India, with a single leather strap between the first and second toes

char
see CHA

charabanc or ***char-à-banc***
from FRENCH *char à bancs* meaning 'carriage with benches'
1 (formerly) a long open vehicle with rows of transverse seats
2 a tourist coach
plural ***charabancs, char-à-bancs*** or ***chars-à-bancs***

charade
FRENCH for 'riddle'
a ridiculous pretence

> in the party game *charades* players act out the syllables of a word, or the words of a phrase, in successive scenes

charcuterie
FRENCH
1 a pork-butcher's shop
2 a delicatessen
3 the meats sold in either of these shops

chargé(-d'affaires)
FRENCH
1 a diplomatic agent of lesser rank
2 the person in charge of a diplomatic mission in the absence of the ambassador
plural ***chargés(-d'affaires)***

charisma
GREEK
1 a personal quality that enables an individual to impress and influence others
2 a similar quality felt to reside in an office or position
3 a spiritual power given by God

charivari
FRENCH
1 a cacophonous mock serenade, originally to newly-weds, using kettles, pans, lids, etc
2 a cacophony of sound, a din

> from LATIN *caribaria* meaning 'headache'

charka or ***charkha***
HINDI
a spinning wheel used in Indian households for spinning cotton

charqui
QUECHUA
beef cut into long strips and dried in the sun

chassé
FRENCH
a gliding step in dancing

chasse(-café)
FRENCH, literally 'chase away (coffee)'
a spirit or liqueur taken after coffee

chasseur
FRENCH
1 a hunter
2 a liveried attendant, especially in hotels
3 *(cookery)* cooked in a sauce containing mushrooms, shallots, white wine, and herbs

chassis
FRENCH
1 the structural framework of a car, to which the working parts and body are attached
2 the framework of a radio, television, etc
3 an aeroplane's landing-carriage

château
FRENCH
1 a castle or large country house, especially in France
2 a vineyard estate around a castle, house, etc, especially in the Bordeaux region

used in the names of wines from specific estates, eg *Château Lafite*, *Château Margaux*, etc

plural ***châteaux***

châteaux en Espagne
FRENCH
castles in Spain, castles in the air

châtelain
FRENCH
the keeper of a castle, lord of the manor

châtelaine
FRENCH
1 a female keeper or mistress of a castle or a large household
2 an ornamental bunch of short chains bearing keys, scissors, etc, attached to a woman's belt

chaton
FRENCH
the setting or stone of a ring

chatoyant
FRENCH
(said of gems, plumage, etc) iridescent, shimmering

chaudfroid
FRENCH, literally 'hot-cold'
(cookery)
1 a jellied sauce
2 a dish of chicken, etc, coated with this sauce

chauffeur
FRENCH, literally 'stoker'
a person employed to drive a car
feminine ***chauffeuse***

chef (de cuisine)
FRENCH, literally 'head (of the kitchen)'
a cook, especially the head cook in a hotel or restaurant

chef d'oeuvre
FRENCH
a masterpiece
plural ***chefs d'oeuvre***

chemin de fer
FRENCH for 'railway'
a variation of the card-game baccarat

chemise
FRENCH
1 a woman's shirt-like undergarment
2 a straight, loose-fitting dress

chenet
FRENCH
an andiron

chenille
FRENCH for 'caterpillar'
1 a thick, velvety cord or yarn of silk or wool
2 a velvet-like material used for table covers, etc

cheongsam
CHINESE (CANTONESE), literally 'long dress'
a tight-fitting, high-necked dress with slits at the sides, worn by Chinese women

cher
FRENCH
dear
feminine **chère**

cherchez la femme
FRENCH, literally 'look for the woman'
there's a woman at the bottom of it

chère amie
FRENCH, literally 'dear friend'
a mistress, a female lover

chéri
FRENCH
darling

chiefly used as a term of address

feminine **chérie**

chernozem
RUSSIAN, literally 'black earth'
a very fertile soil, rich in humus and calcium salts, found in cool regions with low humidity

che sarà sarà
ITALIAN
what will be will be

cheval de bataille
FRENCH for 'warhorse'
a favourite topic or subject, a hobby-horse

chevalier
FRENCH
1 a cavalier
2 a knight
3 a gallant

chevalier d'industrie
FRENCH, literally 'knight of industry'
an adventurer, a swindler, a person who lives by their wits

chevaux-de-frise
FRENCH, literally 'horses of Friesland'
a row of iron spikes or something similar, such as pieces of broken glass, along the top of a wall

originally (in the singular form *cheval-de-frise*) applied to a defensive structure of iron spikes set in wood, used to stop cavalry

chevelure
FRENCH
1 a head of hair
2 a hairstyle

cheville
FRENCH
1 *(music)* the peg of a stringed instrument
2 a redundant word or expression used in a verse or sentence for the purpose of metre or balance only

chevron
FRENCH for 'rafter'
1 a V-shaped band on the sleeve of a military uniform
2 (on a road sign) a horizontal white V-shape on a black background indicating a sharp bend

chez
FRENCH
at the home or establishment of

chez nous
FRENCH
at our house, at home

chi or ***ch'i***
see QI

chiaroscuro
ITALIAN, literally 'bright dark'
(art)
1 the use of strong highlighting and dark shadow in a picture
2 a painting in black and white
plural ***chiaroscuros***

chibouk or ***chibouque***
from TURKISH *chibūk*
a long, straight-stemmed Turkish tobacco pipe

chic
FRENCH
1 style, elegance
2 smart, elegant, and fashionable

chicane
FRENCH, literally 'sharp practice at law'
1 a trick or trickery
2 a series of sharp bends on a motor-racing track

chichi or ***chi-chi***
FRENCH
1 pretentious, fussy, affected
2 stylish, self-consciously fashionable

chiffon
FRENCH for 'rag'
a thin fine fabric of silk, nylon, etc

chiffonnier
FRENCH
1 an ornamental cabinet
2 a chest of drawers

chignon
FRENCH
a soft bun or coil of hair worn at the back of the neck

chilli con carne, chili con carne or ***chile con carne***
NAHUATL
a spicy dish of minced meat, beans, tomatoes, etc, cooked with chillis or chilli powder, originating in Mexico

chimera or ***chimaera***
LATIN, from GREEK *chimaira* meaning 'she-goat'
1 any idle or wild fancy
2 (in Greek mythology) a fire-breathing monster with a lion's head, a serpent's tail, and a goat's body

chiné
FRENCH, literally 'dyed in a (supposedly) Chinese way'
(said of fabric) mottled, with the pattern printed on the warp

chinoiserie
FRENCH
1 a style of design or decoration that uses or copies Chinese motifs or methods
2 an object or ornament in this style

chinovnik
RUSSIAN
1 a high official in the Russian civil service
2 a bureaucrat

chipolata
FRENCH, from ITALIAN *cipollata* meaning 'onion-flavoured sausage'
a small sausage used as a garnish, etc

chiyogami
JAPANESE
hand-printed patterned Japanese paper

chop suey
CHINESE, literally 'mixed bits'
a Chinese-style dish made up of chopped meat, beansprouts, etc, fried in sesame oil

chorizo
SPANISH
a dry, highly-seasoned pork sausage

chose jugée
FRENCH
something already decided or settled, so that any further discussion is futile or unnecessary

chota
ANGLO-INDIAN, from HINDI *chhotá*
1 small, little
2 younger, junior

chota hazri
ANGLO-INDIAN, from HINDI
an early light breakfast of tea, toast, and usually fruit

chou
FRENCH for 'cabbage'
1 a cream bun
2 *(informal)* dear, pet
plural **choux**

> the plural form is also used of a type of very light, rich pastry made with flour, butter, and eggs

chow mein
CHINESE, literally 'fried noodles'
a Chinese-style dish of seasoned shredded meat and vegetables, served with fried noodles

chronique scandaleuse
FRENCH
1 a story full of scandalous events or details
2 unsavoury gossip

chuddah or ***chuddar***
see CHADAR

churidars
HINDI
tight-fitting trousers worn by Indian men and women

chutzpah or ***hutzpah***
HEBREW and YIDDISH
effrontery, brazenness, impudence

Cia.
see COMPAGNIA, COMPAÑÍA

ciao
ITALIAN
an informal greeting or farewell
plural **ciaos**

cicerone
ITALIAN
a guide who shows visitors and sightseers around a place of interest

> from the name of *Cicero*, the Roman orator, statesman, and man of letters

plural **ciceroni** or **cicerones**

cicisbeo
ITALIAN
the acknowledged lover of a married woman
plural **cicisbei**

ci-devant
FRENCH, literally 'before this'
1 former
2 formerly

Cie.
see COMPAGNIE

ci-gît
FRENCH
here lies ...

followed by the name of the dead person on tombstones, monuments, etc

ciment fondu
FRENCH, literally 'cast (or melted) cement'
a type of rapid-hardening cement with a high aluminium content

cinéaste, cineaste or ***cineast***
FRENCH
1 a person who takes an artistic interest in the cinema
2 a film-maker

cinéma vérité or ***ciné vérité***
FRENCH, literally 'cinema truth'
realism in films achieved by filming scenes from real life, or scenes that have the appearance of real life

cinquecento
ITALIAN, literally 'five hundred'
the 16th century, especially with reference to Italian art and architecture of the Renaissance period

the Italian word refers to the 1500s, *mille* meaning 'one thousand' being understood

circa
LATIN
about, around
abbrev **c, ca, cir., circ.**

circuitus verborum
LATIN
a circumlocution

ciré
FRENCH for 'waxed'
a fabric with a highly glazed finish

cire perdue
FRENCH, literally 'lost wax'
a method of casting in metal, the mould being formed round a wax model which is then melted away

clair de lune
FRENCH for 'moonlight'
1 a type of bluish porcelain glaze
2 porcelain glazed with this
3 a type of shiny bluish glass

claque
FRENCH
1 a group of hired applauders
2 sycophantic supporters

claqueur
FRENCH
1 a hired applauder
2 a sycophantic supporter

cliché
FRENCH
1 a stereotyped phrase
2 a hackneyed idea, plot, situation, etc
3 *(printing)* an electrotype or stereotype plate

in France the word is also used of a photographic negative

clique
FRENCH
a group of friends, professional colleagues, etc, who are hostile to outsiders; a faction or coterie

clochard
FRENCH
a tramp

cloche
FRENCH for 'bell'
1 a glass or plastic cover, originally bell-shaped, under which plants are forced or protected from frost, etc
2 a woman's close-fitting hat

cloisonné
FRENCH
1 a type of decorative enamelwork, the pattern being formed in wire and filled with coloured enamel
2 decorated with such enamelwork

cloture
from FRENCH *clôture* meaning 'closure'
a method of ending a debate in a legislative assembly, usually by calling for a vote

> chiefly used in the US

clou
FRENCH for 'nail'
1 the main point of interest, the centre of attraction
2 a dominant idea

cocotte
FRENCH
1 a small ovenproof dish, usually for an individual portion
2 a prostitute

> from a child's word for a hen, from *coq* meaning 'cock'

see also GRANDE COCOTTE

coda
ITALIAN, from LATIN *cauda* meaning 'tail'
1 *(music)* a passage at the end of a piece that brings it to a satisfactory conclusion
2 any similar passage or piece in a story, dance sequence, etc

codex
LATIN
1 a code
2 a manuscript volume
plural ***codices***

cogito, ergo sum
LATIN
I think, therefore I am

> the basic tenet of Descartes' philosophy

cognoscente
ITALIAN
1 a person professing an expert knowledge, especially of art, music, literature, etc
2 a connoisseur

> the modern Italian form is *conoscente*

plural ***cognoscenti***

cognovit
LATIN, literally 'he or she has acknowledged'
(law) an acknowledgement by a defendant that the plaintiff's cause is just

coiffeur
FRENCH
a hairdresser
feminine ***coiffeuse***

coiffure
FRENCH
a hairstyle

coitus interruptus
LATIN
the deliberate withdrawal of the penis from the vagina before ejaculation

collage
FRENCH, literally 'pasting'
1 a picture made from scraps of paper, fabric, etc, glued to a background

2 the art or method of producing such works

➪ first used by Picasso around 1912

coll' arco
see ARCO

collectanea
LATIN
a collection of passages from various sources; a miscellany

col legno
ITALIAN, literally 'with the wood'
(music) an instruction to string players to use the wood of the bow

colloquium
LATIN
a conference; a meeting for discussion; a seminar

plural **colloquia** or **colloquiums**

cologne
see EAU DE COLOGNE

coloratura
ITALIAN for 'colouring'
(music) embellished vocal passages including runs, trills, etc

colporteur
FRENCH
a pedlar, especially one selling religious tracts and books

comble
FRENCH
the acme, the highest point of excellence, success, etc

➪ in French the word usually refers to something undesirable, such as the height of misfortune or stupidity

comédie humaine
FRENCH, literally 'human comedy'
1 the comedy of human life

2 contemporary society

➪ from the title of a series of novels by the 19th-century French writer Honoré de Balzac, intended to form a complete picture of contemporary society

comédie larmoyante
FRENCH
sentimental comedy

comédie noire
FRENCH
black comedy

comme ci comme ça
FRENCH
so-so, neither good nor bad

commedia dell'arte
ITALIAN
Italian Renaissance comedy, mainly improvised with stock characters

comme il faut
FRENCH
1 as it should be; proper; correct; approved by the fashionable world

2 genteel, well-bred

commis
FRENCH
1 an agent or deputy

2 an apprentice waiter, steward, or chef

commode
FRENCH
1 a chair containing a chamberpot

2 an ornamental chest of drawers

➪ not used in sense 1 in France

communautaire or ***communitaire***
FRENCH
in keeping with or appropriate to the aims and principles of the European Community

commune bonum
LATIN
the good of all, the common good

communibus annis
LATIN
on the annual average

communi consensu
LATIN
by common consent

communiqué or ***communique***
FRENCH
an official announcement or bulletin, especially one given to the media

compadre
SPANISH for 'godfather'
a male friend or companion

Compagnia
ITALIAN
Company
abbrev **Cia.**

Compagnie
FRENCH
Company
abbrev **Cie.**

compagnon de voyage
FRENCH
a travelling companion

Compañia
SPANISH
Company
abbrev **Cia.**

compère
FRENCH, literally 'godfather'
a person who presents a radio or television show, introduces performers, etc

> not used in this sense in modern French, where the word means 'partner, accomplice, mate, fellow'

compos mentis
LATIN
of sound mind, sane
see also NON COMPOS MENTIS

compote
FRENCH
(a dessert of) fruit stewed in sugar or syrup

comprador or ***compradore***
PORTUGUESE for 'buyer'
1 (especially in China and the Far East) a native agent through whom a foreign firm trades
2 an agent of a foreign power

compte rendu
FRENCH, literally 'account rendered'
an official report

con.
see CONTRA

con amore
ITALIAN
(music)
1 with love or tenderness
2 heartily

conatus
LATIN
1 an effort or striving
2 a natural impulse or tendency
plural ***conatus***

con brio
ITALIAN
(music)

1 with vivacity
2 forcefully

concertante
ITALIAN
(music)
1 a symphonic composition in which two or more solo instruments or voices take the principal parts alternately
2 (said of a composition) providing an opportunity for brilliant virtuosity

concertino
ITALIAN
a short concerto
plural ***concertinos***

concerto
ITALIAN
a composition for one or more solo instruments and orchestra
plural ***concertos*** or ***concerti***

concerto grosso
ITALIAN
a musical work in which solo parts played by a small group of instruments alternate with passages for the full orchestra
plural ***concerti grossi***

concetto
ITALIAN for 'conceit'
1 an ingenious turn of expression
2 a flash of wit
3 a fanciful, ingenious, or witty idea
plural ***concetti***

conchiglie
ITALIAN for 'seashells'
shell-shaped pasta

concierge
FRENCH
1 a warden
2 a janitor

concours
FRENCH
1 a contest, competition
2 a competitive examination
3 a meeting

concours d'élégance
FRENCH
a competition among cars in which marks are allotted for appearance, not speed

condottiere
ITALIAN
a leader or member of band of mercenaries
plural ***condottieri***

con espressione
ITALIAN
(music) with expression

confer
LATIN
compare
abbrev **cf**

> the abbreviation is the usual form

conférence
FRENCH
a lecture

conférencier
FRENCH
a lecturer

confetti
ITALIAN, plural of *confetto* meaning 'sweet'
1 small pieces of coloured paper thrown at a wedding
2 small pieces of coloured paper (originally sweets) thrown at a carnival in Italy

confrère
FRENCH
a colleague, fellow member, or associate

confrérie
FRENCH
a brotherhood

con fuoco
ITALIAN, literally 'with fire'
(music) spiritedly

congé
FRENCH
1 permission to depart
2 dismissal, discharge
3 leave of absence

congé d'élire
FRENCH
1 permission to elect a nominated candidate
2 formal permission granted to a dean and chapter to elect a certain person as bishop

con moto
ITALIAN, literally 'with movement'
(music) briskly

connoisseur
FRENCH
a person with a well-informed appreciation of fine food and wine, the arts, etc

> the modern French form is *connaisseur*

conquistador
SPANISH
a conqueror, especially one of the 16th-century Spanish conquerors of Mexico and S America
plural ***conquistadors*** or ***conquistadores***

conseil
FRENCH
1 advice
2 council

conseil d'administration
FRENCH
a board of directors

conseil de famille
FRENCH
a family consultation

conseil d'état
FRENCH
a council of state

conservatoire
FRENCH
a school of music

consommé
FRENCH
a clear soup made from meat stock

con sordino
ITALIAN
(music) played with a mute

con spirito
ITALIAN
(music) with spirit

constantia et virtute
LATIN
by constancy and virtue

contadino
ITALIAN
an Italian peasant
plural ***contadini***
feminine ***contadina,*** *plural* ***contadine***

conte
FRENCH
a short story (as a literary genre)

continuum
LATIN
a continuous sequence; an unbroken progression
plural ***continuums*** or ***continua***

contorno
ITALIAN
a contour or outline
plural ***contornos***

contra
LATIN
against
abbrev **con.**

contra bonos mores
LATIN
contrary to good manners or morals
abbrev (informal) **cont. bon. mor.**

contra jus gentium
LATIN
against the law of nations

contralto
ITALIAN
1 the lowest female singing voice
2 a singer with such a voice
3 a part for such a voice
plural ***contralti*** or ***contraltos***

contra mundum
LATIN
against the world

contra pacem
LATIN
against the peace

contrapposto
ITALIAN
(art) a pose of the human body with hips, shoulders, and head in different planes
plural ***contrappostos***

contrat
FRENCH
a contract; an agreement

contrat aléatoire
FRENCH
(in French law) conditional contract

contrat de vente
FRENCH
contract of sale

contrat social
FRENCH
social contract

contrecoup
FRENCH for 'counterblow'
1 repercussion
2 *(medicine)* an injury, especially to the brain within the skull, resulting from a blow on the side opposite to it

contretemps
FRENCH
1 an awkward or embarrassing moment, situation, etc
2 a setback or hitch
3 a slight disagreement

contrôlé
FRENCH
1 registered
2 hallmarked

convenable
FRENCH
conforming to etiquette

convenances
FRENCH
conventional usages or social proprieties, etiquette

conversazione
ITALIAN
a meeting for conversation, especially intellectual discussion
plural ***conversaziones*** or ***conversazioni***

copia verborum
LATIN, literally 'plenty of words'
fluency, prolixity

coq au vin
FRENCH, literally 'cock in wine'
a dish of chicken cooked in red wine with onions, herbs, garlic, etc

coquette
FRENCH
a woman who flirts

coquille
FRENCH
1 a scallop or other seafood served in a scallop shell
2 a dish or pastry case in the shape of a scallop shell

coram
LATIN
before; in the presence of

coram domino rege
LATIN
before our lord the king

coram nobis
LATIN
before us (ie the monarch), in our presence

coram paribus
LATIN
before equals, before one's peers

coram populo
LATIN
in the presence of the people; publicly

cor anglais
FRENCH, literally 'English horn'
a woodwind instrument similar to the oboe, but lower in pitch

> despite the name, the instrument is probably not English

plural ***cors anglais***

cordon bleu
FRENCH, literally 'blue ribbon'
1 a person of distinction, especially a cook of the highest standard
2 (said of a cook or cookery) of the highest standard

> from the blue ribbon worn by the knights of the French Order of the Holy Ghost

cordon sanitaire
FRENCH, literally 'sanitary cordon'
1 a line of sentries posted to restrict passage into and out of an area where there is contagious disease
2 neutral states keeping hostile states apart
3 any barrier isolating a state, etc, that is considered dangerous

corniche
FRENCH
1 a coast road built along the edge of a cliff
2 in Egypt, a boulevard along a bank of the Nile

corno
ITALIAN
1 horn
2 the French horn
plural ***corni***

corona
LATIN
1 a crown or crownlike structure
2 a coloured ring round the sun or moon
3 the outer atmosphere of the sun, observable during total eclipse
plural ***coronas*** or ***coronae***

corona lucis
LATIN, literally 'crown of light'
a round chandelier, as hung from the roof of a church

corps
FRENCH for 'body'
1 a division of an army forming a tactical unit; a branch or department of an army
2 an organized body; a group of people working more or less together
plural ***corps***

corps de ballet
FRENCH
the company of ballet dancers at a theatre

corps d'élite
FRENCH
a small number of people picked out as the best of a group

corps diplomatique
FRENCH
the entire diplomatic staff of all the embassies in a capital or state

Corpus Christi
LATIN, literally 'body of Christ'
the festival in honour of the Eucharist, held on the Thursday after Trinity Sunday

corpus delicti
LATIN, literally 'body of the offence'
(law) the substance or fundamental facts of the crime or offence

> for example, in a murder trial, the fact that someone is actually dead and has been murdered. The phrase is sometimes wrongly used of the corpse itself

corpus juris
LATIN
a body of law, eg of a country or jurisdiction

Corpus Juris Canonici
LATIN
the body of the canon law

Corpus Juris Civilis
LATIN
the body of the civil law

corpus vile
LATIN, literally 'worthless body'
a person or thing considered to be expendable, and therefore a fit subject for experimentation
plural ***corpora vilia***

corral
SPANISH
1 a pen for cattle
2 an enclosure to drive hunted animals into
3 a defensive ring of wagons

corrida (de toros)
SPANISH
a bullfight

corrigendum
LATIN
something to be corrected, especially a correction to be made in a book
plural ***corrigenda***

corruptio optimi pessima
LATIN
the corruption of the best is the worst of all

cortège
FRENCH
1 a train of attendants, a retinue
2 a procession, especially a funeral procession

Cosa Nostra
ITALIAN, literally 'our thing'
the Mafia organization, especially in the US

così fan tutte
ITALIAN
that is what all women do; all women are like that

> the title of an opera by Mozart

côtelette
FRENCH
a cutlet, a chop

coterie
FRENCH
an exclusive group of people with a common interest, especially a social or literary circle

> originally a number of peasants holding land jointly from a lord

cottage orné
FRENCH
an ornately designed small country house built in rustic style

couchette
FRENCH
a sleeping-berth on a train or boat, convertible from and into an ordinary seat

couleur de rose
FRENCH
1 rose-coloured
2 seen or presented in a favourable or optimistic light

> also used as a noun

coulis
FRENCH
a thin purée of fruit, vegetables, fish, or meat

coup
FRENCH
1 a blow, a stroke
2 a sudden action or motion
3 a masterstroke, a clever and successful stratagem
4 a coup d'état

coup de bonheur
FRENCH
1 a stroke of luck
2 a lucky hit or shot

coup d'éclat
FRENCH
a bold stroke

coup de foudre
FRENCH, literally 'stroke of lightning'
1 a sudden and surprising occurrence
2 love at first sight

coup de grâce
FRENCH, literally 'stroke of mercy'
1 a finishing stroke, especially a death blow
2 a death blow to put the victim out of pain

coup de main
FRENCH, literally 'blow with the hand'
a sudden vigorous attack

coup de maître
FRENCH
a masterstroke

coup de poing
FRENCH
a blow or punch with the fist

coup d'essai
FRENCH
1 an experimental work
2 a first attempt

coup d'état
FRENCH, literally 'stroke of state'
the sudden, often violent, overthrow of a government
plural ***coups d'état***

coup de théâtre
FRENCH
1 a sudden and sensational turn of events
2 a dramatic theatrical effect

coup d'oeil
FRENCH, literally 'stroke of the eye'
a general view at a glance

coupe

FRENCH

1 a dessert, usually made with fruit and ice cream, served in a glass bowl

2 a glass container for serving such a dessert, usually with a shallow bowl and a short stem

coupé

FRENCH, literally 'cut'

a two-door car with a sloping roof at the rear

couscous

FRENCH, from ARABIC *kuskus*

1 hard wheat semolina

2 a N African dish of steamed couscous with meat, vegetables, etc

coûte que coûte

FRENCH

cost what it may

couturier

FRENCH

a dressmaker or dress designer

feminine **couturière**

couvert

FRENCH

a cover (at table, ie a place setting)

crambe repetita

LATIN

cold cabbage warmed up; stale repetitions

craquelure

FRENCH

1 the fine cracks that appear in the varnish or pigment of old paintings

2 this effect or pattern

crèche

FRENCH for 'manger'

1 a nursery for the care of young children while their parents are otherwise occupied

2 a model representing the scene of Christ's nativity

credenza

ITALIAN

1 a sideboard

2 a bookcase, especially one without legs

credo

LATIN, literally 'I believe'

a belief or set of beliefs

plural **credos**

crème

FRENCH

cream

> applied to various creamy substances

crème brûlée

FRENCH, literally 'burnt cream'

a dessert made from egg yolks, cream, and vanilla topped with caramelized sugar

crème caramel

FRENCH

an egg custard baked in a dish lined with caramel

crème de la crème

FRENCH, literally 'cream of the cream'

the very best

crème de menthe

FRENCH

a green peppermint-flavoured liqueur

crème fraîche

FRENCH, literally 'fresh cream'

cream thickened with a culture of bacteria

crêpe

FRENCH

a thin pancake

crêpe suzette or ***crêpe Suzette***
FRENCH
a thin pancake in a hot orange-flavoured sauce, usually flambéed
plural ***crêpes suzettes*** or ***crêpes Suzette***

crescendo
ITALIAN for 'increasing'
1 *(music)* gradually increasing in loudness
2 *(music)* an increase of loudness; a passage of increasing loudness
3 *(figurative)* a high point, a climax
plural ***crescendos***

crevasse
FRENCH
a crack or split, especially a cleft in a glacier

crève-coeur
FRENCH
heartbreak

crevette
FRENCH
a shrimp or prawn

criant or ***criard***
FRENCH for 'crying'
garish

cri de coeur
from FRENCH *cri du coeur*
a cry from the heart; a heartfelt appeal, complaint, or reproach

crimen
LATIN
a crime
plural ***crimina***

crimen falsi
LATIN
the crime or charge of perjury

crimen laesae majestatis
LATIN, literally 'crime of injured majesty'
high treason
see also LESE-MAJESTÉ

crime passionnel
FRENCH
a crime prompted by passion, especially sexual desire, jealousy, infidelity, etc

crise (de coeur)
FRENCH
an emotional crisis

crise de conscience
FRENCH
a crisis of conscience, a moral dilemma

crise de foi
FRENCH
an attack of doubt, distrust, or disillusionment

crise de nerfs
FRENCH
an attack of nerves or hysteria

critique
FRENCH
1 the art of criticism
2 a critical analysis of a work of literature, art, etc

crochet
FRENCH for 'little hook'
1 decorative work consisting of loops of wool or thread intertwined with a hooked needle
2 to work in crochet

croissant
FRENCH for 'crescent'
a crescent-shaped bread roll with a flaky consistency, made with a high proportion of butter

croix de guerre
FRENCH
a military decoration for bravery in action

croque-monsieur
FRENCH
a toasted sandwich filled with ham and cheese

croquette
FRENCH
a ball or roll of minced meat or fish, mashed potato, etc, coated in breadcrumbs and fried

croquis
FRENCH
an outline or rough sketch

croupier
FRENCH
a person who presides over a gaming-table, collecting the stakes and paying the winners

croûte
FRENCH for 'crust'
a thick slice of fried bread used as a base or garnish
see also EN CROÛTE

croûton
FRENCH
a small cube of fried bread used in soups and salads

cru
FRENCH
1 a vineyard or group of vineyards
2 a vintage
see also GRAND CRU

crudités
FRENCH
raw vegetables served as an hors d'oeuvre

crux
LATIN for 'cross'
1 a cross
2 a puzzle, problem, or difficulty
3 a decisive, crucial, or essential point
plural ***cruxes*** or ***cruces***

crux ansata
LATIN
a T-shaped cross with a loop at the top, the ankh

crux criticorum
LATIN
a puzzle for the critics

crux decussata
LATIN
an X-shaped cross, such as the cross of St Andrew or St Patrick

crux medicorum
LATIN
a puzzle for the doctors

csárdás or ***czardas***
HUNGARIAN
1 a Hungarian dance
2 music for this dance in two movements, one slow and one fast

cuadrilla
SPANISH for 'gang, troop'
the attendants of a matador

cuesta
SPANISH
a hill ridge with a steep scarp on one side and a gradual slope on the other

cui bono?
LATIN
for whose good is it?; who will gain by it?

> sometimes wrongly used to mean 'for what purpose?'

cui malo?
LATIN
whom will it harm?

cuique suum
LATIN
to each his own

cuir-bouilli
FRENCH
leather that has been boiled or soaked in hot water and moulded, originally used for armour

cuisine
FRENCH
1 a kitchen
2 the art or style of cooking
3 the dishes cooked
see also NOUVELLE CUISINE

cuisine bourgeoise
FRENCH
plain cooking

cuisine minceur
FRENCH, literally 'slimness cookery'
a style of cooking characterized by imaginative use of light, simple ingredients

cul-de-sac
FRENCH, literally 'bottom of bag'
a road that is closed at one end; a dead end

> in France the word *impasse* is preferred

culottes
from FRENCH *culotte* meaning 'breeches'
a divided skirt; women's trousers or shorts designed to look like a skirt
see also SANSCULOTTE

culpa lata
LATIN
gross negligence

culpa levis
LATIN
1 a fault of little importance
2 excusable neglect

cum
LATIN
with

cum grano salis
LATIN, literally 'with a grain of salt'
with a pinch of salt, ie with caution or suspicion

cum laude
LATIN
with distinction (used on a diploma to denote special merit or the lowest grade of honours)
see also MAGNA CUM LAUDE, SUMMA CUM LAUDE

cum multis aliis
LATIN
with many other things

cum notis variorum
LATIN
with the notes of various critics or commentators

> often shortened to *variorum*, as in *a variorum edition*

cum privilegio
LATIN
with privilege

cupola
ITALIAN
1 a spherical vault or concave ceiling on the top of a building
2 a dome or dome-shaped structure
3 a furnace used in iron foundries

curé
FRENCH
a parish priest in France

curia
LATIN
1 the court of the papal see

2 one of the ten divisions of a Roman tribe
3 a building in which the Roman senate met
4 a provincial senate

curia advisari vult

LATIN
(law) the court wishes to be advised, or to consider
abbrev **c.a.v., cur. adv. vult.**

curragh

IRISH GAELIC
a coracle

currente calamo

LATIN, literally 'with a running pen'
written freely and easily, without preparation

curriculum

LATIN
a course, especially the course of study at a school, college, university, etc
plural ***curricula*** or ***curriculums***

curriculum vitae

LATIN, literally 'course of life'
a biographical summary of someone's life, especially written details of education and achievements supplied to potential employers
abbrev **cv, CV**

custos

LATIN
a guardian, custodian, or keeper
plural ***custodes***

custos rotulorum

LATIN
keeper of the rolls

cuvée

FRENCH
1 a vat of blended wine of uniform quality
2 the contents of such a vat

cwm

WELSH
(geography) a deep rounded hollow with steep sides formed through erosion by snow and ice

cy pres

OLD FRENCH, literally 'so near'
(law) the principle of following as closely as possible the wishes of a donor or testator when what is actually specified is impracticable

czar, czarevich, czarevitch, czarevna, czarina, czaritsa

see TSAR, TSAREVICH, etc

czardas

see CSÁRDÁS

D

da capo
ITALIAN, literally 'from the head or beginning'
(music) an indication that the performer must return to the beginning of the piece
abbrev **DC**

d'accord
FRENCH
1 agreed
2 in tune

dacha
RUSSIAN for 'gift (especially from a ruler)'
a country house or cottage in Russia

dacoit or ***dakoit***
from HINDI *dakait*
one of a gang of robbers in India and Burma

daftar
HINDI
1 (in India) an office, especially a military orderly room
2 a bundle of documents

Dáil (Eireann)
IRISH for 'assembly (of Ireland)'
the lower house of the legislature of the Republic of Ireland

daimio
JAPANESE, literally 'great name'
a Japanese territorial noble under the old feudal system
plural ***daimios***

dalai lama
from MONGOLIAN *dalai* meaning 'ocean' and TIBETAN *lama* meaning 'high-priest'
the head of the Tibetan Buddhist hierarchy
see also LAMA

dal segno
ITALIAN, literally 'from the sign'
(music) an indication that the performer must return to the *segno* sign
abbrev **DS**

dame
FRENCH
woman, lady

dame d'honneur
FRENCH
maid of honour

dames de la halle
FRENCH
market women

damnosa haereditas or ***damnosa hereditas***
LATIN, literally 'harmful inheritance'
1 (in Roman law) an inheritance of debts
2 any undesirable inheritance, especially one that entails financial hardship, loss, or ruin

da multos annos
LATIN, literally 'grant many years'
a wish for long life, eg on the birthday of the person concerned

dan
JAPANESE

1 (in Japanese combative sports) a level of proficiency, usually from 1st to 10th
2 a person who has attained such a level

danke schön
GERMAN
thank you very much

danse macabre
FRENCH
dance of death, a series of allegorical paintings symbolizing the universal power of death

danseur
FRENCH
a male ballet dancer

danseur noble
FRENCH, literally 'noble dancer'
a principal male ballet dancer
plural ***danseurs nobles***

danseuse
FRENCH
1 a female dancer
2 a female ballet dancer

darshan
HINDI
(in Hinduism) a blessing conferred by seeing or touching a great or holy person

das heisst
GERMAN
that is

> the equivalent of ID EST

abbrev **dh, d.h.**

dat, dicat, dedicat
LATIN
gives, devotes, and dedicates
abbrev **DDD**

daube
FRENCH
a meat stew

DC
see DA CAPO

DD or *dd*
see DONO DEDIT

DDD
see DAT, DICAT, DEDICAT; DONO DEDIT DEDICAVIT

débâcle or *debacle*
FRENCH
total disorder, defeat, collapse, etc

> originally applied to the breaking up of ice on a river

de bene esse
LATIN, literally 'as being good'
(law) without prejudice; provisionally or conditionally

debonair or *debonnaire*
from FRENCH *débonnaire*
1 of elegant appearance and good manners; charming; courteous
2 carefree

déboutonné
FRENCH for 'unbuttoned'
careless, especially in dress
feminine ***déboutonnée***

débris or *debris*
FRENCH
1 wreckage; ruins
2 rubbish
3 a mass of rocky fragments

début or *debut*
FRENCH
1 a beginning or first attempt
2 a first appearance before the public, or in society

débutant
FRENCH
a male performer making his first appearance

débutante
FRENCH
1 a young woman making her first appearance in society
2 a female performer making her first appearance

decessit sine prole
LATIN
died without issue
abbrev **dsp, d.s.p.**

déchéance
FRENCH
forfeiture

déclassé
FRENCH
having descended in social rank or lost social standing
feminine ***déclassée***

décolletage
FRENCH
1 a low-cut neckline
2 a dress with such a neckline
3 the exposure of the neck and shoulders in such a dress

décolleté
FRENCH
(of clothes) low-cut

décolletée
FRENCH
(of a woman) wearing a low-cut dress

décor or *decor*
FRENCH for 'decoration'
1 the general decorative effect (colour scheme, furnishings, etc) of a room
2 scenery and other stage decorations

découpage or *decoupage*
FRENCH
1 the application of decorative paper cut-outs to wood and other surfaces
2 a picture produced in this way

> the craft originated in the 18th century

decus et tutamen
LATIN
an ornament and a protection

> inscribed round the milled edge of a one-pound coin

de die in diem
LATIN
from day to day; daily

de facto
LATIN
1 actual, if not rightful or legally recognized
2 in fact, actually
compare DE JURE

de fide
LATIN
(of a teaching) in which belief is obligatory

dégagé
FRENCH for 'clear, free'
1 unembarrassed, unconstrained, easy
2 uninvolved
feminine ***dégagée***

dégoût
FRENCH
distaste; disgust; loathing

dégringolade
FRENCH
1 a sudden descent
2 a quick deterioration

de gustibus non est disputandum
LATIN
there is no disputing about tastes

de haut en bas
FRENCH, literally 'downwards, from top to bottom'
with an air of superiority, contemptuously

Dei gratia
LATIN
by the grace of God

de integro
LATIN
anew, again, afresh

déjà vu
FRENCH, literally 'already seen'
1 an illusion that one has experienced before something that one is actually experiencing for the first time
2 (in art, literature, etc) unoriginal material

déjeuner
FRENCH
1 lunch
2 breakfast

de jure
LATIN
by right or law
compare DE FACTO

dekko
from HINDI *dekho* meaning 'see!'
(slang) a look
plural ***dekkos***

délassement
FRENCH
relaxation

del credere
ITALIAN, literally 'of trust'
applied to an agent who sells goods or obtains orders for another and guarantees that the buyers will pay

delicatessen
from GERMAN *Delikatessen* meaning 'delicacies', from FRENCH *délicatesse*
a shop selling prepared foods, especially cooked meats, pâtés, and unusual or foreign foods

delineavit
LATIN
he or she drew this

> sometimes added to the signature of the artist or draughtsman on a drawing

abbrev **del.**

delirium tremens
LATIN, literally 'trembling delirium'
a disorder of the brain caused by persistent overconsumption of alcohol, marked by trembling and hallucinations
abbrev (informal) **DTs**

de luxe or ***deluxe***
FRENCH, literally 'of luxury'
1 sumptuous, luxurious
2 having special features or superior qualities

démarche
FRENCH
a step, measure, or initiative, especially a diplomatic initiative

démenti
FRENCH
a contradiction or denial

demi-jour
FRENCH
half-light, twilight, subdued light

demi-mondaine
FRENCH
a woman of the demi-monde

demi-monde
FRENCH, literally 'half-world'
1 a class of women on the fringes of social respectability, especially the kept mistresses of society men
2 the less respectable section of a profession or group

de minimis non curat lex
LATIN
the law does not concern itself about trifles

demi-pension
FRENCH
(in hotels, etc) half-board, ie the provision of bed, breakfast, and one other meal
see also PENSION

demi-tasse or ***demitasse***
FRENCH, literally 'half-cup'
1 a small cup of coffee, especially black coffee
2 the cup itself

demi-vièrge
FRENCH, literally 'half-virgin'
a woman who frequently engages in sexual activity without losing her virginity

démodé
FRENCH
out of fashion

démon de midi
FRENCH, literally 'midday demon'
the reawakening of sexual desire in middle age

de mortuis nil nisi bonum
LATIN, literally 'nothing but good of the dead'
do not speak ill of the dead

denominazione di origine controllata
ITALIAN
(in the labelling of Italian wines) a guarantee that the wine conforms to certain specified conditions of origin, strength, etc
abbrev **DOC**

de nos jours
FRENCH
of our times

usually follows a name, as in *the Michelangelo de nos jours*

dénouement or ***denouement***
FRENCH
1 (in a novel, play, etc) the final unravelling of the plot
2 the issue, event, or outcome

de novo
LATIN
anew, again from the beginning

deoch-an-doruis or ***doch-an-doris***
GAELIC, literally 'drink of the door'
a stirrup cup, a parting drink

Deo favente
LATIN
with God's favour

Deo gratias
LATIN
thanks to God

Deo Optimo Maximo
LATIN
to God, the best, the greatest (the motto of the Benedictines)
abbrev **DOM**

the abbreviation is used on bottles of Benedictine liqueur

Deo volente
LATIN
God willing
abbrev **DV**

dépêche
FRENCH
dispatch, message

depot
from FRENCH *dépôt*
1 a storehouse or warehouse
2 a bus station or garage
3 a military post where stores are kept and recruits trained
4 the headquarters of a regiment

de profundis
LATIN, literally 'out of the depths'
from the depths of despair

> from Psalm 130

de re
LATIN, literally 'about the thing'
(in the terminology of logic and philosophy) denotes that knowledge, belief, etc, is based on a thing itelf rather than any linguistic or other representation of it

de règle
FRENCH
according to rule or convention

de rigueur
FRENCH, literally 'of strictness'
required by etiquette, fashion, etc

dernier cri
FRENCH, literally 'last cry'
the last word, the latest fashion

dernier ressort
FRENCH
a last resort

derrière
FRENCH for 'behind'
the buttocks

der Tag
GERMAN for 'the day'
the day when the struggle begins

> originally applied to the first day of World War I, when a career of conquest by Germany was to begin

dervish or ***Dervish***
TURKISH, from PERSIAN *darvish* meaning 'a poor man'
a member of a Muslim religious group professing poverty and leading an austere life

> some perform spinning dances as part of their religious ritual

désagrément
FRENCH
something disagreeable

déshabillé or ***dishabille***
FRENCH for 'undressed'
1 carelessness about one's dress, appearance, etc
2 a state of undress
3 informal or scanty attire
see also EN DÉSHABILLÉ

desideratum
LATIN
something greatly desired
plural ***desiderata***

désoeuvré
FRENCH
unoccupied, at a loose end
feminine ***désoeuvrée***

désorienté
FRENCH
disoriented, having lost one's bearings, confused
feminine ***désorientée***

de te fabula narratur
LATIN
the story is about you

détente
FRENCH

relaxation of strained relations (especially between nations)

détenu
FRENCH
a prisoner, especially a political prisoner in India
feminine ***détenue***

détraqué
FRENCH, literally 'upset, out of order'
a deranged person
feminine ***détraquée***

detritus
LATIN for 'worn'
1 loose fragments of rock, produced by disintegration or erosion
2 accumulated débris

de trop
FRENCH
1 superfluous
2 in the way

Deus avertat
LATIN
God forbid

Deus det
LATIN
God grant

deus ex machina
LATIN, literally 'a god from a machine'
1 (in classical drama) a god brought on stage by a mechanical device, usually to resolve the plot
2 a contrived solution of a difficulty in the plot of a play, novel, etc

Deus vobiscum
LATIN
God be with you

Deuxième Bureau
FRENCH, literally 'second office'
the French Department of Military Intelligence

deva
SANSKRIT
(in Hinduism and Buddhism) a god; a good spirit

devanagari
from SANSKRIT *devanāgari* meaning 'town-script of the gods'
the script in which Sanskrit and Hindi are usually written and printed
see also NAGARI

> also used for other Indian languages

dévot
FRENCH
a person wholly or superstitiously devoted to religion
feminine ***dévote***

dewan
see DIWAN

dextro tempore
LATIN
at a lucky moment

dh or ***d.h.***
see DAS HEISST

dharma
SANSKRIT
1 (in Hinduism) virtue or righteousness arising from observance of social and moral law
2 truth as laid down in the Buddhist scriptures
see also ADHARMA

dharna
HINDI
a means of calling attention to injustice, etc, by sitting or standing in a place where one will be noticed

> especially sitting and fasting at the door of an offender

dhobi
HINDI
an Indian washerman

dhoti
HINDI
1 the Hindu loincloth
2 a cotton fabric used for this

diable
FRENCH for 'devil'
an unglazed earthenware casserole with a handle, a wide base, and a narrow neck

diablerie
FRENCH
1 magic; sorcery
2 mischief

dialogue des sourds
FRENCH, literally 'dialogue of the deaf'
a conversation or discussion in which neither party pays attention to the other

diamanté
FRENCH
1 (said of a fabric, garment, etc) decorated with small sparkling ornaments
2 fabric so decorated

Diaspora
GREEK
1 the dispersion of the Jewish people after the Babylonian captivity
2 the dispersed Jews themselves, or any Jewish communities outside Israel
3 (usually *diaspora*) a similar dispersion or migration of other peoples or communities

dictum
LATIN
1 a popular maxim or saying
2 an authoritative statement or pronouncement
plural **dicta**

dictum de dicto
LATIN
hearsay

dictum sapienti sat est
see VERBUM SAPIENTI SAT EST

dies
LATIN
day
plural **dies**

dies faustus
LATIN
lucky day

dies festi or ***dies feriae***
LATIN
days of actual festival

dies infaustus
LATIN
unlucky day

dies irae
LATIN
1 the day of wrath, the day of judgement
2 the Latin hymn that begins with these words, used in the mass for the dead

dies non (juridicus)
LATIN
a day on which judges do not sit, or one on which normal business is not conducted

Dieu avec nous
FRENCH
God with us

Dieu défend le droit
FRENCH
God defends the right

Dieu et mon droit
FRENCH
God and my right

> the royal motto since the reign of Henry VI

Dieu vous garde
FRENCH
God keep you

Diktat or ***diktat***
GERMAN, literally 'something dictated'
1 an order or statement that must be obeyed
2 a harsh settlement forced on the defeated

dilettante
ITALIAN
a dabbler in art, science, or literature; a person whose interest in a subject is superficial and without serious purpose
plural ***dilettanti***

diminuendo
ITALIAN for 'diminishing'
(music)
1 letting the sound die away
2 a passage in which the sound dies away
plural ***diminuendoes*** or ***diminuendos***

dim sum
CHINESE
a selection of Chinese foods, often eaten as an appetizer, usually including steamed dumplings with various fillings

Ding an sich
GERMAN
(in the philosophy of Kant) the thing-in-itself, the noumenon, an object regarded as having a status independent of its attributes

di penates
LATIN
household gods

Directoire
FRENCH
1 the French Directorate of 1795–9
2 of the fashion in dress or furniture prevailing at that time
3 (said of knickers) knee-length, with elastic at the waist and knees

dirigisme
FRENCH
state control in social and economic affairs

dirndl
GERMAN DIALECT, literally 'little girl'
1 an Alpine peasant woman's dress with a close-fitting bodice and a full skirt
2 an imitation of this, especially a full skirt with a tight, often elasticated, waistband

dis aliter visum
LATIN
the gods have adjudged otherwise

di salto
ITALIAN
at a leap

discothèque or ***discotheque***
FRENCH for 'record-library'
1 a club or party where music for dancing is provided by pop records, usually played by a disc jockey, and often accompanied by special lighting effects
2 the equipment used to provide such music and effects
abbrev (informal) **disco,** *plural* **discos**

diseur
FRENCH
a reciter or entertainer
feminine ***diseuse***

dishabille
see DÉSHABILLÉ

disjecta membra
LATIN, literally 'scattered limbs'
fragments of literary work

distingué
FRENCH
1 distinguished
2 striking
feminine ***distinguée***

distrait
FRENCH
absent-minded
feminine ***distraite***

dit
FRENCH
1 named, called
2 reputed, said

ditto
ITALIAN, literally 'said'
1 the same thing
2 as before or above
3 in the same manner, likewise
4 (said as a rejoinder) same here

> the modern Italian past participle is *detto*

diva
ITALIAN
a great female singer, especially an operatic prima donna

divertimento
ITALIAN
(music) a light composition intended primarily for entertainment, especially a suite for orchestra or chamber ensemble
plural ***divertimenti***

divertissement
FRENCH
a diversion or entertainment, especially a short entertainment between the acts of a play, opera, ballet, etc

divide et impera
LATIN
divide and rule

divisim
LATIN
separately

divorcé
FRENCH
a divorced person
feminine ***divorcée***

> the anglicized form *divorcee* may be used of either sex

diwan or ***dewan***
PERSIAN
1 in India, a financial minister or a state prime minister
2 the native steward of a business house

dixi
LATIN
I have spoken

djebel
see JEBEL

djellaba, djellabah, jellaba or ***jelab***
from ARABIC *jallabah*
a cloak with a hood and wide sleeves

djibbah
see JUBBAH

djinn
see JINN

doab
PERSIAN, literally 'two waters'
a strip of land between two rivers (especially the Ganges and Jumna)

DOC
see DENOMINAZIONE DI ORIGINE CONTROLLATA

doch-an-doris
see DEOCH-AN-DORUIS

doctrinaire
FRENCH
1 a theorist who carries principles to logical but unworkable extremes
2 adhering rigidly to theories or principles, often regardless of practicality or suitability

dojo
JAPANESE
a place where judo, karate, etc, are taught or practised
plural **dojos**

dolce
ITALIAN
sweet or sweetly

dolce far niente
ITALIAN, literally 'sweet doing nothing'
pleasant idleness

dolce vita
ITALIAN, literally 'sweet life'
a life of luxury and self-indulgence

> used by the Italian director Federico Fellini in the title of his film *La Dolce Vita* (1960)

dolma
TURKISH
(in Greek cookery) a vine or cabbage leaf with a savoury stuffing
plural **dolmas** or **dolmades**

doloroso
ITALIAN
(music) in a soft and pathetic manner

DOM
see DEO OPTIMO MAXIMO

Domine, dirige nos
LATIN
Lord, direct us

> the motto of London

Dominus illuminatio mea
LATIN
the Lord is my light

> the motto of Oxford University

donnée
FRENCH
1 a datum
2 a basic assumption on which a work of literature is founded

Donnerwetter
GERMAN for 'thunderstorm'
an exclamation of annoyance, etc

dono dedit
LATIN
gave as a gift
abbrev **DD, dd**

dono dedit dedicavit
LATIN
gave and dedicated as a gift
abbrev **DDD**

dopatta or dupatta
HINDI
a silk or muslin shawl or headscarf

Doppelgänger, doppelgänger or doppelganger
GERMAN, literally 'double-goer'
1 a ghostly double of a person
2 an apparition

doppio movimento
ITALIAN
(music) double speed

dossier
FRENCH
a set of documents relating to a person, event, or case

douane
FRENCH
a customs house

douanier
FRENCH
a customs officer

double entendre
FRENCH
1 a word or phrase with two meanings, one of which is usually sexually suggestive
2 the use of such a word or phrase

douceur
FRENCH for 'sweetness'
a conciliatory present, a bribe or tip

douche
FRENCH
1 a jet of water directed onto or into the body
2 an apparatus for producing such a jet

douma
see DUMA

doyen
FRENCH
a senior member of a profession, organization, etc
feminine ***doyenne***

dragée
FRENCH
1 a nut, raisin, etc, with a hard sugar coating
2 a sugar-coated drug
3 a small round sweet, often silvered, for decorating a cake

dramatis personae
LATIN
1 the characters of a play, etc
2 a list of these characters

Drang nach Osten
GERMAN, literally 'eastward thrust'
the policy of German expansionists

dressage
FRENCH
1 the training of a horse in deportment, obedience, and set manoeuvres
2 the performance of these manoeuvres in competition
3 the manoeuvres themselves

droit
FRENCH
right, legal claim

droit au travail
FRENCH
right to work

droit des gens
FRENCH
international law

droit du seigneur or ***droit de seigneur***
FRENCH, literally 'lord's right'
1 the alleged right of a feudal lord to take the virginity of a vassal's bride
2 any excessive or unreasonable demand made of a subordinate
see also JUS PRIMAE NOCTIS

droshky or ***drosky***
from RUSSIAN *drozhki*
1 a low four-wheeled open carriage used in Russia
2 a German four-wheeled cab

DS
see DAL SEGNO

dsp or ***d.s.p.***
see DECESSIT SINE PROLE

DTs
see DELIRIUM TREMENS

duce
ITALIAN for 'leader'
the title assumed by the Italian dictator Benito Mussolini

duende
SPANISH for 'ghost, goblin, demon'
inspiration, magnetism, ardour
plural ***duendes***

duenna
from SPANISH *dueña*
1 an older woman who chaperons a younger one in Spain or Portugal
2 a governess

dulce est desipere in loco
LATIN
it is pleasant to play the fool on occasion

dulce et decorum est pro patria mori
LATIN
it is sweet and noble to die for one's country

> the Latin phrase *dulce et decorum* has been variously translated as 'pleasant and proper', 'sweet and glorious', 'lovely and honourable', etc

duma or ***douma***
RUSSIAN
an elected council, especially the Russian parliament of 1906–17

dumka
CZECH
(music)
1 a lament
2 a slow movement or piece
plural ***dumky***

Dummkopf
GERMAN
blockhead

dum spiro, spero
LATIN, literally 'while I breathe, I hope'
while there is life there is hope

dum vivimus, vivamus
LATIN
let us live while we are alive

> the equivalent of the English saying 'eat, drink, and be merry (for tomorrow we die)', which is of biblical origin

d'un certain âge
FRENCH, literally 'of a certain age'
middle-aged; no longer young

> chiefly used of women, politely or euphemistically

duomo
ITALIAN
a cathedral, especially in Italy
plural ***duomos*** or ***duomi***

dupatta
see DOPATTA

durante vita
LATIN
during life

duumvir
from LATIN *duumvirī* meaning 'two men'
one of two men in the same office or post
plural ***duumvirs*** or ***duumviri***

duvet
FRENCH for 'down'

1 a quilt stuffed with feathers or man-made fibres, used on a bed in place of blankets, etc
2 a quilted coat or jacket

➪ the French term for sense 1 is *couette*

DV
see DEO VOLENTE

dvornik
RUSSIAN
a caretaker or porter

E

eau de Cologne
FRENCH, literally 'Cologne water'
a perfumed mixture of alcohol and essential oils, first made at Cologne in 1709 by Johann Farina

often shortened to *cologne* in English

eau de Javelle
FRENCH, literally 'Javel water'
a solution of potassium chloride and hypochlorite used for bleaching, disinfecting, etc

eau de Nil
FRENCH, literally 'Nile water'
a pale green colour, Nile green

eau de vie
FRENCH, literally 'water of life'
brandy

ébauche
FRENCH
a rough draft or sketch

ébéniste
FRENCH
a cabinetmaker

Eboracensis
LATIN
of York
abbrev **Ebor.**

écarté
FRENCH for 'discarded'
a card game in which cards may be discarded for others

ecce
LATIN
behold

ecce homo
LATIN, literally 'behold the man'
(art) a portrayal of Christ crowned with thorns

from the Vulgate (John 9.5)

ecce signum
LATIN, literally 'behold the sign'
here is the proof

ecco
ITALIAN
1 here is
2 there
3 look there

échappé
FRENCH for 'escaped'
(ballet) a double leap from two feet, starting in fifth position, landing in second or fourth, and finishing in fifth

echelon
from FRENCH *échelon* meaning 'rung, step'
1 a level or rank in the hierarchy of an organization
2 the people at this level
3 an arrangement of troops, ships, planes, etc, as if in steps

echt
GERMAN
genuine, authentic

éclair
FRENCH for 'lightning'
a long cake made of choux pastry,

filled with cream and usually topped with chocolate icing

➪ the name may allude to the speed with which it is eaten

éclaircissement
FRENCH
the act of clearing up a misunderstanding; explanation

éclat
FRENCH
1 a striking effect
2 showy splendour
3 distinction
4 applause

école
FRENCH
school

e contra
LATIN
on the other hand, conversely

e contrario
LATIN
on the contrary

e converso
LATIN
conversely, by logical conversion

écorché
FRENCH for 'flayed'
a figure in which the muscular system is displayed for the purposes of artistic study

écritoire or ***escritoire***
FRENCH
a writing-desk

ecru
from FRENCH *écru*
the off-white or greyish-brown colour of unbleached linen

écurie
FRENCH for 'stable'
a team of racing cars under individual or joint ownership

Edenburgensis
LATIN
of Edinburgh
abbrev **Edenburgen.**

edite, bibite
LATIN
eat, drink

édition de luxe
FRENCH
an expensive edition of a book, usually prepared with high-quality materials and workmanship

editio princeps
LATIN
the first printed edition of a work, especially one known previously in manuscript
plural ***editiones principes***

effendi
TURKISH
1 (in Turkey) a former title for civil officials, abolished in 1934 and now used as the equivalent of 'Mr'
2 a title of respect for educated or high-ranking people in E Mediterranean countries

effleurage
FRENCH, literally 'glancing, grazing'
a stroking movement in massage

effluvium
LATIN
an unpleasant smell or exhalation, such as that given off by decaying matter
plural ***effluvia***

eg or ***e.g.***
see EXEMPLI GRATIA

égarement
FRENCH
confusion, bewilderment

ego
LATIN for 'I'
1 self-image; personal pride; conceit
2 the part of the conscious mind concerned with perception, memory, and reasoning

eirenicon or ***irenicon***
from GREEK *eirēnikon*
a proposition or scheme for peace

Eisen und Blut
see BLUT UND EISEN

eisteddfod
WELSH for 'session'
a Welsh arts festival with competitions in music, poetry, drama, etc

> originally a competitive gathering of Welsh bards and musicians

plural ***eisteddfods*** or ***eisteddfodau***

ejusdem generis
LATIN
of the same kind

ek dum
from HINDI *ek dam*
at once

élan
FRENCH
1 impetuosity
2 dash or style

élan vital
FRENCH
the creative force responsible for the growth and evolution of organisms

> from the philosophy of Henri Bergson

El Dorado, Eldorado or ***eldorado***
SPANISH
1 the golden land or city sought by the Spanish conquerors of America
2 any place where wealth is easily acquired

> from SPANISH *el dorado* meaning 'the gilded man', the king of the legendary city of Manoa who covered himself with gold-dust. The name was later transferred to the city itself

Eliensis
LATIN
of Ely
abbrev **Elien.**

élite or ***elite***
FRENCH
the best or most powerful people within society, or within a profession or organization; a select group

elixir
LATIN, from ARABIC *al-iksīr* meaning 'the philosopher's stone'
1 an alchemical preparation that was formerly claimed to prolong life or to change metals into gold
2 a sweetened, flavoured, or alcoholic liquid containing an otherwise unpalatable medicine
3 a panacea

embargo
SPANISH
1 an official order, usually temporary, forbidding the arrival or departure of merchant ships
2 the resulting stoppage of trade
3 any similar restriction or prohibition
plural ***embargoes***

embarras de choix or ***embarras du choix***
FRENCH, literally 'embarrassment of choice'
a perplexing or disconcerting number of things to choose from

embarras de richesses, embarras des richesses or ***embarras de richesse***
FRENCH, literally 'embarrassment of riches'
a superfluity of wealth, fine details, or other good things

from the title of a play by the Abbé d'Allainval (1726)

embonpoint
FRENCH, from *en bon point* meaning 'in good form'
stoutness or plumpness

embouchure
FRENCH
1 the mouth of a river
2 the mouthpiece of a wind instrument
3 the way the mouth is used to play a wind instrument

embroglio
see IMBROGLIO

embusqué
FRENCH
1 in ambush
2 a slacker or shirker
3 a person who evades military service

emeritus
LATIN
retired or honourably discharged but retaining one's former title, especially in the phrase *professor emeritus*

émigré
FRENCH
1 an emigrant, especially a political emigrant
2 a royalist who fled from France during the Revolution

éminence grise
FRENCH, literally 'grey eminence'
someone who has great influence over a ruler, government, etc, without occupying an official position of power

from the nickname given to Père Joseph, Cardinal Richelieu's private secretary and alter ego

Empfindung
GERMAN
sensation or feeling

empressé
FRENCH
eager or enthusiastic
feminine ***empressée***

empressement
FRENCH
1 demonstrative warmth of manner
2 assiduous attention

en ami
FRENCH
as a friend

en arrière
FRENCH
behind or in the rear

en attendant
FRENCH, literally 'while waiting'
in the meantime

en avant
FRENCH
forward

en badinant
FRENCH
jocularly

en beau
FRENCH
in a flattering style

said of the way a person is depicted in a portrait, etc

en bloc
FRENCH
all together; as one unit

en brochette
FRENCH
(cookery) on a skewer

en brosse
FRENCH, literally 'like a brush'
(said of hair) cut short and standing up stiffly

en caballo
SPANISH
on horseback

en cabochon
FRENCH
(said of a gem) rounded on top and flat on the back, without facets
see also CABOCHON

enceinte
FRENCH
1 pregnant
2 an enclosure, a fortified place

enchanté
FRENCH for 'delighted, enchanted'
pleased to meet you
feminine ***enchantée***

encheiridion or ***enchiridion***
GREEK
a handbook or manual

enchilada
SPANISH, literally 'seasoned with chilli'
a Mexican dish consisting of a rolled tortilla filled with meat and served with a chilli-flavoured sauce

encierro
SPANISH for 'enclosure'
an event in which bulls are driven through the streets of a Spanish town to the bull-ring
plural ***encierros***

en clair
FRENCH
not in code

enclave
FRENCH
part of a country entirely enclosed within foreign territory

encomium or ***encomion***
LATIN, from GREEK *enkōmion* meaning 'song of praise'
1 high commendation
2 a eulogy

encore
FRENCH for 'again, still'
1 an enthusiastic call for a repeated performance or additional item at the end of a concert, etc
2 the performance given in response to such a call

not used in this sense in France, where the equivalent interjection is *bis*

en croûte
FRENCH
(cookery) wrapped in pastry and baked
see also CROÛTE

en déshabillé
FRENCH
in a state of undress
see also DÉSHABILLÉ

en effet
FRENCH
in effect; in fact

en face
FRENCH
1 in front
2 opposite
3 facing forwards

en famille
FRENCH
1 among one's family; at home
2 informally, without ceremony

enfant de la maison
FRENCH, literally 'child of the house'
a person who is quite at home

enfant de son siècle
FRENCH, literally 'child of his or her century'
a person who reflects the spirit of their time

enfant gâté
FRENCH
a spoilt child
feminine ***enfant gâtée***

enfants perdus
FRENCH, literally 'lost children'
a body of soldiers selected for a particularly dangerous mission or duty

enfant terrible
FRENCH, literally 'terrible child'
a person with a reputation for indiscreet, embarrassing, or unconventional behaviour, remarks, etc

enfant trouvé
FRENCH
a foundling, an abandoned child of unknown parents

en fête
FRENCH
in festive mood, attire, etc

enfilade
FRENCH, from *enfiler* meaning 'to thread on a string'
a series of rooms with the doors in line, providing a continuous passage or uninterrupted view from one end to the other

engagé
FRENCH
committed to a social or political cause or movement
feminine ***engagée***

engagement
FRENCH
commitment to a social or political cause or movement

en garçon
FRENCH
like a bachelor; in bachelor style

en garde
FRENCH
(fencing) a warning to assume a defensive position in readiness for an attack

en grande tenue
FRENCH
in full dress, especially military or evening dress

en grand seigneur
FRENCH
like a great lord

engrenage
FRENCH for 'gearing'
a series of events, decisions, etc, each of which leads inevitably to another

enjambement or ***enjambment***
FRENCH
in verse, the continuation of the sense without a pause beyond the end of the line

en l'air
FRENCH, literally 'in the air'
1 under discussion
2 without substance

en masse
FRENCH
in a body; all together

ennui
FRENCH
1 a feeling of weariness or languor
2 boredom or discontent caused by lack of activity or stimulation

ennuyé
FRENCH
bored
feminine ***ennuyée***

ennuyeux
FRENCH
1 boring
2 annoying

enosis
from GREEK *henosis*
union, especially the reunion of Cyprus with Greece, the goal of the Greek Cypriot movement
plural ***enoses***

en pantoufles
FRENCH, literally 'in slippers'
unconstrained, at one's ease

en papillote
FRENCH
(said of food) cooked and served in an envelope of oiled or greased paper or foil
see also PAPILLOTE

en passant
FRENCH
in passing; by the way

en pension
FRENCH
at a fixed rate for board and lodging

en plein air
FRENCH
in the open air

en plein jour
FRENCH
in broad daylight

en poste
FRENCH
(said of a diplomat) resident at a place in an official capacity

en prince
FRENCH
in princely style

en principe
FRENCH
in principle

en prise
FRENCH
(said of a piece in chess) exposed to capture

en queue
FRENCH, literally 'like a tail'
1 in a string or line
2 (said of hair) tied at the nape of the neck, in a pigtail or ponytail

en rapport
FRENCH
1 in direct relation
2 in sympathy or harmony

en règle
FRENCH
1 in due order
2 according to regulations

en retraite
FRENCH
in retirement; on a pension

en revanche
FRENCH
in return

en route
FRENCH
on the way

ens
LATIN
(metaphysics)
1 being or existence
2 an entity, as opposed to an attribute
plural **entia**

ensemble
FRENCH for 'together'
1 all parts of a thing taken together
2 a group of musicians playing together
3 the performance of such a group
4 a combined or general effect
5 an outfit consisting of several matching garments
see also TOUT ENSEMBLE

en suite
FRENCH
1 forming a unit or set
2 (said of a bathroom) connecting directly with a bedroom
3 an en suite bathroom
4 (said of a bedroom) having an en suite bathroom
5 in succession

entente
FRENCH
an understanding

entente cordiale
FRENCH
a friendly agreement or relationship between states, especially the understanding reached between Britain and France in 1904

entêté
FRENCH
1 infatuated
2 opinionated
feminine **entêtée**

entourage
FRENCH
1 followers, attendants
2 surroundings

en-tout-cas
from FRENCH *en tout cas* meaning 'in any case'
a parasol that can be used as an umbrella

entr'acte
FRENCH
1 the interval between acts in a play
2 a piece of music or other entertainment intended to occupy this interval

entrain
FRENCH
liveliness or spirit

en train
FRENCH
in progress

en travesti
FRENCH
(said especially of a dancer, singer, etc) wearing the clothes of the opposite sex

entrechat
FRENCH
(ballet) a leap during which the heels are struck together or the feet crossed and uncrossed

entrecôte
FRENCH
a steak cut from between two ribs

entre deux âges
FRENCH, literally 'between two ages'
middle-aged

entre deux guerres
FRENCH, literally 'between two wars'

(the period) between World War I and World War II

entrée

FRENCH

1 entry, access, admittance, introduction

2 a formal entrance, or music for it

3 a dish served at dinner between the fish course and the meat course

4 (especially in the US) a main course

5 (especially in Australia) a starter

entremets

FRENCH

1 a light dish served at table between courses

2 a side dish

3 a dessert

entre nous

FRENCH

between ourselves

entrepôt or ***entrepot***

FRENCH

1 a storehouse

2 a bonded warehouse

3 a port through which exports and imports pass, especially one from which imported goods are re-exported without duty being paid on them

entrepreneur

FRENCH

a person who engages in a commercial enterprise, often at personal financial risk

> the French feminine form *entrepreneuse* is rarely if ever used in English

entresol

FRENCH

a low storey between two main ones, usually between the ground floor and the first floor of a building

entrez

FRENCH

come in!

en ventre sa mère

FRENCH

(law) in their mother's womb

> referring to the rights of the unborn child

en vérité

FRENCH

in truth

en ville

FRENCH

1 in town

2 not at home

eo nomine

LATIN

by that name, on that claim

épée

FRENCH

a narrow-bladed sword used in duelling and fencing

éperdument amoureux

FRENCH

desperately in love

feminine ***éperdument amoureuse***

e pluribus unum

LATIN

one out of many

> (former) motto of the US

eppur si muove

ITALIAN

and yet it does move

> allegedly said by Galileo after recanting his theory that the earth moves round the sun

épris
FRENCH
captivated or smitten
feminine ***éprise***

épuisé
FRENCH
worn out
feminine ***épuisée***

équipe
FRENCH
(in motor-racing and other sports) a team

Erdgeist
GERMAN, literally 'earth-spirit'
the active spiritual force of the world

e re nata
LATIN
1 according to the demands or requirements of the case
2 as things stand

ergo
LATIN
therefore

> used to introduce the conclusion of a syllogism

erotica
from GREEK *erōtika*
erotic literature

errare humanum est or ***humanum est errare***
LATIN
to err is human

erratum
LATIN
an error in writing or printing, especially one noted in a list supplied with a book
plural ***errata***

ersatz
GERMAN
1 substitute
2 fake

Erziehungsroman
see BILDUNGSROMAN

escalier
FRENCH
a staircase

escalier dérobé
FRENCH
a private staircase

escamotage
FRENCH
juggling

escargot
FRENCH
an edible snail

esclandre
FRENCH
1 notoriety; scandal
2 a public quarrel or disturbance

escribano
SPANISH
a notary
plural ***escribanos***

escritoire
see ÉCRITOIRE

escroc
FRENCH
a swindler

espada
SPANISH
1 a sword
2 a swordfish
3 a matador

espadrille
FRENCH
a rope-soled shoe

espiègle
FRENCH
1 roguish
2 frolicsome

espièglerie
FRENCH
1 roguishness
2 frolicsomeness

espresso or ***expresso***
ITALIAN for 'expressed'
1 coffee made in a machine that forces steam or boiling water through ground coffee beans
2 such a machine

also used as an adjective

plural ***espressos*** or ***expressos***

esprit
FRENCH
1 wit
2 liveliness; spirit

esprit de corps
FRENCH
loyalty to or pride in the group or body to which one belongs; a sense of fellowship with other members of the group

esprit de l'escalier or ***esprit d'escalier***
FRENCH, literally 'staircase wit'
an apt or witty remark or retort that comes to mind after the opportunity to use it has gone by

esprit follet
FRENCH
a mischievous goblin

esprit fort
FRENCH
a freethinker

espumoso
SPANISH
a sparkling wine
plural ***espumosos***

esquisse
FRENCH
a sketch or outline

esse
LATIN, literally 'to be'
(philosophy)
1 actual existence
2 essence
see also IN ESSE

estancia
SPANISH
a large estate or cattle ranch in Spanish America

estro
ITALIAN
1 enthusiasm
2 poetic inspiration

étage
FRENCH
a floor, a storey

étagère
FRENCH
a display stand with shelves for small objects or ornaments

étalage
FRENCH
a display, especially of goods in a shop window

et alibi
LATIN
and elsewhere
abbrev **et al**

et alii
LATIN
and other people or things
abbrev **et al**

the abbreviation is the usual form

feminine ***et aliae***
neuter ***et alia***

étape
FRENCH
1 a storehouse
2 a stopping-place
3 a day's march
4 a stage, eg of a cycle race

état
FRENCH
state or rank
see also L'ÉTAT, C'EST MOI

étatisme
FRENCH
extreme state control over the individual citizen

état-major
FRENCH
the staff of an army, regiment, etc

et cetera or ***etcetera***
LATIN
and the rest, and so on
abbrev **etc, &c**

> the abbreviation *etc* (pronounced in full) is the usual form. The variant form *etcetera* is also used as a noun, often in the plural meaning 'additional people or things'

et hoc genus omne
LATIN
and all that sort of thing

ethos
GREEK for 'custom, character'
1 the distinctive character or spirit of an individual, group, race, etc
2 moral significance

étoile
FRENCH
1 a star
2 a star-shaped object

étourderie
FRENCH
1 heedlessness
2 a stupid blunder

étourdi
FRENCH
thoughtless; foolish; scatterbrained
feminine ***étourdie***

étranger
FRENCH
1 foreign
2 a foreigner
feminine ***étrangère***

et sequens
LATIN
and the following (page, chapter, etc)
plural ***et sequentes*** or ***et sequentia***
abbrev **et seq.**

et sic de ceteris
LATIN
and so of the rest

et sic de similibus
LATIN
and so of the like

et tu, Brute
LATIN
you too, Brutus

> Caesar's alleged exclamation when he saw Brutus amongst his assassins. In modern usage the phrase is addressed to a friend who joins with others to betray, desert, disparage, or attack the speaker

étude
FRENCH for 'study'
(music) a composition intended to train or test the player's technical skill

étui
FRENCH
a small case for holding needles or other small objects

eureka
from GREEK *heurēka* meaning 'I have found it'
an exclamation of triumph on making a discovery or solving a problem

> the cry of Archimedes when he discovered a method of determining the adulteration of the gold in Hiero's crown, allegedly while taking a bath

événement
FRENCH
1 an event or happening
2 a political strike or demonstration

Ewigkeit
GERMAN
eternity

ex
LATIN for 'out of, from'
1 direct from (as in *ex stock, ex works*)
2 without (as in *ex dividend, ex interest*)

ex abundanti cautela
LATIN
from excessive caution

ex aequo
LATIN
1 equally
2 equitably

ex animo
LATIN
from the heart, earnestly

ex ante
LATIN, literally 'from before'
based on prediction and extrapolation

ex auctoritate mihi commissa
LATIN
by the authority entrusted to me

ex cathedra
LATIN, literally 'from the chair'
1 with authority, especially the full authority of the pope
2 (said of a papal pronouncement) stating an infallible doctrine

exceptis excipiendis
LATIN
making the appropriate exceptions

excerpta
LATIN
extracts, selections

ex concessis or ***ex concesso***
LATIN
from what has been conceded

ex consequenti
LATIN
by way of consequence

ex curia
LATIN
out of court

excursus
LATIN
an incidental digression from the main topic under discussion, in which some detail is discussed at length

ex debito justitiae
LATIN
as a legal obligation

ex delicto
LATIN
resulting from or owing to a crime

ex dono
LATIN
as a gift (from)

exeat
LATIN, literally 'let him or her go out'

formal leave of absence, especially from a school, college, or university

exegesis
GREEK
a critical interpretation of a text, especially a biblical text

exempli gratia
LATIN, literally 'for the sake of example'
for example, for instance
abbrev **eg, e.g., ex gr**

> the abbreviation *eg* or *e.g.* is the usual form

exemplum
LATIN
1 an example
2 a short story or anecdote illustrating a moral

exeunt
LATIN
(stage direction) they go out or leave the stage

exeunt omnes
LATIN
(stage direction) all go out

ex gratia
LATIN
1 as an act of grace
2 (said of a payment, etc) given as a favour, not out of obligation, and with no acceptance of liability
abbrev **ex gr**

ex hypothesi
LATIN
from the hypothesis

exigeant
FRENCH
exacting
feminine ***exigeante***

exit
LATIN
(stage direction) he or she goes out or leaves the stage

ex libris
LATIN
from the books of ...

> used on bookplates, followed by the name of the owner. The term is also used as a noun, denoting such a bookplate or inscription

abbrev **ex lib**

ex mero motu
LATIN, literally 'from mere impulse'
of his, her, or its own accord

ex natura rei
LATIN
from the nature of the case

ex natura rerum
LATIN
from the nature of things

ex nihilo
LATIN
out of nothing, as in *creation ex nihilo*

ex nihilo nihil fit
LATIN, literally 'from nothing, nothing is made'
nothing comes from nothing

ex officio
LATIN
by virtue of office or position
abbrev **ex off**

Exoniensis
LATIN
of Exeter
abbrev **Exon.**

ex parte
LATIN
(law) on one side only, or in the interests of one party only; partial; prejudiced

experientia docet (stultos)
LATIN
experience teaches (fools)

experimentum crucis
LATIN
a crucial test

expertise
FRENCH
expert knowledge; expertness

experto crede or ***experto credite***
LATIN
trust one who has tried, or who has experience

explication de texte
FRENCH
a method of literary criticism based on a detailed analysis of the text of the work

exposé
FRENCH
1 an article or programme exposing a crime, scandal, etc
2 a formal statement or exposition

ex post facto
LATIN, literally 'from what is done after'
1 retrospective
2 retrospectively

expressis verbis
LATIN
in express terms

expresso
see ESPRESSO

ex professo
LATIN
avowedly

ex propriis
LATIN
from one's own resources

ex proprio motu
LATIN
of one's own accord

ex quocunque capite
LATIN
from whatever source

ex tacito
LATIN
silently

extempore or ***ex tempore***
from LATIN *ex tempore* meaning 'out of time'
1 on the spur of the moment
2 without preparation
3 composed and delivered or performed impromptu
4 sudden

extra
LATIN
outside

extrait
FRENCH
extract

extrait de naissance
FRENCH
birth certificate

extra modum
LATIN
beyond measure, extravagant

extra muros
LATIN
outside the walls

ex utraque parte
🔊 LATIN
on either side

ex voto
🔊 LATIN
1 (said of an offering, etc) in accordance with a vow, or in recognition of a prayer being answered; votive
2 a votive offering

F

f
see FORTE

façade or ***facade***
FRENCH
1 the exterior front or face of a building
2 *(figurative)* a false or superficial outward appearance

facetiae
LATIN
witty or humorous sayings or writings

facile princeps
LATIN
1 obviously pre-eminent
2 easily first

façon de parler
FRENCH
a manner of speaking, a mere form of words

facta non verba
LATIN
deeds, not words

factotum
LATIN, literally 'do all'
a person employed to do all kinds of work for another
plural ***factotums***

fade
FRENCH
insipid, colourless

fado
PORTUGUESE for 'fate'
a type of Portuguese folk-song or dance
plural ***fados***

faex populi
LATIN, literally 'dregs of the people'
the common people, the mob

faïence or ***faience***
FRENCH
glazed coloured earthenware

probably from *Faenza* in Italy

fainéant
FRENCH, literally 'do-nothing'
1 idle
2 an idler
see also ROI FAINÉANT
feminine ***fainéante***

fainéantise
FRENCH
idleness

fait accompli
FRENCH, literally 'accomplished fact'
something already done, or done before obtaining permission, especially something that cannot be changed or undone

faites vos jeux
FRENCH
(in roulette, etc) place your bets

fakir
from ARABIC *faqīr* meaning 'poor man'
a wandering Muslim or Hindu holy man who depends on begging for survival

Falange
SPANISH
a Spanish fascist movement established in 1933

faldetta
ITALIAN
a combined hood and cape worn by Maltese women

falsetto
ITALIAN
1 an artificially high voice, especially one produced by a male singer above his natural range
2 a person who uses such a voice

falsi crimen
LATIN
the crime of falsification, especially forgery

fama clamosa
LATIN, literally 'noisy rumour'
1 (especially in Scotland) a rumour ascribing immoral conduct to a minister of the church
2 any similar rumour or scandal

fandango
SPANISH
1 an old Spanish dance for two, performed with castanets
2 the music for such a dance
plural ***fandangos***

fan-tan
CHINESE
a Chinese gambling game in which players try to guess the number of objects remaining after some have been removed

farandole
FRENCH
1 a Provençal dance performed in a long line
2 the music for such a dance

farceur
FRENCH
a joker or buffoon
feminine ***farceuse***

farci
FRENCH
(cookery) stuffed

farouche
FRENCH for 'wild, shy, savage'
1 shy or ill at ease
2 sullen and unsociable
3 socially inexperienced and lacking refinement

farrago
LATIN for 'mixed fodder'
a confused mixture; a hotchpotch

farruca
SPANISH
a Spanish gypsy dance with abrupt variations of tempo and mood

fartlek
SWEDISH, literally 'speed play'
alternate fast and slow running, done as training for marathons and other long-distance races

fascia
LATIN for 'band, bandage'
1 the board above the entrance to a shop that bears the name of the shop
2 an instrument panel, especially the dashboard of a car or other motor vehicle

fascio
ITALIAN for 'bundle, group'
an organized political group or club
plural ***fasci***

Fascismo
ITALIAN
1 the authoritarian form of government in Italy from 1922–43, characterized by extreme nationalism, militarism, anti-communism, and restrictions on individual freedom
2 (usually *fascismo*) fascism

Fascista
ITALIAN
1 a member of the ruling party in Italy from 1922–43, or a similar party elsewhere
2 (usually *fascista*) a fascist
plural **Fascisti**

fata Morgana
ITALIAN, literally 'fairy Morgan'
a striking kind of mirage seen most often in the Strait of Messina

> supposed to be caused by Morgan le Fay, half-sister of King Arthur

fatwa or ***fatwah***
ARABIC
a formal legal opinion or decision issued by a Muslim judicial authority, eg that someone should be killed

> a well-known example is the *fatwa* issued in 1989 by Ayatollah Khomeini of Iran against the writer Salman Rushdie for his book *The Satanic Verses*

faubourg
FRENCH
a suburb

fauna
LATIN
all forms of animal life of a region or period, especially as distinct from plant life
compare FLORA

> from *Fauna*, goddess of living creatures

plural ***faunas*** or ***faunae***

faute de mieux
FRENCH
for want of anything better

fauteuil
FRENCH
1 an armchair, especially a president's chair
2 a theatre stall

faux
FRENCH
false

faux ami
FRENCH for 'false friend'
a word in one language that has a different meaning from a similar word in another

> an example is the French verb *assister*, which does not mean 'to assist'

faux-naïf
FRENCH
a person who seems or pretends to be simple and unsophisticated

> also used as an adjective

faux pas
FRENCH for 'false step'
a mistake or blunder, especially a social indiscretion

FD
see FIDEI DEFENSOR

fecit
LATIN
he or she made or did this

> sometimes added to the signature of the artist on a work of art

abbrev **fec.**

fée
FRENCH
a fairy

féerie
FRENCH

1 fairyland
2 *(theatre)* an extravaganza

feldsher
RUSSIAN
1 (in Russia and parts of E Europe) a partly trained person who practises medicine
2 a person who assists a doctor, especially on the battlefield

feliciter
LATIN
1 happily
2 successfully

fellah
ARABIC
a peasant, especially in Egypt
plural ***fellahs***, ***fellaheen*** or ***fellahin***

felo de se
LATIN, literally 'felon of oneself'
1 suicide
2 a person who commits suicide
plural ***felos de se*** or ***felones de se***

feme covert
OLD FRENCH
(law) a married woman

feme sole
OLD FRENCH
(law) a spinster, a widow, or a married woman who is in the legal position of an unmarried woman

femme de chambre
FRENCH
1 a lady's-maid
2 a chambermaid

femme du monde
FRENCH
1 a woman of the world
2 a society woman

femme fatale
FRENCH
an irresistibly attractive woman who brings difficulties or disaster to the men who succumb to her charms

femme incomprise
FRENCH
a woman who is misunderstood or not appreciated

femme savante
FRENCH
a highly educated woman

ferae naturae
LATIN
(said of animals) wild, undomesticated

fermata
ITALIAN
(music) a pause
plural ***fermatas*** or ***fermate***

festa
ITALIAN
1 a holiday
2 a festival
3 a saint's day

festina lente
LATIN, literally 'make haste slowly'
more haste, less speed

Festschrift
GERMAN, literally 'festival writing'
a celebratory publication, usually a collection of learned papers, presented by their authors and published in honour of some person

fête
FRENCH
1 an outdoor entertainment with stalls, competitions, refreshments, etc, often in aid of a charity
2 a festival or holiday
3 the festival of the saint whose name one bears

fête champêtre
FRENCH
a rural festival or garden party

Fête-Dieu
FRENCH
the festival in honour of the Eucharist; Corpus Christi

fettuccine, fettucine or ***fettucini***
ITALIAN
pasta made in long ribbons, tagliatelle

feu d'artifice
FRENCH
a firework
plural ***feux d'artifice***

feu de joie
FRENCH
a bonfire
plural ***feux de joie***

feuilleté
FRENCH
puff pastry

feuilleton
FRENCH
a serial story or critical article in a newspaper, magazine, etc

ff
see FORTISSIMO

fiacre
FRENCH
a hackney carriage or cab

> from the Hôtel de St Fiacre in Paris, where such carriages were first used

fiançailles
FRENCH
engagement, betrothal

fiancé
FRENCH
the person one is engaged to, one's betrothed
feminine ***fiancée***

fianchetto
ITALIAN
(chess) the development of a bishop on a diagonal following the movement of the adjacent knight's pawn
plural ***fianchetti***

fiasco
ITALIAN for 'flask, bottle'
1 a complete failure
2 a failure in a musical or dramatic performance
plural ***fiascos*** or ***fiascoes***

fiat
LATIN, literally 'let it be done'
1 a formal or solemn command
2 an official sanction or authorization for some procedure

fiat justitia, ruat caelum
LATIN
let justice be done, though the heavens fall

fiat lux
LATIN
let there be light

fiche
FRENCH for 'a slip of paper'
a card or strip of film containing miniaturized data

fide et amore
LATIN
by faith and love

fide et fiducia
LATIN
by faith and confidence

fide et fortitudine
LATIN
by faith and fortitude

fidei defensor
LATIN
defender of the faith, a title held by the sovereigns of England since Henry VIII
abbrev **FD, Fid Def**

> the abbreviation *Fid Def* was used on coins before decimalization in 1971; *FD* has been used on coins since decimalization

fide non armis
LATIN
by faith, not arms

fides et justitia
LATIN
fidelity and justice

fides implicita
LATIN
implicit unquestioning faith

fides Punica
LATIN
Punic faith, ie treachery

fidus Achates
LATIN, literally 'faithful Achates'
a close and reliable friend

> Achates was Aeneas's friend in the Aeneid

fidus et audax
LATIN
faithful and bold

fieri facias
LATIN, literally 'cause to be done'
the name of a writ commanding the sheriff to distrain the defendant's goods

fiesta
SPANISH
1 a saint's day
2 a holiday
3 a carnival or festivity

figurine
FRENCH
a small carved or moulded figure

filet
FRENCH
1 a fillet, especially of beef
2 a kind of lace

filet mignon
FRENCH
a small, tender, boneless cut of beef from the underside of a sirloin

filius nullius
LATIN, literally 'son of nobody'
an illegitimate child

filius populi
LATIN
a son of the people

filius terrae
LATIN, literally 'son of the soil'
a person of low birth

fille
FRENCH
1 a girl
2 a daughter

fille de chambre
FRENCH
a chambermaid

fille de joie
FRENCH
a prostitute

fille d'honneur
FRENCH
a maid of honour

film noir
FRENCH, literally 'black film'
a style of film, popular in US

cinema of the 1940s and 1950s, in which the darker side of human nature is presented in a bleak setting

fils
FRENCH
1 son
2 (following a name) junior
compare PÈRE

finale
ITALIAN for 'final'
1 the end or climax
2 the last movement in a musical composition
3 a spectacular conclusion to any performance, such as the last song or dance in a show

fin de siècle
FRENCH
1 the end of the 19th century, or of any era
2 characteristic of the ideas, etc, of the late 19th century; modernistic or decadent

fines herbes
FRENCH
(cookery) a mixture of herbs used as a garnish or seasoning

finesse
FRENCH
1 subtlety of invention or design
2 skill or expertise
3 (in bridge) an attempt by a player holding a higher card to take the trick with a lower card

fini
FRENCH
1 finished or completed
2 ruined or broken

finis
LATIN
the end; the conclusion
plural ***fines***

finis coronat opus
LATIN
the end crowns the work

fino
SPANISH for 'fine, excellent'
a dry sherry

fioritura
ITALIAN for 'flowering'
(music) a florid embellishment
plural ***fioriture***

fjord or ***fiord***
NORWEGIAN
a long, narrow, rock-bound inlet

fl.
see FLORUIT

flagrante bello
LATIN
while war is raging

flagrante delicto or ***in flagrante delicto***
LATIN, literally 'while the crime is blazing'
in the very act of committing the crime, red-handed

flair
FRENCH for 'sense of smell'
1 intuitive discernment
2 a natural aptitude

flambé
FRENCH
(cookery) prepared or served with flaming brandy or other liquor

flambeau
FRENCH
a flaming torch
plural ***flambeaux*** or ***flambeaus***

flamenco
SPANISH
1 an emotionally intense gypsy song
2 the dance performed to it,

originally from the region of Andalusia
plural ***flamencos***

Flammenwerfer
GERMAN
a flame-thrower

flânerie
FRENCH
idling

flâneur
FRENCH
1 a person who saunters about, a stroller
2 a lounger or idler

flèche
FRENCH for 'arrow'
a church spire, especially a slender spire rising from the intersection of the nave and transepts

flecti non frangi
LATIN
to be bent, not broken

fleur-de-lis or ***fleur-de-lys***
FRENCH, literally 'lily flower'
1 an ornament and heraldic design based on the lily or iris, borne by the kings of France
2 the iris
plural ***fleurs-de-lis*** or ***fleurs-de-lys***

fleuret
FRENCH
1 a small flowerlike ornament
2 a fencing foil

fleuron
FRENCH
a flowerlike ornament in architecture, printing, etc

flic
FRENCH
(slang) a policeman

flora
LATIN
all forms of plant life of a region or period, especially as distinct from animal life
compare FAUNA

> from *Flora*, goddess of flowers

plural ***floras*** or ***florae***

floreat
LATIN
may he, she, or it flourish

florilegium
LATIN
an anthology; a collection of the finest passages of literature

> the Latin word literally refers to the gathering of flowers, as does the Greek word from which the noun *anthology* is derived

floruit
LATIN for 'he or she flourished'
indicating the period during which a person was most active, produced most works, etc

> often used when the person's birth and death dates are not known

abbrev **fl., flor.**

Föhn, föhn, Foehn or ***foehn***
GERMAN
a hot dry wind blowing down a mountain valley, especially in the Alps

foie gras
FRENCH
fattened goose liver made into pâté

folie
FRENCH
madness, insanity, folly

folie à deux
FRENCH
a form of mental illness in which two people, generally close to one another, share the same delusion

folie de doute
FRENCH
mental illness characterized by a total inability to make decisions, however trifling

folie de grandeur
FRENCH
delusions of grandeur

fonctionnaire
FRENCH
an official; a civil servant

fond
FRENCH
1 basis, foundation
2 background

fonda
SPANISH
an inn

fonds
FRENCH
1 landed property
2 capital; money; fund

fondue
FRENCH, literally 'melted'
1 a hot sauce made from cheese and wine into which pieces of bread are dipped
2 a dish consisting of small cubes of meat cooked at the table on forks in hot oil

fons et origo
LATIN
the source and origin

foo yong or ***foo yung***
see FU YUNG

forçat
FRENCH
a convict condemned to hard labour

force de frappe
FRENCH
a strike force, especially a nuclear one

force majeure
FRENCH
1 superior power
2 an unforeseeable or uncontrollable course of events that excuses a party from fulfilling a contract

forte
ITALIAN
(music) loud
abbrev **f**

fortissimo
ITALIAN
(music) very loud
abbrev **ff**

fortiter et recte
LATIN
bravely and uprightly

foulard
FRENCH
1 a soft untwilled silk fabric
2 a silk handkerchief, neckerchief, or headscarf

fou rire
FRENCH
wild laughter, helpless giggling

foyer
FRENCH for 'hearth'
the entrance hall of a theatre, hotel, etc

fra
ITALIAN
brother or friar

fracas
FRENCH
1 uproar
2 a noisy quarrel

fraîcheur
FRENCH
freshness or coolness

franchise
FRENCH
candour or frankness

franco
ITALIAN
1 post-free
2 franked

franc-tireur
FRENCH
a sniper or guerrilla

Frankfurter or ***frankfurter***
from GERMAN *Frankfurter Wurst* meaning 'Frankfurt sausage'
a small smoked sausage

frappant
FRENCH
striking
feminine ***frappante***

frappé
FRENCH
1 (said of drinks) iced or artificially cooled
2 an iced drink
feminine ***frappée***

frate
ITALIAN
a friar, a mendicant Franciscan
plural ***frati***

Frau
GERMAN
1 (also *frau*) a married woman, a lady
2 (also *frau*) a wife
3 (prefixed to a name) Mrs

Frauendienst
GERMAN
courtly love

Fräulein
GERMAN
1 (also *fräulein*) an unmarried woman
2 (also *fräulein*) a German governess
3 (as a form of address) miss
4 (prefixed to a name) Miss

fraus est celare fraudem
LATIN
it is fraud to conceal a fraud

fraus pia
see PIA FRAUS

fredaine
FRENCH
an escapade or prank

frère
FRENCH
a brother

fresco
ITALIAN for 'fresh'
a picture painted on a wall while the plaster is still damp
plural ***frescoes*** or ***frescos***

fricassée or ***fricassee***
FRENCH
(cookery)
1 a dish of chicken, rabbit, etc, cut into pieces and served in sauce
2 to prepare as a fricassée

frigorifico
SPANISH
a slaughtering and meat-freezing establishment
plural ***frigorificos***

fripon
FRENCH

a rascal or rogue

frisée
FRENCH
a variety of curly endive

frisette
FRENCH
a fringe of curls on the forehead

frisson
FRENCH
a shiver; a shudder; a thrill

fritto misto
ITALIAN
a mixed dish of fried food, especially seafood

friture
FRENCH
1 fried food
2 a fritter

frizzante
ITALIAN
(said of wine) sparkling

fromage frais
FRENCH, literally 'fresh cheese'
a light creamy cheese with the consistency of whipped cream, sold in tubs

frottage
FRENCH for 'rubbing'
1 the use of a technique similar to brass-rubbing to obtain a textured effect in a work of art
2 a type of sexual activity in which gratification is obtained by rubbing against someone or something

frou-frou
FRENCH
1 the rustling of silk
2 elaborate trimmings or frills
3 fussy decoration

fruits de mer
FRENCH
seafood

Führer
GERMAN for 'leader, guide'
the title taken by Adolf Hitler as dictator of Nazi Germany

fumetto
ITALIAN
1 a cartoon or comic-strip
2 a balloon in a cartoon
plural ***fumetti***

functus officio
LATIN
having completed a term of office; no longer having official power to act

fundamentum relationis
LATIN, literally 'basis of relation'
the principle or nature of a connection

funèbre
FRENCH
mournful

furioso
ITALIAN
1 a mad or furious person
2 *(music)* with fury
plural ***furiosos***

furor
LATIN
1 fury, rage, frenzy
2 wild excitement or enthusiasm
3 a furore

furore
ITALIAN
1 a general outburst of indignation or protest
2 a craze
3 furor

furor loquendi

LATIN

1 a passion for speaking

2 the urge to speak

furor poeticus

LATIN

1 poetic frenzy

2 a passion for writing poetry

furor scribendi

LATIN

1 a passion for writing

2 the urge to write

fuselage

FRENCH

the body of an aeroplane

futon

JAPANESE

a mattress designed to be laid on the floor or on a low frame

fu yung, foo yung or ***foo yong***

CHINESE for 'hibiscus'

a Chinese omelette-like dish containing bean sprouts, meat, etc

G

gaffe
FRENCH
a blunder, especially a social indiscretion

gagaku
JAPANESE, literally 'graceful (or noble) music'
a type of Japanese classical music played mainly on ceremonial occasions at the Japanese court

galantine
FRENCH
a dish of poultry, veal, etc, served cold in jelly

galère
FRENCH for 'galley'
1 a group of people, especially undesirable people
2 an unpleasant situation

galette
FRENCH
a round, flat, sweet or savoury cake

galop
FRENCH
1 a lively dance
2 the tune for such a dance

gamin
FRENCH
a street urchin

gamine
FRENCH
a girl of a pert, boyish, impish appearance and disposition

garam masala
HINDI, literally 'hot mixture'
a mixture of spices used to make curry

garçon
FRENCH
1 a boy
2 a male servant, especially a waiter in a restaurant

often used vocatively in sense 2

garni
FRENCH
(cookery) trimmed, garnished
see also BOUQUET GARNI

Gastarbeiter
GERMAN, literally 'guest-worker'
a migrant worker, especially one who does menial work

Gasthaus or ***Gasthof***
GERMAN
a hotel or guesthouse

gâteau or ***gateau***
FRENCH for 'cake'
a rich cake, usually filled with cream and decorated with chocolate, fruit, nuts, etc
plural ***gâteaux*** or ***gateaus***

gauche
FRENCH for 'left'
1 clumsy
2 tactless
3 awkward

gaucherie
FRENCH
1 clumsiness
2 tactlessness
3 awkwardness

gaucho
SPANISH
a cowboy of the pampas, usually of mixed Spanish and Indian descent

gaudeamus igitur
LATIN
let us rejoice therefore

the opening words of a students' drinking song

gaudium certaminis
LATIN
the joy of combat, the pleasure of a good contest or argument

gaufrette
FRENCH
a wafer biscuit

Gauleiter or ***gauleiter***
GERMAN, literally 'district leader'
1 the chief official of a district under the Nazi régime
2 *(informal)* a person who wields petty authority in an overbearing manner

gavotte
FRENCH
1 a lively dance
2 the music for such a dance

originally a dance of the *Gavots*, people of the French Alps

gazpacho
SPANISH
a spicy vegetable soup, served cold
plural ***gazpachos***

Gegenschein
GERMAN
counterglow

geisha
JAPANESE, literally 'art person'
a Japanese girl trained to provide entertainment, such as conversation and dancing, for men
plural ***geisha*** or ***geishas***

Geist or ***geist***
GERMAN for 'spirit'
any inspiring or dominating principle

Gemeinschaft
GERMAN for 'community'
a social group united by friendship, kinship, etc

gemütlich
GERMAN
1 amiable
2 comfortable; cosy

Gemütlichkeit
GERMAN
1 kindness
2 comfort; cosiness

gendarme
FRENCH, from *gens d'armes* meaning 'armed people'
a member of an armed police force in France and elsewhere

gendarmerie
FRENCH
1 an armed police force
2 a police station or barracks

gêne or ***gene***
FRENCH
embarrassment

genius loci
LATIN, literally 'spirit of the place'
1 a local deity or guardian spirit
2 the distinctive atmosphere of a place

genre
FRENCH
1 kind, sort
2 a particular type of literature, music, or other artistic work
3 a style of painting that features scenes from everyday or rustic life

gens de bien
FRENCH
honest, respectable people

gens de condition
FRENCH
people of rank

gens d'église
FRENCH
churchmen

gens de guerre
FRENCH
military men

gens de lettres
FRENCH
men and women of letters

gens de loi
FRENCH
lawyers

gens de peu
FRENCH
people of humble condition

gens du monde
FRENCH
people of fashion

gentilhomme
FRENCH
1 a nobleman
2 a gentleman

Gesellschaft
GERMAN
1 an association of people united by individual commitment to a common cause
2 a commercial company

gesso
ITALIAN
plaster used as a medium for sculpture or as a surface for painting
plural ***gessoes***

Gestalt or ***gestalt***
GERMAN
1 form, shape, pattern
2 an organized whole that is more than the sum of its parts
3 denoting a form of psychotherapy that works towards self-discovery through self-expression, self-analysis, etc

Gesundheit
GERMAN
your health!

said to someone who has just sneezed; also used as a drinking toast

geta
JAPANESE
a Japanese wooden sandal with a thong between the big toe and the other toes
plural ***geta*** or ***getas***

gharri or ***gharry***
from HINDI *gārī* meaning 'cart'
(especially in India) a wheeled vehicle, usually for hire

ghat or ***ghaut***
HINDI for 'descent'
(in India)
1 a mountain pass
2 a set of steps leading down to a river
3 a place of cremation

ghazi
ARABIC for 'fighting'
1 a veteran Muslim warrior, a killer of infidels
2 a Turkish title

ghee or ***ghi***
from HINDI *ghī*
clarified butter made from cow's or buffalo's milk, used in Indian cookery

gherao
HINDI for 'siege'
(in India) a form of industrial action in which employers are trapped in a room, building, etc, until they meet the workers' demands
plural ***gheraos***

ghetto
ITALIAN for 'foundry'
1 the Jewish quarter in an Italian or other city
2 a deprived inner-city area densely populated by any ethnic or minority group

> from a foundry that previously occupied the site of the Jewish ghetto in Venice

plural ***ghettoes*** or ***ghettos***

gigolo
FRENCH
1 a professional male dancing partner or escort
2 a young man who lives at the expense of a rich older woman in return for companionship and sexual favours
plural ***gigolos***

gigot
FRENCH
1 a leg of mutton, etc
2 a leg-of-mutton sleeve

gigue
FRENCH
1 a dance derived from the English jig
2 the music for such a dance, often used to complete 18th-century dance suites

gilet
FRENCH
1 a waistcoat
2 part of a woman's dress shaped like a waistcoat

giocoso
ITALIAN
(music) in a lively or humorous manner

girandole
FRENCH, from ITALIAN *girandola*
1 a branched chandelier or similar candle-holder
2 a pendant or earring with a central jewel surrounded by smaller jewels
3 a rotating firework

> the Italian form *girandola* is sometimes used in English

gitano
SPANISH
a gypsy
plural ***gitanos***
feminine ***gitana***

gîte or ***gite***
FRENCH
a farmhouse, cottage, etc, in France, especially one providing simple holiday accommodation

glacé
FRENCH
1 frozen or iced
2 coated with icing
3 candied
4 glossy, lustrous

glasnost
RUSSIAN, literally 'openness, publicity, speaking aloud'
1 the policy of openness and willingness to provide information followed by the former Soviet government under the premiership of Mikhail Gorbachev
2 any similar policy of increased openness

Gleichschaltung
GERMAN for 'co-ordination'
(in politics, culture, etc) elimination

of all opposition, enforcement of strict conformity

glissade
FRENCH
1 a gliding movement in dancing
2 (in mountaineering) the act of sliding down a snowy or icy slope

glissando
ITALIAN
(music)
1 the effect produced by sliding the finger along the keyboard or strings of an instrument
2 a similar effect on the trombone, etc
plural ***glissandos*** or ***glissandi***

glockenspiel or ***Glockenspiel***
from GERMAN *Glockenspiel* meaning 'play of bells, carillon, chimes'
a musical instrument consisting of a set of bells or metal bars struck by hammers, with or without a keyboard

glogg
from SWEDISH *glögg*
a hot spiced drink containing wine, brandy, fruit, etc, often served at Christmas

gloire
FRENCH
glory

gloria
LATIN
1 glory
2 any doxology beginning with the word 'Gloria'

gloria in excelsis (Deo)
LATIN
glory (to God) on high

gnocchi
ITALIAN
a dish of small dumplings made from flour, semolina, or cooked potatoes, served with a sauce

gnomon
GREEK for 'carpenter's square'
1 the pin of a sundial, which casts a shadow pointing to the hour
2 an upright rod for measuring the sun's altitude by its shadow

gnōthi seauton
GREEK
know thyself
see also NOSCE TEIPSUM

> inscribed on the temple of Apollo at Delphi

go
JAPANESE
a Japanese board game for two, played with black and white stones or counters, the object being to capture one's opponent's stones and gain control of the larger part of the board

gobbo
ITALIAN
a hunchback
plural ***gobbi***

gobe-mouches
FRENCH
1 a flycatcher
2 an insectivorous plant
3 a credulous person

gopak
RUSSIAN
a high-leaping folk-dance from the Ukraine

Götterdämmerung
GERMAN, literally 'twilight of the gods'
(in German mythology) the ultimate defeat of the gods by evil

Gott mitt uns
GERMAN
God with us

➪ motto of the Hohenzollern family, rulers of Prussia and Germany

gouache
FRENCH
1 a method of watercolour painting using opaque colours mixed with water, honey, and gum, giving a matt surface
2 a painting so produced
3 the paint itself

gourmand
FRENCH
1 a person who eats greedily; a glutton
2 a lover of good food

gourmet
FRENCH
a connoisseur of good food and wines

goût or ***gout***
FRENCH
1 taste
2 relish

goutte
FRENCH
a drop of liquid

goutte à goutte
FRENCH
drop by drop

goy
HEBREW for 'people, nation'
a non-Jew, a Gentile
plural ***goyim*** or ***goys***

grâce à Dieu
FRENCH
thanks to God

gracioso
SPANISH for 'gracious'
a clown in Spanish comedy
plural ***graciosos***

gradatim
LATIN
step by step

gradus ad Parnassum
LATIN, literally 'a step (or stairs) to Parnassus'
a Latin or Greek poetical dictionary

Graf
GERMAN
a title of nobility equivalent to that of a count or earl
feminine ***Gräfin***

graffiti
ITALIAN
words or drawings, often obscene or political, found on the walls of public buildings, in lavatories, etc
singular ***graffito***

grand amateur
FRENCH
a collector of beautiful objects on a large scale

grand coup
FRENCH
1 a successful stroke
2 (in bridge or whist) the trumping of a trick that could have been trumped by the winner's partner

grand cru
FRENCH
wine from a famous vineyard or group of vineyards
see also CRU

grande amoureuse
FRENCH
a woman greatly involved in love affairs

grande cocotte
FRENCH
a high-class prostitute, usually one kept by a rich lover
see also COCOTTE

grande dame
FRENCH
a dignified aristocratic lady

> now usually ironic, like its masculine equivalent GRAND SEIGNEUR

grande école
FRENCH
a prestigious French college of higher education with a competitive entrance examination

grande marque
FRENCH
(said of cars, etc) a famous make

grande passion
FRENCH
a serious love affair or intense infatuation

grande tenue
FRENCH
full dress, especially military or evening dress

grande toilette
FRENCH
full dress, especially women's evening dress

grande vedette
FRENCH
a leading star of stage or screen

Grand Guignol
FRENCH
1 short horror plays
2 anything intended to horrify

> from the name of a small theatre in Paris that specialized in such plays

grand luxe
FRENCH
great luxury

grand mal
FRENCH, literally 'great ill'
a violently convulsive form of epilepsy
compare PETIT MAL

grand merci
FRENCH
many thanks

grand monde
FRENCH
high society

grand prix or ***Grand Prix***
FRENCH, literally 'great prize'
1 any of several international motor races
2 any competition of similar importance in other sports

> from the Grand Prix de Paris, a famous horse race

plural ***grands prix*** or ***Grands Prix***

grand seigneur
FRENCH
a dignified aristocratic gentleman

> now usually ironic, like its feminine equivalent GRANDE DAME

Grand Siècle
from FRENCH *le Grand Siècle* meaning 'the great century'
the classical age of French literature during the reign of Louis XIV

granita
from ITALIAN *granito* meaning 'grainy'
a flavoured water ice with a grainy texture

gran turismo
ITALIAN, literally 'grand touring'
(said of a car) designed for touring

in luxury and at high speed
abbrev **GT**

> the abbreviation often indicates a model that is of higher performance and greater comfort than the standard car

grappa
ITALIAN, literally 'grape stalk'
a brandy of Italian origin made from the residue of a winepress

gratia placendi
LATIN
the joy of pleasing

gratin
FRENCH
(cookery) a topping of buttered breadcrumbs and/or cheese browned until crisp
see also AU GRATIN

> in French the term originally referred to the (burnt) scrapings from a pan, casserole, etc, from *gratter* meaning 'to scratch or scrape'

gratiné
FRENCH
cooked or served au gratin
feminine ***gratinée***

gratis
LATIN
for nothing; without payment or recompense

gravamen
LATIN
1 a grievance
2 *(law)* the chief ground of complaint or accusation
plural ***gravamina***

graviora manent
LATIN
greater dangers remain; the worst is yet to come

gravitas
LATIN
1 seriousness
2 weight, importance

gravlax or ***gravadlax***
SWEDISH, literally 'buried salmon'
a Scandinavian dish of salmon dry-cured with dill (or other herbs and spices), sugar, salt, and pepper

grazioso
ITALIAN
(music)
1 graceful
2 gracefully

gregatim
LATIN
in flocks

greige or ***grège***
from FRENCH *(soie) grège* meaning 'raw (silk)'
1 (said of cloth) undyed
2 of a greyish-beige colour

Grenzgänger
GERMAN
a person who crosses a national or political border, especially from a communist country to the West
plural ***Grenzgänger***

grex venalium
LATIN, literally 'herd of hirelings'
the corrupt or mercenary crowd

gringo
SPANISH
in the Spanish-speaking countries of Latin America, someone whose first language is not Spanish, especially an English speaker

> probably from SPANISH *Griego* meaning 'Greek'

grosgrain
FRENCH
a heavy corded silk fabric or tape used especially for ribbons and hatbands

gros point
FRENCH
1 a large diagonal or cross stitch covering two vertical and two horizontal threads of the canvas
2 embroidery or tapestry using this stitch
compare PETIT POINT

grossièreté
FRENCH
rudeness, coarseness

GT
see GRAN TURISMO

guacamole
AMERICAN SPANISH, from NAHUATL *ahuacamolli*
a dish of mashed avocado with tomatoes, onions, and seasoning

guano
SPANISH
the droppings of seabirds, used as a fertilizer
plural ***guanos***

guéridon
FRENCH
a small ornate table or stand

guerre à mort
FRENCH
war to the death

guerre à outrance
FRENCH
war to the bitter end

guerrilla or ***guerilla***
SPANISH, literally 'little war'
a member of a small irregular armed force, often politically motivated

also used as an adjective

guichet
FRENCH
1 a hatch or other small opening in a wall, door, etc
2 a ticket-office window

guillotine
FRENCH
1 an instrument for beheading, with a heavy oblique blade that descends between two upright posts
2 a manually or electrically operated machine used for cutting or trimming paper, card, metal, etc
3 a time limit set to speed up discussion and voting in parliament, etc

sense 1 named after the French physician Joseph Ignace *Guillotin* (1738–1814) and adopted during the French Revolution, though a similar apparatus had already been used in Scotland, Germany, and Italy. The word is also used as a verb (in all three senses) in English

guipure
FRENCH
a kind of heavy lace with a large open pattern and no background, the pattern sections being fixed by interlacing threads

gulag
RUSSIAN
a Soviet forced-labour camp

an acronym of *Glavnoye Upravleniye Ispravitelno-Trudovykh Lagerei* meaning 'main administration for corrective labour camps'

gung-ho
from CHINESE *kung ho* meaning 'work together'
(slang) excessively or irrationally enthusiastic, eager, or zealous

guru
HINDI
1 (in Hinduism) a spiritual teacher

2 a highly respected and influential leader, expert, adviser, or instructor

gusto
ITALIAN
exuberant enjoyment, zest

guten Abend
GERMAN
good evening

gute Nacht
GERMAN
goodnight

guten Morgen
GERMAN
good morning

guten Tag
GERMAN
good day

gutta cavat lapidem
LATIN
the drop wears away the stone

Gymnasium
GERMAN
a top-grade secondary school in Germany and other European countries, which prepares pupils for higher education, especially in academic rather than vocational subjects

> in this sense the German pronunciation, including the hard initial G, is usually retained in English

plural ***Gymnasiums*** or ***Gymnasien***

H

ha or ***h.a.***
see HOC ANNO

habeas corpus
LATIN, literally 'have the body'
a writ requiring that a prisoner be brought to court for the judge to decide if their imprisonment is lawful

habitué
FRENCH
a regular or frequent visitor or customer
feminine ***habituée***

hacienda
SPANISH
(in Spanish America)
1 a landed estate
2 a ranch or farm
3 a main dwelling-house on an estate
4 a country house
5 a stock-rearing, manufacturing, or mining establishment in the country

hac lege
LATIN
with this law, under this condition

hadj, haj or ***hajj***
from ARABIC *hajj* meaning 'effort, pilgrimage'
a pilgrimage, especially the pilgrimage to Mecca that all Muslims are required to make at least once in their life

hadji, haji or ***hajji***
from ARABIC *hājī*
1 someone who has performed a hadj
2 a Christian who has visited Jerusalem

haec olim meminisse juvabit
LATIN
some day we shall be glad to remember these things

> referring to something unpleasant

haiku, haikai or ***hokku***
JAPANESE
a Japanese poem in three lines of 5, 7, and 5 syllables, usually humorous, incorporating a word or phrase that symbolizes one of the seasons

Hakenkreuz
GERMAN, literally 'hooked cross'
swastika

halal or ***hallal***
ARABIC for 'lawful'
1 to slaughter animals according to Muslim law
2 meat from animals that have been so slaughtered, which may lawfully be eaten by Muslims

> also used as an adjective

Halbstarker
GERMAN
a juvenile delinquent

Hammerklavier
GERMAN
a pianoforte

hapax legomenon
GREEK, literally 'said once'

a word or phrase that is found only once in all the written works of a language

hara-kiri
JAPANESE, literally 'belly-cut'
ritual suicide by cutting open the belly with a sword, formerly practised in Japan to avoid dishonour

> the practice is also called *seppuku*

hasta la vista
SPANISH, literally 'until we meet again'
goodbye

hasta luego
SPANISH, literally 'until then'
see you later

hasta mañana
SPANISH
see you tomorrow

hatha yoga
SANSKRIT
a form of yoga that uses exercises, positions, and breathing control to promote physical and mental wellbeing
see also YOGA

Hausfrau or ***hausfrau***
GERMAN
a housewife, especially a woman exclusively interested in domestic matters

haute bourgeoisie
FRENCH
the wealthier and more influential section of the middle class

haute couture
FRENCH
the work or products of the leading fashion designers

haute cuisine
FRENCH
cookery of a very high standard

haute école
FRENCH
horsemanship of the most difficult kind

haute époque
FRENCH
the period during which Louis XIV, XV, and XVI reigned in France

> used in relation to architecture, furniture, etc

haute politique
FRENCH
the higher reaches of politics

hauteur
FRENCH
haughtiness; arrogance

haute vulgarisation
FRENCH
popularization of scholarly subjects

haut monde
FRENCH
high society

haut-relief
FRENCH for 'high relief'
sculpture in which the figures project by at least half their thickness from the background on which they are formed

> the Italian equivalent is *alto-rilievo*

haut ton
FRENCH
high fashion

heft or ***Heft***
from GERMAN *Heft*
1 a number of sheets or pages fastened together

2 an instalment of a serial publication

hegira, hejira, hejra or ***hijra***
from ARABIC *hijrah*
1 the flight of Mohammed from Mecca in AD622, marking the beginning of the Muslim era
2 any similar flight

heil
GERMAN
hail!

Heimat
GERMAN
1 home
2 homeland
3 birthplace

Heimweh
GERMAN
homesickness

Herr
GERMAN
1 lord, master
2 (as a form of address) sir
3 (prefixed to a name) Mr
plural ***Herren***

Herrenvolk
GERMAN for 'master race'
those who believe themselves to be superior to other races, and therefore entitled and qualified to rule the world

hiatus
LATIN
1 a gap; an opening
2 a break in continuity
plural ***hiatuses***

hibachi
JAPANESE, literally 'fire bowl'
a portable barbecue for cooking food out of doors
plural ***hibachi*** or ***hibachis***

hic et ubique
LATIN
here and everywhere

hic jacet
LATIN
here lies ...

> followed by the name of the dead person on tombstones, monuments, etc

hidalgo
from SPANISH *hijo de algo* meaning 'son of something'
1 a Spanish nobleman of the lowest class
2 a gentleman
plural ***hidalgos***
feminine ***hidalga***

hijra
see HEGIRA

hinc illae lacrimae
LATIN, literally 'hence those tears'
that is the cause of the trouble

hinterland
from GERMAN *Hinterland*
a region lying inland from a port or around a centre of influence

Hizbollah or ***Hizbullah***
ARABIC, literally 'party of God'
an organization of militant Shiite Muslims

hoc anno
LATIN
in this year
abbrev **ha, h.a.**

hoc genus omne
LATIN
all that sort (of thing or people)

hoc loco
LATIN
in this place

hoc monumentum posuit
LATIN
he or she erected this monument
abbrev **HMP**

hoc tempore
LATIN
at this time

hodie mihi, cras tibi
LATIN
me today, you tomorrow

Hof
GERMAN
1 yard
2 manor
3 court

hoi polloi
GREEK, literally 'the many'
(derogatory) the masses; the rabble

> usually prefixed by 'the', although the English definite article is redundant, since *hoi* means 'the'

hokku
see HAIKU

hola
SPANISH
an informal greeting; hello!

hombre
SPANISH
man

homme
FRENCH
man

homme d'affaires
FRENCH
1 a businessman
2 an agent, a steward

homme de bien
FRENCH
a good man

homme de lettres
FRENCH
a man of letters

homme d'épée
FRENCH, literally 'man of sword'
a military man

homme d'esprit
FRENCH
a man of wit

homme d'état
FRENCH
a statesman

homme du monde
FRENCH
1 a man of the world
2 a society man; a man of fashion

homme moyen sensuel
FRENCH, literally 'average sensual man'
the ordinary man; the man in the street

homme sérieux
FRENCH
a serious, earnest man

homo
LATIN
man

Homo sapiens
LATIN, literally 'wise man'
the species that constitutes the human race

homo trium litterarum
LATIN, literally 'man of three letters'
a thief

> the three letters are *fur*, Latin for 'thief'

homo unius libri
LATIN

a man of one book, ie ignorant of all others

honi soit qui mal y pense
OLD FRENCH
shame on him who thinks ill of it

the motto of the Order of the Garter

honorarium
from LATIN *honōrārium (donum)* meaning 'honorary (gift)'
a voluntary fee, especially one paid to a professional person for their services
plural **honorariums** or **honoraria**

honoris causa or ***honoris gratia***
LATIN
as an honour, as a token of respect

used eg of a degree conferred without examination

hookah or ***hooka***
from ARABIC *huqqah* meaning 'bowl, casket'
a tobacco-pipe used by Arabs, Turks, etc, in which smoke is inhaled through water

horae canonicae
LATIN
the canonical hours

horas non numero nisi serenas
LATIN
I number none but shining hours

a common inscription on sundials

horresco referens
LATIN
I shudder in relating it

horribile dictu
LATIN
horrible to tell

horribile visu
LATIN
horrible to see

hors concours
FRENCH, literally 'out of competition'
1 (said of an exhibitor, etc) not competing
2 unrivalled

hors de combat
FRENCH
out of action; unfit to fight, compete, take part, etc

hors de saison
FRENCH
out of season

hors d'oeuvre
FRENCH
a savoury snack served as an appetizer
plural ***hors d'oeuvre*** or ***hors d'oeuvres***

hors la loi
FRENCH
outlawed

hors série
FRENCH
not included in a series, added later

hors texte
FRENCH
an illustration inserted into a book on a separate leaf

as opposed to one printed on a page of text

hortus siccus
LATIN
a collection of dried plants; a herbarium

hôtel de ville
FRENCH
town hall

houri
▮ from PERSIAN *hūrī*
1 a nymph of the Muslim paradise
2 a voluptuously alluring woman

howdah or ***houdah***
▮ from ARABIC *haudaj*
a seat, often with a canopy, used for riding on an elephant's back

hubris or ***hybris***
▮ from GREEK *hybris*
arrogance or over-confidence, especially bringing disaster or ruin

hula-hula or ***hula***
▮ HAWAIIAN
a Hawaiian dance

huma
▮ PERSIAN for 'phoenix'
a fabulous bird

humanum est errare
see ERRARE HUMANUM EST

hummus, hoummos or ***houmus***
▮ TURKISH
a Middle Eastern hors d'oeuvre of puréed chickpeas and sesame oil with garlic and lemon

hutzpah
see CHUTZPAH

hwyl
▮ WELSH
1 divine inspiration in oratory
2 emotional fervour

hyperbole
▮ GREEK for 'excess'
the use of overstatement or exaggeration to produce an effect

hypotheses non fingo
▮ LATIN
I do not frame hypotheses, I do not make unverifiable speculations

➪ said by Isaac Newton

hysteron-proteron
▮ GREEK, literally 'latter-former'
an inversion of the natural or logical sequence of ideas, words, etc

I

ibidem
LATIN
in the same place

referring to a book, chapter, passage, etc, already cited

abbrev **ib., ibid.**

ich dien
GERMAN
I serve

the motto of the Prince of Wales

I Ching
CHINESE, literally 'book of changes'
an ancient Chinese system of divination, consisting of a set of symbols and the text used to interpret them

ich kann nicht anders
GERMAN
I can do no other

from a speech by Martin Luther at the Diet of Worms in 1521. In modern usage the phrase may be said by or of anyone who stands by their principles in the face of opposition

id
LATIN for 'it'
the part of the subconscious mind that is regarded as the source of primitive instincts and urges for survival and reproduction

idée fixe
FRENCH
a fixed idea, an obsession or monomania

idée reçue
FRENCH
1 an accepted idea
2 a conventional outlook

idem
LATIN
the same
abbrev **id**

idem quod
LATIN
the same as
abbrev **iq, i.q.**

idem sonans
LATIN
sounding the same

used of a misspelt word in a legal document that can be accepted as the intended word

id est
LATIN
that is, that is to say
abbrev **ie, i.e.**

the abbreviation is the usual form

idiot savant
FRENCH, literally 'knowing idiot'
a mentally subnormal person who demonstrates remarkable talent in a particular area, such as memorizing or rapid calculation

ie or ***i.e.***
see ID EST

igloo
from ESKIMO *iglu* meaning 'house'

1 originally, a dome-shaped hut made of blocks of hard snow

2 a dwelling made of other materials

ignis fatuus

LATIN, literally 'foolish fire'

1 will-o'-the-wisp, a light produced by combustion of marsh gas, which may lead a traveller into danger

2 any ideal or delusion that may lead one astray

plural ***ignes fatui***

ignoramus

LATIN, literally 'we are ignorant, we ignore'

an ignorant person

plural ***ignoramuses***

ignorantia juris neminem excusat or ***ignorantia legis neminem excusat***

LATIN

ignorance of the law excuses nobody

ignoratio elenchi

LATIN, literally 'ignorance of proof'

(logic) the fallacy of appearing to refute a proposition by proving an irrelevant proposition

ignotum per ignotius

LATIN

the unknown by the still more unknown

> referring to an attempt to explain something that is little known or understood by means of something that is even less known or understood

ignotus

LATIN

unknown

abbrev **ign.**

ijtihad

ARABIC, literally 'exerting oneself'

the use of reasoning in Islamic law

ikebana

JAPANESE, literally 'living flowers'

the Japanese art of flower arranging

il faut cultiver notre jardin

FRENCH, literally 'we must cultivate our garden'

we must attend to our own affairs

> the closing words of Voltaire's *Candide* (1759)

il faut souffrir pour être belle

FRENCH

it is necessary to suffer in order to be beautiful

> usually referring to painful cosmetic procedures

illustrissimo

ITALIAN

most illustrious

il n'y a que le premier pas qui coûte or ***ce n'est que le premier pas qui coûte***

FRENCH

it is only the first step that counts

> Mme du Deffand's comment (in a letter of 1763) on the legend that St Denis walked two leagues after his decapitation

il penseroso

ITALIAN

the pensive (or melancholy) man

> the modern Italian form is *il pensieroso*

ils ne passeront pas

FRENCH

they shall not pass

➪ first used at Verdun in 1916

ils n'ont rien appris ni rien oublié
FRENCH
they have learned nothing and forgotten nothing

➪ said of the French émigrés, often of the Bourbons

imago
LATIN for 'image'
the final stage in the life cycle of an insect
plural ***imagines, imagos*** or ***imagoes***

imam or ***imaum***
ARABIC for 'chief'
1 the person who leads the devotions in a mosque
2 a title for various Muslim leaders and potentates

imaret
TURKISH
(in Turkey) an inn or refuge for travellers

imbroglio or ***embroglio***
ITALIAN for 'confusion'
1 a confused mass or heap
2 a complicated situation
3 a misunderstanding or disagreement
plural ***imbroglios*** or ***embroglios***

immortelle
from FRENCH *(fleur) immortelle*
an everlasting flower, ie one that keeps its shape and colour when dried

impair
FRENCH
any of the odd numbers in roulette
compare PAIR

impasse
FRENCH
a situation from which further progress is impossible; deadlock, stalemate

impasto
ITALIAN
(art)
1 paint or pigment applied thickly, especially to create surface texture
2 the technique of applying paint or pigment in this way
plural ***impastos***

impedimenta
LATIN
encumbrances, especially baggage, luggage, etc

imperium
LATIN
sovereignty, absolute authority, supreme power
plural ***imperia***

imperium in imperio
LATIN
absolute authority within the realm of a higher authority

impetus
LATIN
1 momentum
2 impulse
3 incentive
plural ***impetuses***

impresario
ITALIAN
1 the manager of an opera or theatre company
2 a producer or organizer of public entertainments
plural ***impresarios*** or ***impresari***

imprimatur
LATIN, literally 'let it be printed'
a licence to publish a book, etc

imprimis
LATIN
in the first place

impromptu
LATIN, from *in promptū* meaning 'in readiness'
1 improvised, spontaneous, unrehearsed
2 makeshift
3 without preparation
4 on the spur of the moment
5 an extempore or improvised composition, performance, speech, etc
6 *(music)* a composition with the character of an extemporization

improvvisatore
ITALIAN
someone, especially a performer, who improvises
feminine ***improvvisatrice***

in absentia
LATIN
in his, her, or their absence

in abstracto
LATIN
in the abstract

inamorato or ***innamorato***
from ITALIAN *innamorato*
a person in love with or loved by another
plural ***inamoratos*** or ***innamoratos***
feminine ***inamorata*** or ***innamorata***

in articulo mortis
LATIN
at the point or moment of death

in banco
LATIN
(law) in full court

in bianco
ITALIAN, literally 'in white'
blank

in bonam partem
LATIN
in a favourable manner

in camera
LATIN
1 in a judge's private room
2 in secret
3 in private

incipit
LATIN
here begins

> often used as an introduction in medieval manuscripts

incognito
ITALIAN for 'unknown'
1 concealing one's identity, usually by means of an assumed name, a disguise, etc
2 unknown, unidentified
3 a person concealing their identity
4 an assumed name, a disguise
plural ***incognitos***

incommunicado
from SPANISH *incomunicado*
1 without means of communication
2 in solitary confinement

inconnu
FRENCH
an unknown person
feminine ***inconnue***

incubus
LATIN
1 a devil supposed to assume a male body and have sexual intercourse with women in their sleep
2 a nightmare
3 any oppressive person or thing
compare SUCCUBUS

plural ***incubuses*** or ***incubi***

incunabula

LATIN for 'swaddling-clothes'
early printed books, especially those printed before 1501
singular ***incunabulum***

in deposito

LATIN
on deposit, as a pledge

index auctorum

LATIN
an index of authors

Index Expurgatorius

LATIN
a former list of books from which certain passages had to be removed before the books could be read by Roman Catholics

Index Librorum Prohibitorum

LATIN
a former list of books prohibited to Roman Catholic readers

index locorum

LATIN
an index of places

index rerum

LATIN
1 an index of matters or subjects
2 a reference notebook

index verborum

LATIN
an index of words

in Domino

LATIN
in the Lord

in esse

LATIN
in existence
see also ESSE
compare IN POSSE

in excelsis

LATIN
1 on high
2 in the highest degree

in extenso

LATIN
at full length

in extremis

LATIN
1 in the last extremity
2 in desperate circumstances
3 at the point of death

inf.

see INFRA

in facie curiae

LATIN
in the presence of, or before, the court

infanta

SPANISH and PORTUGUESE
1 a princess of the royal family of Spain or Portugal
2 the wife of an infante

infante

SPANISH and PORTUGUESE
a prince of the royal family of Spain or Portugal, especially a son of the king other than the heir-apparent

inferiae

LATIN
offerings to the spirits of the dead

inferno

ITALIAN for 'hell'
1 a raging fire
2 any place or situation of horror and confusion
plural ***infernos***

in fieri

LATIN

(law) in course of completion; pending

in flagrante delicto
see FLAGRANTE DELICTO

in forma pauperis
LATIN
(law) as a poor person, not liable to costs

in foro conscientiae
LATIN, literally 'in the court of conscience'
judged by one's own conscience

infra
LATIN
1 below
2 lower down on the page, or further on in the book
abbrev **inf.**

infra dignitatem
LATIN
beneath one's dignity; unbecoming
abbrev (informal) **infra dig**

ingénue
FRENCH
1 a naive or inexperienced young woman
2 an actress portraying such a type
masculine ***ingénu***

in gremio legis
LATIN, literally 'in the bosom of the law'
under the protection of the law

in limine
LATIN
on the threshold

in loc. cit.
see LOCO CITATO

in loco
LATIN
in its place
abbrev **in loc.**

in loco citato
see LOCO CITATO

in loco parentis
LATIN
in the place of a parent

> said of one who temporarily assumes the role and responsibilities of a parent while working with, supervising, or caring for children

in malam partem
LATIN
in an unfavourable manner

in medias res
LATIN
into the midst of things

in memoriam
LATIN
in memory of, to the memory of

innamorato, innamorata
see INAMORATO

innuendo
LATIN, literally 'by nodding at'
1 insinuation
2 an indirect reference or allusion
plural ***innuendos*** or ***innuendoes***

in pace
LATIN
in peace

in partibus infidelium
LATIN
in the lands of the unbelievers

> applied to titular bishops in countries where no Catholic hierachy has been set up, or to those bearing the title of an extinct see

in perpetuum

LATIN

for ever

in personam

LATIN

(law) (said of a proceeding, enforceable right, etc) against a specific person

compare IN REM

in petto

ITALIAN, literally 'within the breast'

1 in one's own mind but not yet disclosed

2 in secret

3 in reserve

in pleno

LATIN

in full

in posse

LATIN

potentially; possibly

see also POSSE

compare IN ESSE

in principio

LATIN

in the beginning

in propria persona

LATIN

in person; personally

in puris naturalibus

LATIN

stark naked

inqilab

URDU

(in India, Pakistan, etc) revolution

in re

LATIN

in the matter of; concerning

see also RE

> chiefly used in legal proceedings

in rem

LATIN

(law) (said of a proceeding, enforceable right, etc) against all persons or against a thing

compare IN PERSONAM

in rerum natura

LATIN

in the nature of things

in rixa

LATIN, literally 'in a quarrel'

(law) in the heat of the moment

> used as a defence in cases of defamation

inro

JAPANESE, literally 'seal-box'

a small container for pills and medicines, once part of traditional Japanese dress

plural ***inro***

in saecula saeculorum

LATIN

for ever and ever

in se

LATIN

in itself

insignia

LATIN

1 emblems or badges of office, honour, membership, occupation, etc

2 marks by which anything is known

> sometimes treated as singular, especially in the US

in situ

LATIN

1 in position

2 in the original, intended, or designated position

insouciance
FRENCH
1 indifference
2 nonchalance
3 heedlessness
4 apathy

insouciant
FRENCH
1 indifferent, unconcerned
2 nonchalant
3 heedless
4 apathetic
feminine ***insouciante***

instar omnium
LATIN
worth all of them

Cicero's description of Plato in relation to other men

in statu pupillari
LATIN
as a pupil or ward

in statu quo
LATIN
in the same state as formerly or at present, unchanged
see also STATUS QUO

intaglio
ITALIAN
1 a stone or gem in which the design is hollowed out
2 a design cut into any substance
3 the production of such designs, stones, or gems

intelligentsia
RUSSIAN, from LATIN *intelligentia* meaning 'intelligence'
the intellectual or cultured classes

inter alia
LATIN
among other things

inter alios
LATIN
among other people

intermezzo
ITALIAN
1 a short dramatic or musical entertainment performed as an entr'acte
2 *(music)* a short intermediate movement separating sections of a symphonic work
plural ***intermezzi*** or ***intermezzos***

in terminis
LATIN
definitely; in express terms

inter nos
LATIN
between ourselves

inter partes
LATIN
(law) between parties

inter pocula
LATIN, literally 'between cups'
in the course of drinking, over drinks

interregnum
LATIN
1 the time between two reigns, governments, etc
2 any breach of continuity in order, etc
plural ***interregnums*** or ***interregna***

in terrorem
LATIN
as a warning

inter se
LATIN
between or among themselves

inter vivos
LATIN, literally 'among the living'
(law) (said of gifts, etc) from one living person to another

intifada
ARABIC, literally 'shaking off'
the uprising in 1987 and subsequent resistance by Palestinians to Israeli occupation of the Gaza Strip and West Bank of the Jordan

intime
FRENCH
1 intimate
2 small and cosy

intonaco
ITALIAN
in fresco painting, the final coat of plaster onto which the paint is applied

in totidem verbis
LATIN
in so many words

in toto
LATIN
entirely, completely, totally

intra
LATIN
within

intrada
ITALIAN
(music) an introductory piece, a prelude

intra muros
LATIN
within the walls

in transitu
LATIN
in passage, in transit, on the way

intra vires
LATIN
within the legal power of

intra vitam
LATIN
during life

in usum Delphini
LATIN, literally 'for the use of the Dauphin'
bowdlerized or expurgated for young readers

from an edition of Latin classics prepared for Louis XIV's son

in utero
LATIN
in the womb

in utroque jure
LATIN
under both laws (civil and canon)

in utrumque paratus
LATIN
prepared for either event

in vacuo
LATIN
1 in a vacuum
2 unrelated to a context, without specific application

in vadio
LATIN
in pledge

invenit
LATIN
he or she devised or designed this
abbrev **inv.**

in vino veritas
LATIN, literally 'in wine is truth'
truth is told under the influence of alcohol

in vitro

LATIN, literally 'in glass'
(medicine) outside the living organism, eg in a test tube
compare IN VIVO

often found in the phrase *in-vitro fertilization*, referring to the technique whereby a 'test-tube baby' is conceived outside the mother's body

in vivo

LATIN
(medicine) within the living organism
compare IN VITRO

ipecacuanha

PORTUGUESE, from TUPÍ
the dried root of various South American plants, used as a purgative, emetic, and expectorant
abbrev **ipecac**

ippon

JAPANESE, literally 'one point'
(in judo and karate) a winning point awarded for a perfectly executed move

ipse dixit

LATIN, literally 'he himself said it'
a dogmatic pronouncement; a dictum

ipsissima verba

LATIN
the very words

ipsissimis verbis

LATIN
quoted exactly

ipso facto

LATIN
by that very fact; thereby

iq or ***i.q.***

see IDEM QUOD

irenicon

see EIRENICON

issei

JAPANESE, literally 'first generation'
a Japanese immigrant in the US or Canada
see also NISEI, SANSEI

ita est

LATIN
it is so

iterum

LATIN
again; anew

iure

see JURE

ius

see JUS

ivresse

FRENCH
drunkenness

izvestiya or ***izvestia***

RUSSIAN
1 news
2 information

izzat

URDU
public esteem; honour, reputation, prestige

J

jabot
FRENCH
a lace frill or ruffle on the front of a garment, especially on a man's shirt-front as part of full Highland dress

j'accuse
FRENCH, literally 'I accuse'
any publication that makes an accusation of intolerance, injustice, etc

> originally the title of a open letter from Emile Zola, published in *L'Aurore* (13 January 1898), in connection with the Dreyfus case

Jacquerie
FRENCH
1 the revolt of the French peasants in 1358
2 any peasant revolt

> from *Jacques Bonhomme*, a name derisively applied to the peasants

jacta est alea, alea jacta est or ***jacta alea est***
LATIN
the die is cast

> said by Caesar at the crossing of the Rubicon

j'adoube
FRENCH, literally 'I adjust'
(chess) a warning that only an adjustment is intended, not a move

> said by a player touching a piece

Jäger, jäger or ***jaeger***
GERMAN
1 a huntsman
2 a German or Austrian rifleman or sharpshooter

jai alai
SPANISH, from BASQUE, literally 'merry festival'
a game resembling handball but played with a long curved basket strapped to the wrist; a type of pelota

jalousie
FRENCH
an outside shutter with slats

jambalaya
from PROVENÇAL *jambalaia*
a Creole or Cajun dish consisting of rice mixed with seafood or chicken, seasonings, etc

jambiya or ***jambiyah***
ARABIC
a Middle Eastern curved, double-edged dagger

jamdani
PERSIAN
a variety of Dacca muslin woven in a flowery design

japonaiserie
FRENCH
1 Japanese decoration
2 a Japanese ornament
3 Japanese bric-à-brac

jardinière
FRENCH
1 an ornamental pot or stand for flowers

2 a style of drapery, especially curtains, with raised centre and full-length ends
3 *(cookery)* a mixture of diced or sliced cooked vegetables, usually served with a meat dish

jaspé or ***jaspe***
FRENCH
mottled, variegated, or veined

jataka
SANSKRIT
the birth-story of Buddha

ja wohl
GERMAN
yes indeed

jebel or ***djebel***
ARABIC
(in Arab countries) a hill or a mountain

jehad
see JIHAD

jellaba or ***jelab***
see DJELLABA

je m'en fous
FRENCH
(slang) I don't care, I don't give a damn

je-m'en-foutisme
FRENCH
a couldn't-care-less attitude or philosophy

je ne regrette rien
FRENCH
I regret nothing
the title of a song popularized by Edith Piaf

je ne sais quoi
FRENCH, literally 'I don't know what'
a special unknown ingredient or quality

jet d'eau
FRENCH
a jet of water, eg in an ornamental fountain

jeté
FRENCH for 'thrown'
(ballet) a leap from one foot to the other, landing with the free leg extended forwards, backwards, or sideways

jeu
FRENCH
a game
plural ***jeux***
see also FAITES VOS JEUX, LES JEUX SONT FAITS

jeu de mots
FRENCH
a play on words, a pun
plural ***jeux de mots***

jeu d'esprit
FRENCH
a witticism
plural ***jeux d'esprit***

jeune amour
FRENCH
young love

jeune fille
FRENCH
a girl

jeune premier
FRENCH
(theatre) a juvenile lead
feminine ***jeune première***

jeunesse dorée
FRENCH, literally 'gilded youth'
wealthy, stylish, and sophisticated young people

jibbah
see JUBBAH

jihad or ***jehad***
ARABIC for 'struggle'
1 a holy war (for the Muslim faith)
2 a fervent crusade

jinn or ***djinn***
ARABIC
in Muslim theology and folklore, a class of spirits able to adopt human or animal form
singular ***jinni, jinnee*** or ***djinni***

jinricksha or ***jinrickshaw***
see RICKSHA

jiu-jitsu
see JU-JITSU

jnana
from SANSKRIT *jñāna*
(Hinduism) spiritual knowledge

joie de vivre
FRENCH, literally 'joy of living'
exuberance

jojoba
MEXICAN SPANISH
a desert shrub of the box family, growing in Mexico, Arizona, and California, whose seeds yield a waxy oil used in cosmetic preparations, etc

jolie laide or ***belle laide***
FRENCH
a woman whose ugliness is part of her charm
plural ***jolies laides*** or ***belles laides***

jour
FRENCH
a day

jour de fête
FRENCH
a feast day, especially a saint's day

journal intime
FRENCH
a personal diary

jubbah, djibbah or ***jibbah***
ARABIC
a long loose outer garment worn by Muslims

Judenhetze
GERMAN
Jew-baiting

judo
JAPANESE, literally 'gentle way'
a sport and physical discipline based on unarmed self-defence techniques, a modern variety of ju-jitsu

judogi
JAPANESE
the costume (jacket and trousers) worn for judo

judoka
JAPANESE
1 a person who practises judo
2 an expert in judo

Jugendstil
GERMAN, literally 'youth style'
the German term for art nouveau

> from *Jugend*, the name of a magazine that first appeared in 1896

ju-jitsu or ***jiu-jitsu***
from JAPANESE *jū-jutsu*
1 a system of unarmed combat developed by the samurai in Japan
2 a martial art founded on this system
see also JUDO

julienne
FRENCH
1 a clear soup containing shredded vegetables
2 shredded vegetable or other foodstuffs

Junker
🕪 GERMAN
1 a young German noble
2 an overbearing, narrow-minded, reactionary aristocrat

junta
🕪 SPANISH
1 a government formed by a group of military officers after a coup d'état
2 a meeting or council
3 a Spanish grand council of state
4 a body of people joined or united for some secret intrigue

jure
🕪 LATIN
by right or by law
see also JUS

jure divino
🕪 LATIN
by divine right or law

jure humano
🕪 LATIN
by human law

jure mariti
🕪 LATIN
by a husband's right

jure propinquitatis
🕪 LATIN
by right of relationship

jure sanguinis
🕪 LATIN
by right of blood
see also JUS SANGUINIS

jus
🕪 LATIN
law; a legal right
see also JURE
plural ***jura***

jus canonicum
🕪 LATIN
canon law

jus civile
🕪 LATIN
civil law

jus divinum
🕪 LATIN
divine right or law

jus gentium
🕪 LATIN
law of nations
see also CONTRA JUS GENTIUM

jus mariti
🕪 LATIN
the right of a husband

jus naturale
🕪 LATIN
natural law; the fundamental shared human conception of what constitutes justice

jus primae noctis
🕪 LATIN, literally 'law of the first night'
the alleged right of a feudal lord to take the virginity of a vassal's bride on her wedding night
see also DROIT DU SEIGNEUR

jusqu'au bout
🕪 FRENCH
to the very end

jusqu'auboutisme
🕪 FRENCH
the practice of carrying on to the bitter end

jus sanguinis
🕪 LATIN, literally 'right of blood'
the principle that a person's nationality is that of their natural parents

jus soli
🕪 LATIN, literally 'right of soil'
the principle that a person's

nationality is that of the country in which they were born

juste milieu

FRENCH

the happy medium

juvenilia

LATIN, literally 'youthful things'

writings or works produced in the childhood or youth of the author, artist, etc

j'y suis, j'y reste

FRENCH

here I am, here I stay

attributed to Marshal MacMahon at Malakoff, 1855, during the Crimean War

K

kabab
see KEBAB

kabaya
▶ MALAY, from PERSIAN or ARABIC
a loose tunic

kabob
see KEBAB

kabuki
▶ JAPANESE, literally 'song-dance skill'
a popular, traditional, stylized form of Japanese drama, with singing and dancing, in which men play all the roles

kaccha
▶ PUNJABI
the short trousers traditionally worn by Sikhs

kachahri or ***kacheri***
▶ HINDI
an Indian magistrate's office or courthouse

Kaffeeklatsch
▶ GERMAN
1 gossip, especially among women, over a cup of coffee
2 a coffee party at which gossip is exchanged

kaffiyeh, keffiyeh or ***kufiyah***
▶ ARABIC
an Arab headdress comprising a cloth folded and held by a cord around the head

kaftan
see CAFTAN

kago
▶ JAPANESE
a Japanese basketwork palanquin
plural ***kagos***

kagoule
see CAGOULE

kahal
▶ HEBREW
1 any of the Jewish communities scattered across Europe
2 the local governing body of any of these communities

kai
▶ MAORI and POLYNESIAN LANGUAGES
(in New Zealand, etc)
1 food
2 a meal

kaif
see KIF

kaimakam
▶ from TURKISH *kaymakam*
a Turkish lieutenant-colonel or lieutenant-governor

Kaiser or ***kaiser***
▶ GERMAN, from LATIN *Caesar*
an emperor, especially a German emperor

kajawah
▶ PERSIAN
a camel saddle or pannier

kakemono
▶ JAPANESE, literally 'hanging thing'
a Japanese wall-picture or calligraphic inscription on a roller
plural ***kakemonos***

kali
PERSIAN
1 a carpet with long nap
2 the large carpet covering the centre of a Persian room

kalpa or ***calpa***
SANSKRIT for 'formation'
(Hinduism) a day of Brahma, a period of 4320 million years

kalpak, calpac or ***calpack***
TURKISH
a triangular Turkish or Tatar felt cap

kama
SANSKRIT for 'love'
(Hinduism) earthly desire

Kama Sutra or ***Kamasutra***
SANSKRIT
an ancient Sanskrit text on sexual love
see also SUTRA

kamerad
from GERMAN *Kamerad* meaning 'comrade'
a German shout of surrender or appeal for mercy

kami
JAPANESE
1 a lord
2 (in Shintoism) a divine being or object of worship

kamikaze
JAPANESE, literally 'divine wind'
1 a Japanese aircraft loaded with explosives deliberately crashed by its pilot on an enemy target
2 a pilot making such an attack
3 of or engaged in such an attack
4 of or engaged in any act of certain or deliberate self-destruction in pursuit of a particular cause
5 *(informal)* reckless, foolhardy

kana
JAPANESE
Japanese syllabic writing, as distinguished from Japanese written in Chinese characters
see also KANJI

kang
CHINESE
a Chinese sleeping-platform that can be warmed by a fire underneath

kanga or ***khanga***
SWAHILI
(in E Africa) a piece of cotton cloth, usually brightly decorated, wound around the body as a woman's dress

kanji
JAPANESE, from CHINESE, literally 'a Chinese work'
1 in the Japanese writing system, the set of characters derived from Chinese ideographs
2 one of these characters
see also KANA
plural ***kanji*** or ***kanjis***

kantha
BENGALI
an embroidered cloth quilt

Kapellmeister or ***kapellmeister***
GERMAN
the director of an orchestra or choir, especially formerly in the household of a German prince

kaputt or ***kaput***
GERMAN
(slang)
1 ruined
2 broken
3 not working

Karabiner, karabiner or ***carabiner***
GERMAN

(mountaineering) a steel link with a spring clip on one side, used to attach a climber to a rope, etc

karaoke
JAPANESE, literally 'empty orchestra'
a form of entertainment of Japanese origin, popular at public venues and parties, in which people sing pop songs to the accompaniment of pre-recorded backing music provided by a karaoke machine

karate
JAPANESE, literally 'empty hand'
a traditional Japanese form of unarmed self-defence using blows and kicks, now a popular sport

karateka
JAPANESE
an expert in karate

karma
SANSKRIT for 'act'
(in Hinduism and Buddhism)
1 the actions of one's lifetime, regarded as determining the nature of a future life
2 the concept of such transcendental retribution
3 fate, destiny

kasbah or ***casbah***
from ARABIC DIALECT *kasba*
a castle or fortress in a N African town or the area round it, especially in Algiers

kasha
RUSSIAN
a dish resembling porridge or gruel, usually made from crushed buckwheat

kata
JAPANESE
(in karate) a formal sequence of practice exercises and movements

katabasis
GREEK, literally 'a going down'
a military retreat

katabothron or ***katavothron***
MODERN GREEK
an underground water-channel

katana
JAPANESE
a long single-edged samurai sword, slightly curved towards the tip

kathak
SANSKRIT, literally 'professional storyteller'
a classical dance of N India in which brief passages of mime alternate with rapid, rhythmic dancing

kathakali
MALAYALAM for 'drama'
a classical dance drama of S India

katorga
RUSSIAN
hard labour, especially in the labour camps of Joseph Stalin

Katzenjammer or ***katzenjammer***
GERMAN, literally 'cats' misery'
1 a hangover
2 a state of emotional distress
3 an uproar, clamour

kayak
ESKIMO
1 an Eskimo sealskin canoe
2 a canoe of canvas, fibreglass, etc, built in this style

kebab, kabab or ***kabob***
from ARABIC *kabab*
small pieces of meat cooked with vegetables, etc, usually on a skewer

keef or ***kef***
see KIF

keffiyeh
see KAFFIYEH

kelim
see KILIM

kendo
JAPANESE, literally 'way of the sword'
the Japanese art of swordsmanship practised with bamboo staves, in 18th-century-style armour

kepi
from FRENCH *képi*
a flat-topped French military cap with a straight peak

khaki
URDU and PERSIAN for 'dusty'
1 dust-coloured, dull brownish or greenish yellow
2 cloth of this colour used for military uniforms, etc

khan
TURKISH
(in Central Asia)
1 a title for a prince or chief
2 such a prince or chief

khanga
see KANGA

khanum
TURKISH
(in the Middle East)
1 (a title for) a lady of rank
2 Mrs

khidmutgar or ***khitmutgar***
URDU
a servant at table

khurta
see KURTA

khutbah, khotbah or ***khotbeh***
ARABIC
a Muslim prayer and sermon delivered in the mosques on Fridays

kia-ora
MAORI
good health!

kibbutz
HEBREW
a Jewish communal agricultural settlement in Israel
plural ***kibbutzim***

kibitka
RUSSIAN
1 a Russian covered wagon or sledge
2 a Central Asian felt tent

kiblah
from ARABIC *qiblah*
the point towards which Muslims turn in prayer, the direction of Mecca

kif, kaif, keef or ***kef***
from ARABIC *kaif* meaning 'pleasure'
1 a state of dreamy repose
2 a drug such as marijuana, smoked to produce this state

kikumon
JAPANESE
the chrysanthemum badge of the Japanese imperial family

kilim, kelim or ***khilim***
TURKISH, from PERSIAN
a woven rug traditionally made in the Middle East

kimchi
KOREAN
a very spicy Korean dish made with a variety of raw vegetables, especially cabbage, radish, cucumber, garlic, ginger, etc

kimono
JAPANESE
1 a loose robe with wide sleeves, fastening with a sash, a traditional outer garment in Japan
2 a dressing-gown of similar form
plural ***kimonos***

kindergarten
from GERMAN *Kindergarten* meaning 'children's garden'
a school or class for young children, usually aged between four and six

Kinder, Kirche, Küche or ***Kirche, Küche, Kinder*** or ***Küche, Kirche, Kinder***
GERMAN
children, church, cooking

formerly said to be the proper interests of a German woman

kirimon
JAPANESE
one of the two imperial crests of Japan, bearing three leaves and three flowers of the paulownia tree

kirsch, kirschwasser, Kirsch or ***Kirschwasser***
from GERMAN *Kirschwasser* meaning 'cherry water'
a liqueur made from the wild cherry

kismet
from TURKISH *qismet*
fate, destiny

kissel
from RUSSIAN *kisel*
a Russian dessert of thickened fruit purée

kitsch
from GERMAN *Kitsch*
sentimental or vulgar tastelessness in art, design, etc

Klangfarbe or ***klangfarbe***
GERMAN
tone-colour, timbre

klutz
YIDDISH, from GERMAN *Klotz*
an awkward or stupid person

knackwurst or ***knockwurst***
GERMAN, from *knacken* meaning 'to crack' and *Wurst* meaning 'sausage'
a kind of highly seasoned sausage

knish
YIDDISH, from RUSSIAN
(in Jewish cookery) baked or fried dough with a filling of potatoes, meat, etc

koan
JAPANESE for 'public proposal or plan'
(in Zen Buddhism) a nonsensical question given to students as a subject for meditation

kobold
from GERMAN *Kobold*
(in German folklore)
1 a spirit of the mines
2 a domestic brownie

kofta
HINDI
(in Indian cookery) minced and seasoned meat or vegetables, shaped into balls and fried

kohl
from ARABIC *koh'l*
a cosmetic, of oriental origin, in the form of a black powder used to darken the area around the eyes

kolkhoz
RUSSIAN, from *kollektivnoe khozyaistvo*
a Soviet collective farm

Kol Nidre
ARAMAIC, literally 'all the vows'
the prayer that opens the evening service of Yom Kippur

komitaji
from TURKISH *qomitaji* meaning 'committee-man, bandit'
1 originally, a member of the Bulgarian Revolutionary Committee in Macedonia
2 any Balkan guerrilla

kore
GREEK for 'maiden'
a Greek statue of a draped young woman
compare KOUROS

korma
HINDI
a mild-flavoured Indian dish of meat or vegetables braised in water, stock, yoghurt, or cream

kosher
YIDDISH, from HEBREW *kāshēr* meaning 'right'
1 pure or clean according to Jewish law
2 (said of food) prepared according to Jewish law
3 *(informal)* legitimate, proper, genuine

koto
JAPANESE
a Japanese musical instrument consisting of a long box with thirteen silk strings
plural ***kotos***

koumiss
see KUMISS

kouros
GREEK for 'boy'
a Greek statue of a naked young man
compare KORE

kraal
DUTCH
1 a S African village of huts surrounded by a fence
2 a corral

kraken
NORWEGIAN
a fabulous sea-monster

the *-n* is the definite article

kriegspiel, kriegsspiel, Kriegspiel or Kriegsspiel
from GERMAN *Kriegsspiel*
1 a war game played on a map to train officers
2 a form of chess in which the players use separate boards and are allowed only limited communication

kris
MALAY
a Malay dagger with a wavy scalloped blade
plural ***krises***

Küche, Kirche, Kinder
see KINDER, KIRCHE, KÜCHE

Kuchen
GERMAN
a cake or cakes

kudos
from GREEK *kȳdos* meaning 'glory'
credit, fame, renown, prestige

kufiyah
see KAFFIYEH

kukri
HINDI
a curved Gurkha knife or short sword

kulak
RUSSIAN for 'fist'
a rich peasant, regarded in the Communist period as an exploiter of others and a class traitor

Kultur
GERMAN
culture, civilization, especially German civilization regarded by outsiders as imperialistic and arrogant

Kulturgeschichte
GERMAN
the history of civilization

Kulturkampf
GERMAN
a war of culture, a struggle for cultural supremacy

> used by Rudolf Virchow in 1873 of the conflict between Bismarck and the Roman Catholic Church

Kulturkreis
GERMAN
1 an area regarded as a centre of diffusion of cultural elements
2 one of the waves of culture spreading out from such a centre

kumiss or ***koumiss***
from RUSSIAN *kumis*
fermented mare's milk

kümmel or ***Kümmel***
from GERMAN *Kümmel*
a liqueur flavoured with cumin and caraway seeds

kung fu
CHINESE, literally 'combat skill'
a Chinese martial art dating from the 16th century, used for both armed and unarmed combat and self-defence

kurgan
RUSSIAN
a prehistoric burial mound

Kurhaus or ***kurhaus***
GERMAN, literally 'cure-house'
a building in which a spa is housed

Kursaal or ***kursaal***
GERMAN, literally 'cure-room'
the reception room of a spa

kurta or ***khurta***
HINDI
a loose-fitting collarless shirt or tunic worn in India

kvass
from RUSSIAN *kvas*
a weak rye beer made in E European countries

kyogen
JAPANESE for 'play, drama'
a comic interlude between Noh plays

Kyrie eleison
from GREEK *Kȳrie, eleēson* meaning 'Lord, have mercy'
a form of prayer of ancient Greek origin, used in Roman Catholic and Anglican services

kyu
JAPANESE
(judo)
1 one of the six novice grades, the lowest being 6th kyu
2 a novice in one of these grades

L

£
see LIBRA

la
FRENCH for 'the'
prefixed to the name of a famous or notorious woman

> the term may be used with admiration or contempt

laager
from AFRIKAANS *lager*
(in S Africa)
1 a defensive ring of ox-wagons
2 any makeshift fortification
3 an encampment
4 *(figurative)* any defensive group of people

laborare est orare
LATIN
work is prayer

labore et honore
LATIN
by labour and honour

labor improbus
LATIN
persistent, dogged labour

labuntur et imputantur
LATIN
the moments slip away and are laid to our account

> an inscription on sundials

lacrimae rerum
LATIN, literally 'tears of things'
the sorrows of life

lacrimoso or ***lagrimoso***
ITALIAN for 'tearful'
(music)
1 plaintive
2 plaintively

lacuna
LATIN
1 a gap or hiatus
2 a cavity or depression
plural **lacunae**

la dolce vita
see DOLCE VITA

la donna è mobile
ITALIAN
woman is changeable

> the title of a song from Verdi's *Rigoletto*

laesa majestas
see LESE-MAJESTÉ

lagniappe or ***lagnappe***
LOUISIANA FRENCH, from AMERICAN SPANISH
a bonus or gratuity

laissez-aller or ***laisser-aller***
FRENCH, literally 'let go'
lack of constraint; relaxed freedom

laissez-faire or ***laisser-faire***
FRENCH, literally 'let do'
a general policy of not interfering in the affairs or activities of others

laissez-passer
FRENCH, literally 'let pass'
a pass or permit allowing one to travel in a restricted area, etc

lama
TIBETAN
a Buddhist priest in Tibet
see also DALAI LAMA

lamé
FRENCH
a fabric in which gold or silver threads are interwoven

➪ also used as an adjective

Land
GERMAN for 'land'
a state or province in Germany and Austria functioning as a unit of local government
plural ***Länder***

Landammann, landammann or ***landamman***
GERMAN
the chief magistrate in some Swiss cantons

lande
FRENCH
a tract of moorland, now largely forested, along the coast in SW France

Ländler or ***ländler***
GERMAN, from *Landl*, a nickname for Upper Austria
1 a German and Austrian dance similar to a slow waltz
2 the music for such a dance

Landsturm
GERMAN, literally 'land storm'
1 conscription in time of national emergency
2 a reserve force called up at such a time

➪ the force was originally summoned by storm-warning bells

Landtag
GERMAN, literally 'land assembly'
1 the legislative assembly of a German state
2 the Diet of the Holy Roman Empire

Landwehr
GERMAN, literally 'land defence'
an army reserve

Langlauf or ***langlauf***
GERMAN, literally 'long run'
cross-country skiing

langouste
FRENCH
spiny lobster

langue de chat
FRENCH, literally 'cat's tongue'
a thin finger-shaped biscuit or piece of chocolate

lapis lazuli
LATIN
a beautiful stone coloured deep blue by lazurite and other minerals and often spangled with iron pyrites

lapsus
LATIN
a slip

lapsus calami
LATIN
a slip of the pen

lapsus linguae
LATIN
a slip of the tongue

lapsus memoriae
LATIN
a slip of the memory

lares et penates
LATIN
1 household gods

2 valued personal or household objects

largesse or ***largess***
FRENCH
1 gifts, especially of money, given generously
2 generosity or magnanimity

larghetto
ITALIAN
(music)
1 rather slow, but not as slow as largo
2 rather slowly
3 a rather slow movement
plural ***larghettos***

largo
ITALIAN for 'broad'
(music)
1 broad and slow
2 broadly and slowly
3 a movement to be performed in this manner
plural ***largos***

l'art pour l'art
FRENCH
art for art's sake

larva
LATIN for 'spectre, mask'
an animal in an immature but active state markedly different from the adult, eg a caterpillar
plural ***larvae***

lasagne or ***lasagna***
ITALIAN
1 flat sheets of pasta
2 a baked dish of this, usually layered with meat and tomatoes and a cheese sauce

lasciate ogni speranza, voi ch'entrate
ITALIAN
abandon all hope, ye who enter

> the inscription over the gates of hell in Dante's *Inferno*

lashkar
HINDI
a body of armed Indian tribesmen

latet anguis in herba
LATIN
a snake lies hidden in the grass; there is a concealed drawback or danger
see also ANGUIS IN HERBA

laus Deo
LATIN
praise to God

laus Deo semper
LATIN
praise be to God always
abbrev **LDS**

lavabo
LATIN, literally 'I shall wash'
1 in the Roman Catholic mass, the ritual washing of the priest's hands after the offertory
2 a fixed basin or washstand
3 a lavatory

> from the opening of Psalm 26.6 in the Vulgate. The word is also used in French, meaning 'washbasin'

layette
FRENCH
a complete set of clothing, etc, for a baby

lazaretto or ***lazaret***
from ITALIAN *lazzaretto*
1 a hospital for infectious diseases, especially leprosy
2 a place of quarantine
3 a place for keeping stores on a ship
plural ***lazarettos*** or ***lazarets***

lazzarone
ITALIAN
a Neapolitan beggar
plural ***lazzaroni***

lb
see LIBRA

lc or ***l.c.***
see LOCO CITATO

Lebensabend
GERMAN
the evening of life

Lebensraum
GERMAN
1 space inhabited by living things
2 room to live and, if necessary, to expand
3 territory claimed by the Nazis as necessary for economic growth

lector benevole
LATIN
kind reader

Lederhosen or ***lederhosen***
GERMAN
short leather trousers with braces

legato
ITALIAN for 'bound, tied'
(music)
1 smooth or smoothly, the notes running into each other without a break
2 a legato passage or manner
plural ***legatos***

legerdemain
from FRENCH *léger de main* meaning 'light of hand'
dexterous trickery or conjuring, sleight-of-hand

> not used in French

légèreté
FRENCH
1 lightness
2 nimbleness
3 frivolity

lei
HAWAIIAN
a garland or wreath, especially of flowers, shells, or feathers

leitmotiv or ***leitmotif***
from GERMAN *Leitmotiv* meaning 'leading motif'
1 (in opera) a musical theme associated with a person, etc, recurring when the person appears on the stage
2 a recurring theme in literature
3 any recurring theme

le mieux est l'ennemi du bien
FRENCH, literally 'better is the enemy of good'
leave well alone

lento
ITALIAN
(music)
1 slow
2 slowly
3 a slow passage or movement
plural ***lentos*** or ***lenti***

lese-majesté or ***lese-majesty***
from FRENCH *lèse majesté*, from LATIN *laesa majestas* meaning 'injured majesty'
1 an offence against the sovereign power, high treason
2 any attack on authority, or on someone in a position of authority
see also CRIMEN LAESAE MAJESTATIS

> the Latin form *laesa majestas* is also used in English

les jeux sont faits
FRENCH
(in roulette, etc) the bets have been placed

➪ usually followed by RIEN NE VA PLUS

l'état, c'est moi
FRENCH
I am the state

➪ attributed to Louis XIV

lettre
FRENCH
a letter

lettre de cachet
FRENCH
1 a letter under the royal signet
2 a royal warrant for arrest and imprisonment

lettre de change
FRENCH
a bill of exchange

lettre de marque
FRENCH
a letter of reprisal, a privateer's licence to commit acts of hostility

levée en masse
FRENCH
a levy of all able-bodied men for military service; conscription or general mobilization

lever de rideau
FRENCH
a curtain-raiser; a short play, etc, before the main performance

lex
LATIN
law

lex non scripta
LATIN
unwritten law, ie common law

lex scripta
LATIN
statute law

lex talionis
LATIN
the law of retaliation

liaison
FRENCH for 'link, connection'
1 communication with another unit, force, department, organization, etc
2 a secret or illicit love affair

liber
LATIN
a book
abbrev **lib.**

liberté, égalité, fraternité
FRENCH
liberty, equality, fraternity

➪ slogan of the French Revolution

libido
LATIN for 'desire'
1 sexual desire
2 *(psychology)* a vital urge, especially the sexual impulse
plural ***libidos***

libra
LATIN
1 a pound in weight
2 a pound in money
abbrev **lb** (sense 1), **£** (sense 2)

libraire
FRENCH
a bookseller

librairie
FRENCH
a bookshop

libretto
ITALIAN, literally 'little book'
the words or text of an opera, oratorio, etc
plural ***libretti*** or ***librettos***

licentia vatum
LATIN
poetic licence

lied
from GERMAN *Lied*
a German lyric or song
plural ***lieder***

lied ohne worte
from GERMAN *Lied ohne Worte*
a song without words

limbo
LATIN, from the phrase *in limbo* meaning 'on the border'
1 the borderland between heaven and hell, reserved for the unbaptized
2 a place of consignment, neglect, or oblivion
3 any uncertain or intermediate state
plural ***limbos***

lingerie
FRENCH
women's underwear

> the term originally referred to linen goods

lingua franca
ITALIAN, literally 'Frankish language'
1 a language chosen as a means of communication among speakers of different languages
2 any hybrid language used for the same purpose
3 the familiar conventions of any style, especially in the arts, readily understood by devotees

> the phrase originally referred to a mixed Italian trade jargon used in the Levant

plural ***lingue franche*** or ***lingua francas***

liqueur
FRENCH
a strong alcoholic drink, usually heavily flavoured and sweetened, eg Benedictine, chartreuse, cherry brandy, curaçao, etc

> usually drunk at the end of a meal

lit de justice
FRENCH, literally 'bed of justice'
1 the king's throne in the Parlement de Paris
2 a sitting at which the king was present, chiefly for the registration of his own decrees

lite pendente
LATIN
(law) while the case is pending

literati
LATIN or ITALIAN
men and women of letters; learned people
singular ***literatus*** (Latin) or ***literato*** (Italian)

literatim
LATIN
letter for letter

litotes
GREEK for 'simplicity'
(in rhetoric, etc) understatement, especially affirmation by negation of the contrary (as in *not a little angry* meaning 'furious')

litterae humaniores or ***literae humaniores***
LATIN, literally 'the more humane letters'
the humanities, Latin and Greek
abbrev **lit. hum.**

littera scripta manet
LATIN
what is written down is permanent
see also VOX AUDITA PERIT, LITTERA SCRIPTA MANET

littérateur
FRENCH
a literary man

livraison
FRENCH for 'delivery'
a number of a book published in parts

llano
SPANISH
one of the vaste steppes or plains in the northern part of S America
plural ***llanos***

locale
from FRENCH *local*
the scene of some event, etc

> the French noun does not have the final *-e*, added in English to show that the second syllable is stressed

loco citato or ***in loco citato***
LATIN
in the place or passage cited
abbrev **loc. cit., lc, l.c., in loc. cit.**

locum tenens
LATIN, literally 'holding the place'
a person who temporarily takes the place or performs the duties of another, especially in the medical profession

> usually shortened to *locum*

locus
LATIN
1 a place, locality, or location
2 a passage in a book, piece of writing, etc
plural ***loci***

locus classicus
LATIN
the classical passage, the stock quotation

locus paenitentiae
LATIN
1 a place of penitence
2 time for repentance

locus sigilli
LATIN
the place where the seal is affixed on a document, etc

locus standi
LATIN
(law) the right to appear in court

loden
from GERMAN *Loden*
1 a thick waterproof woollen cloth with a short pile
2 a coat made of this cloth

loge
FRENCH
a box in the theatre or opera house

loggia
ITALIAN
a covered gallery or arcade on the side of a building, open to the garden
plural ***loggias*** or ***loggie***

Londiniensis
LATIN
of London
abbrev **Londin.**

longueur
FRENCH
1 a tedious passage, eg in a book
2 prolixity, long-windedness
3 a period or instance of dullness or tedium

loquitur
LATIN
he or she speaks

➪ used with a person's name as stage direction, etc

abbrev **loq.**

lorgnette
FRENCH
eyeglasses or opera-glasses with a long handle

lorgnon
FRENCH
a monocle or a pair of glasses

louche
FRENCH
1 squinting
2 ambiguous
3 shady, sinister, shifty, or disreputable

luau
from HAWAIIAN *lu'au*
1 a Hawaiian dish made of coconut, taro, octopus, etc
2 a Hawaiian feast or party

Luftwaffe
GERMAN
air force

luge
SWISS FRENCH
a light toboggan

lumpen
from GERMAN *Lumpen* meaning 'rag'
1 poor, poverty-stricken, dispossessed
2 stupid

Lumpenproletariat or ***lumpen proletariat***
GERMAN
the poorest down-and-outs

lupus in fabula
LATIN, literally 'the wolf in the fable'
talk of the devil

➪ referring to a person who appears, coincidentally, as they are spoken of

lusus naturae
LATIN
a freak of nature

luxe
FRENCH
luxury
see also DE LUXE

lux mundi
LATIN
light of the world

lycée
FRENCH
a state secondary school in France

M

M
see MONSIEUR

macabre
FRENCH
gruesome; ghastly
see also DANSE MACABRE

macaroni
from NEAPOLITAN DIALECT
maccaroni
pasta in the form of long thin tubes

> the modern Italian form is *maccheroni*

macédoine
FRENCH, from *Macédoine* meaning 'Macedonia'
a mixture of diced vegetables or fruit in syrup or jelly

machete
SPANISH
a heavy knife used as a tool or weapon, especially in S America

machismo
MEXICAN SPANISH
the cult of male virility and masculine pride

macho
SPANISH for 'male'
1 aggressively male; ostentatiously virile
2 a man of this type
3 machismo
plural ***machos***

Machtpolitik
GERMAN
power politics, especially the doctrine that a state should use force to attain its ends

madame
FRENCH
1 (as a form of address) madam
2 (*Madame*; prefixed to a name) Mrs
3 (usually *Madame*) a title for a woman in an artistic profession, a fortune-teller, etc
abbrev **Mme** (senses 2 & 3)
plural ***mesdames*** or ***Mesdames***

madeleine
FRENCH
a small, plain sponge cake, often baked in the shape of a shell

> possibly named after *Madeleine* Paulmier, a 19th-century French pastrycook

mademoiselle
FRENCH
1 (as a form of address) miss
2 (*Mademoiselle*; prefixed to a name) Miss
3 a French governess or teacher
abbrev **Mlle** (sense 2)
plural ***mesdemoiselles*** or ***Mesdemoiselles***

maelstrom
DUTCH
1 a particularly powerful whirlpool
2 a confused or disordered state of affairs
3 any overpowering influence for destruction

> the modern Dutch form is *maalstroom*

maestoso
ITALIAN
(music) with dignity or majesty

maestro
ITALIAN
a master, especially an eminent musical conductor or composer
plural ***maestros*** or ***maestri***

mafioso or ***Mafioso***
ITALIAN
a member of the Mafia
plural ***mafiosi*** or ***Mafiosi***

ma foi
FRENCH, literally 'my faith'
my goodness!

Magi
LATIN
the three wise men who brought gifts to the infant Christ
see also MAGUS

magisterium
LATIN for 'mastery'
1 the philosopher's stone
2 teaching authority or function

Magna Carta or ***Magna Charta***
LATIN
1 the Great Charter obtained from King John at Runnymede in 1215, the basis of English political and personal liberty
2 any document establishing rights

magna cum laude
LATIN
with great distinction
see also CUM LAUDE, SUMMA CUM LAUDE

magna est veritas et praevalebit
LATIN
truth is great and will prevail

Magnificat
from LATIN *magnificat anima mea Dominum* meaning 'my soul doth magnify the Lord'
1 the song of the Virgin Mary, Luke 1.46–55, beginning in the Vulgate with this word
2 a song of praise or thanksgiving

magnum
LATIN
a large bottle of champagne or other wine, holding twice as much as a normal bottle
plural ***magnums***

magnum opus
LATIN
1 a great work, especially of literature or learning
2 a writer's greatest achievement or the culmination of their efforts

magus
LATIN
1 (in ancient Persia) a priest or a member of a priestly class
2 a magician
plural ***magi***
see also MAGI

maharaja or ***maharajah***
HINDI, literally 'great king'
a great Indian prince, especially a ruler of a state

maharani or ***maharanee***
HINDI, literally 'great queen'
1 the wife or widow of a maharaja
2 a woman with the rank of a maharaja in her own right

maharishi
from SANSKRIT *mahat* meaning 'great' and *rishi* meaning 'sage'
a leading instructor in the Hindu faith

mahatma
from SANSKRIT *mahat* meaning 'great' and *atman* meaning 'soul'
a religious sage; a wise and holy leader

Mahayana
▸ SANSKRIT, literally 'great vehicle'
the most widespread form of Buddhism, practised especially in China, Japan, Tibet, and the Himalayas, that seeks enlightenment for all humanity and recognizes many texts as scripture

maha yoga or ***siddha yoga***
▸ SANSKRIT
a form of yoga practised with a master, incorporating all eight classical yogas
see also YOGA

mah-jong or ***mah-jongg***
▸ CHINESE
a Chinese game for four, played with small painted bricks or tiles

> ➪ from a dialect word meaning 'sparrows', perhaps from the sound of the tiles during play

mahout
▸ from HINDI *mahāut*
the keeper and driver of an elephant

maidan
▸ URDU
1 an open plain
2 an open space near a town, used for sports or as a parade-ground in India, Pakistan, etc

maigre
▸ FRENCH for 'lean'
1 relating to food that contains no animal flesh and can therefore be eaten on a fast-day
2 designating a fast-day

maiko
▸ JAPANESE
an apprentice geisha
plural ***maiko*** or ***maikos***

maillot jaune
▸ FRENCH
the yellow jersey worn by the leading cyclist in the Tour de France

maison
▸ FRENCH for 'house'
(said of a dish) prepared or cooked to a recipe that is a speciality of the restaurant in which it is served

> ➪ placed after the noun, as in *pâté maison*

maison de ville
▸ FRENCH
a town house, a residence in town

maisonnette or ***maisonette***
▸ FRENCH
a small house or flat

maître d'hôtel
▸ FRENCH
1 a head waiter
2 the manager of a hotel or restaurant
see also À LA MAÎTRE D'HÔTEL
abbrev (informal) **maître d'**

majorat
▸ FRENCH
primogeniture

makimono
▸ JAPANESE, literally 'rolling thing'
a long, painted scroll, often with narrative text, designed to be unrolled from right to left
plural ***makimonos***

mal
see GRAND MAL, PETIT MAL

mala fide
▸ LATIN
in bad faith, treacherously

mala fides
LATIN
bad faith

malaise
FRENCH
1 uneasiness, discomfort
2 a feeling of debility or of impending sickness
3 a general air of depression or despondency

malapropos or ***mal à propos***
from FRENCH *mal à propos*
1 out of place
2 unsuitable, inappropriate
3 inopportune, untimely

also used as an adverb

mal de mer
FRENCH
seasickness

mal du pays
FRENCH
homesickness, nostalgia

mal du siècle
FRENCH
depression about the state of the world

used by the French critic Sainte-Beuve in 1833 and current in the 20th century

malentendu
FRENCH
a misunderstanding

malgré lui
FRENCH
1 in spite of himself
2 against his will
3 in spite of his efforts
4 willy-nilly

other personal pronouns may be substituted for *lui*

malgré tout
FRENCH
nevertheless, all things considered

mal soigné
FRENCH
badly groomed, unkempt

mal vu
FRENCH
looked upon with disapproval

mamma mia
ITALIAN, literally 'my mother'
an exclamation of surprise, wonder, exasperation, etc

mañana
SPANISH
1 tomorrow
2 (at) an unspecified time in the future

mandala
SANSKRIT
1 (in Buddhism and Hinduism) a pictorial symbol of the universe, usually a circle enclosing images of deities or geometric designs, used as an aid to religious meditation
2 (in Jungian psychology) a symbol of the self, the wholeness or symmetry of the image corresponding to the degree of harmony in the self

mandamus
LATIN, literally 'we command'
(law) a writ or command issued by a higher court to a lower court
plural ***mandamuses***

mandir or ***mandira***
HINDI
a Hindu or Jain temple

manège
FRENCH
1 the art of horsemanship or of training horses
2 a riding-school

manet
LATIN
(stage direction) he or she remains on stage
plural ***manent***

manga
JAPANESE
a type of adult comic book popular in Japan

mangetout
FRENCH, literally 'eat-all'
a type of pea cooked and eaten with its pod

manifesto
ITALIAN
a public written declaration of the intentions, opinions, or motives of a leader, party, or body
plural ***manifestos*** or ***manifestoes***

mannequin
FRENCH
1 a dummy figure used to display clothes in shop windows, etc
2 a fashion model

ma non troppo
ITALIAN
(music) but not too much
see also TROPPO

manqué
FRENCH for 'missed'
having ambition or potential that has never been fulfilled; would-be

> placed after the noun, as in *poet manqué*

feminine ***manquée***

mantilla
SPANISH
1 a small cloak
2 a kind of veil covering the head and shoulders

mantra or ***mantram***
SANSKRIT, literally 'instrument of thought'
1 (in Hinduism and Buddhism) a word, phrase, etc, chanted or repeated inwardly in meditation
2 (in Hinduism) a Vedic hymn

manzanilla
SPANISH
a very dry, light sherry

> the Spanish word also means 'camomile'

maquiladora
MEXICAN SPANISH
a factory or assembly plant owned by a US company in Mexico, operating under a free-trade agreement to allow duty-free export of finished products for sale in the US
plural ***maquiladoras***

maquillage
FRENCH
1 cosmetics, make-up
2 the art of using cosmetics or make-up

marabout
FRENCH, from ARABIC *murābit*
1 a Muslim hermit, especially in N Africa
2 a type of witch-doctor

marc
FRENCH
1 grapeskins and other refuse from wine-making
2 brandy made from this
3 any fruit refuse, eg from the making of cooking oil

marcato
ITALIAN
(music) marked; emphatic; strongly accented

> also used as an adverb

Märchen
GERMAN
a story, fable, or folk-tale
plural ***Märchen***

Mardi Gras
FRENCH
Shrove Tuesday, celebrated with a carnival in many places

mare clausum
LATIN
a closed sea; a sea within the jurisdiction of one state

mare liberum
LATIN
a sea open to free navigation by ships of any nation

marginalia
LATIN
notes written in a margin

mariachi
MEXICAN SPANISH
1 designating a form of Mexican dance music played traditionally by strolling musicians
2 a musician playing mariachi music
plural ***mariachis***

mariage blanc
FRENCH, literally 'white marriage'
an unconsummated marriage

mariage de convenance
FRENCH
a marriage of convenience, a marriage entered into for reasons of expediency rather than love

mari complaisant
FRENCH, literally 'obliging husband'
a husband who condones his wife's infidelity

marionnette or ***marionette***
FRENCH
a puppet with jointed limbs moved by strings

marivaudage
FRENCH
preciosity in literary style or expression

> from the style of the French novelist and dramatist Pierre de *Marivaux* (1688–1763)

marmite
FRENCH
a metal or earthenware cooking pot with a lid

maror
HEBREW
a dish of bitter herbs, especially horseradish, eaten during the Jewish Passover, symbolizing the bitterness of the Egyptian oppression of the Israelites

marque
FRENCH
a brand or make, especially of car

marquisette
FRENCH
an open-weave fabric used for clothing, curtains, mosquito nets, etc

marrons glacés
FRENCH
chestnuts poached in syrup and coated with a sugar glaze

martellato
ITALIAN
(music) played with a hammering touch, or with short quick detached strokes of the bow

> also used as an adverb

masa
SPANISH
(in Mexican cookery) a dough made from ground dried maize, used to make tamales, etc

mascara
from SPANISH *máscara*
a cosmetic for colouring and thickening the eyelashes, applied with a brush

mashallah
from ARABIC *mā shā'llāh*
what God will

> an interjection used among Muslims

masjid
ARABIC
a mosque

maskirovka
RUSSIAN
1 the use or practice of deception as a military stratagem
2 camouflage

massage
FRENCH
a technique of easing pain or stiffness, especially in the muscles, by stroking, pressing, tapping, kneading, friction, etc

massé
FRENCH
(in billiards, etc) a stroke made with the cue vertical or nearly so, causing the cue ball to swerve sharply

masseur
FRENCH
a person trained to carry out massage
feminine ***masseuse***

massif
FRENCH
a central mountain mass

mastaba
from ARABIC *mastabah* meaning 'bench'
an ancient Egyptian tomb with sloping sides and a flat roof

matador
SPANISH
the man who kills the bull in a bullfight
feminine ***matadora***

matelassé, ***matelasse*** or ***matellasse***
FRENCH, from *matelas* meaning 'mattress'
a fabric with a raised pattern that resembles quilting

> also used as an adjective

matelot or ***matlo***
FRENCH
a seaman, a sailor
plural ***matelots*** or ***matlos***

matelote
FRENCH
fish cooked in wine with onions, herbs, etc

mater
LATIN
(slang) mother

> chiefly facetious

materfamilias
LATIN
the mother of a family or household
plural ***matresfamilias*** or ***materfamiliases***

materia medica
LATIN, literally 'medical material'
1 drugs and other medicinal substances
2 the science of their properties and use

matériel
FRENCH
material or equipment, especially the baggage and munitions of an army

as opposed to PERSONNEL

matinée or ***matinee***
FRENCH, literally 'morning'
a daytime performance of a play, showing of a film, concert, etc, usually in the afternoon

matricula
LATIN
a register of members, students, etc

matryoshka
RUSSIAN, literally 'little mother'
a hollow wooden doll containing a series of smaller dolls, each fitting inside the next largest

matsuri
JAPANESE
a Shinto festival or public ceremony held at a shrine

matzo
from YIDDISH *matse*
1 unleavened bread, now usually in the form of large square crackers, eaten during Passover
2 one of these crackers
plural ***matzoth*** or ***matzos***

maurikigusari
JAPANESE
a weapon consisting of a series of weights on a chain

mauvaise honte
FRENCH, literally 'bad shame'
1 false modesty
2 bashfulness

mauvais goût
FRENCH
bad taste, lack of taste

mauvais moment
FRENCH
a bad or unpleasant moment

mauvais quart d'heure
FRENCH, literally 'bad quarter of an hour'
a brief but unpleasant experience

mauvais sang
FRENCH
bad blood, ill feeling

mauvais sujet
FRENCH
a worthless person

mauvais ton
FRENCH
bad style, bad form

maxima cum laude
see SUMMA CUM LAUDE

maxixe
PORTUGUESE
1 a Brazilian dance resembling the tango
2 the music for this dance

maya
SANSKRIT
1 illusion
2 *(philosophy)* the world of phenomena

mayonnaise
FRENCH
1 a cold sauce made from raw egg yolk, vegetable oil, lemon juice or vinegar, and seasoning
2 any cold dish of which this sauce is an ingredient, such as *shrimp mayonnaise*

mazeltov or ***mazel tov***
YIDDISH
a Jewish interjection conveying congratulations or best wishes

mazhbi
HINDI
a Sikh of low caste

mazurka
POLISH
1 a lively Polish dance
2 the music for this dance

mea culpa
LATIN, literally 'my fault'
I am to blame

an acknowledgement of one's guilt or mistake

medina
ARABIC for 'town'
the ancient, native quarter of a N African city

medio tutissimus ibis
LATIN, literally 'you will go safest in the middle'
the middle course is the safest

megillah
HEBREW for 'roll, scroll'
1 *(Judaism)* a scroll containing a book of the Old Testament, especially the Book of Esther, read on certain feast days
2 *(slang)* a lengthy or tedious account
plural ***megillahs*** or ***megilloth***

meishi
JAPANESE
in Japan, a calling card or business card

Meistersinger
GERMAN, literally 'mastersinger'
a member of a guild of German poets or musicians of the 14th–16th centuries, usually burghers or master craftsmen, successors of the Minnesingers
plural ***Meistersinger*** or ***Meistersingers***

me judice
LATIN
in my opinion

melancholia
GREEK
a mental state characterized by dejection and misery

mélange or ***melange***
FRENCH
a mixture; a medley

mêlée or ***melee***
FRENCH
a confused or noisy brawl involving a large number of people

membrum virile
LATIN
the penis

memento
LATIN, literally 'remember!'
something kept or given as a reminder
plural ***mementos*** or ***mementoes***

memento mori
LATIN, literally 'remember that you must die'
a skull or other object intended as a reminder of the inevitability of death

memorabilia
LATIN
1 things worth remembering
2 objects associated with a person or event, often collected or kept as souvenirs

memoria technica
LATIN
1 artificial memory
2 a mnemonic device

ménage
FRENCH
1 a household
2 the management of a house

ménage à trois
FRENCH
a household composed of three people, especially a husband and wife and the lover of one of them

menhir
BRETON, literally 'long stone'
a prehistoric megalith or standing stone

meno mosso
ITALIAN
(music) not so fast

menorah or ***Menorah***
HEBREW
a candelabrum, usually with seven branches, used in Jewish religious ceremony

mens rea
LATIN, literally 'guilty mind'
(law)
1 a wrongful purpose
2 criminal intent
3 knowledge of the unlawfulness of an act

mens sana in corpore sano
LATIN
a healthy mind in a healthy body

Mensur
GERMAN for 'measurement' (from the measured distance of the participants)
a fencing contest between students at some universities, where it is fashionable to sport a duelling scar
plural ***Mensuren***

menuisier
FRENCH
a joiner

meo periculo
LATIN
at my own risk

meringue
FRENCH
1 a crisp baked mixture of beaten egg whites and sugar, used as a pie topping or to form cakes or moulds
2 a small cake or filled mould of meringue

merum sal
LATIN, literally 'pure salt'
genuine Attic wit

mesa
SPANISH
a flat-topped hill with steep sides, especially in the southwestern US

mésalliance
FRENCH
an unsuitable marriage; marriage with someone of lower social rank

mesclun or ***mesclum***
FRENCH, from NIÇOIS *mesclumo* meaning 'mixture'
a mixed green salad of young leaves and shoots, eg of rocket, chicory, fennel, etc

mesdames or ***Mesdames***
see MADAME

mesdemoiselles or ***Mesdemoiselles***
see MADEMOISELLE

meshuga, meshugah, meshugga or ***meshuggah***
YIDDISH
(slang) mad; crazy

mesquin
FRENCH
mean, ungracious
feminine ***mesquine***

mesquinerie
FRENCH
meanness

messieurs or ***Messieurs***
see MONSIEUR

Messrs
see MONSIEUR

mestizo
SPANISH
a person of mixed parentage, especially the offspring of Spanish and American Indian parents
plural ***mestizos***
feminine ***mestiza***

métairie
FRENCH
a piece of land cultivated under the system of métayage

métayage
FRENCH
a system whereby a tenant farmer gives a fixed proportion of the crops, rather than money, in payment for rent

métayer
FRENCH
a tenant farmer under the system of métayage

métier
FRENCH
1 a person's profession or trade
2 something at which one is particularly skilled; one's forte

métis
FRENCH
a person of mixed descent
plural ***métis***
feminine ***métisse***

meum et tuum
LATIN
mine and thine

meze, ***mezze*** or ***mézé***
TURKISH
a type of appetizer or hors d'oeuvre served in Greece, Turkey, Lebanon, etc, especially with an apéritif before dinner

mezuza or ***mezuzah***
HEBREW for 'doorpost'
a parchment scroll containing scriptural texts which is fixed to the doorpost by some Jewish families as a sign of their faith
plural ***mezuzahs*** or ***mezuzoth***

mezza voce
ITALIAN, literally 'half voice'
(music)
1 with medium volume or tone
2 played or sung in this style

mezzo-forte
ITALIAN
(music)
1 rather loudly
2 rather loud

mezzo-piano
ITALIAN
(music)
1 rather softly
2 rather soft

mezzo-rilievo
ITALIAN
1 a form of sculptural relief halfway between high and low relief
2 a carving or sculpture in this form

mezzo-soprano
ITALIAN
1 a singing voice between soprano and contralto
2 a part for such a voice
3 a singer with such a voice
plural ***mezzo-sopranos***

miasma
GREEK
1 foul-smelling vapours, as given off by rotting matter
2 an unwholesome atmosphere or evil influence
plural ***miasmata*** or ***miasmas***

midinette
FRENCH
a young female worker, especially a shop assistant, in the Paris fashion business

from *midi* meaning 'midday' and *dînette* meaning 'snack': such workers are often seen in cafés at lunchtime

mignon
FRENCH
small and dainty
feminine ***mignonne***

migraine
FRENCH
a severe throbbing headache affecting only one side of the head or face and usually accompanied by nausea

ultimately from GREEK *hemikrania* meaning 'half skull'

mihrab
ARABIC
a niche or slab in a mosque marking the direction of Mecca

mikado
JAPANESE, literally 'exalted gate'
a title given by foreigners to the emperor of Japan
plural ***mikados***

miles gloriosus
LATIN
a boastful or self-important soldier, used as a stock character in comedy

from the eponymous hero of a play by Plautus

plural ***milites gloriosi***

milieu
FRENCH for 'middle'
social environment or setting
plural ***milieus*** or ***milieux***

millefeuille or ***millefeuilles***
FRENCH, literally 'thousand leaves'
a layered cake made with puff pastry, cream, etc

millefiori
ITALIAN, literally 'thousand flowers'
1 an ornamental glass-making technique in which thin glass rods of various colours are fused together, cut into sections, then embedded in clear glass
2 glass produced in this way

millefleurs
FRENCH, literally 'thousand flowers'
1 a perfume prepared from many kinds of flowers
2 a pattern of small scattered flowers, used as a background in tapestry, on porcelain, etc

minauderie
FRENCH
a display of affectation

minceur
FRENCH for 'slimness'
(said of food or cooking) lean, low-fat
see also CUISINE MINCEUR

minestrone
ITALIAN
a thick mixed vegetable soup containing pasta or rice

Minnesinger
GERMAN, literally 'courtly-love singer'
any of the aristocratic German lyric poets and musicians of the 12th–13th centuries
see also MEISTERSINGER
plural ***Minnesinger*** or ***Minnesingers***

minshuku
JAPANESE
a Japanese guesthouse

minutia
LATIN for 'smallness'
a minute particular or detail
plural ***minutiae***

> the plural is the more frequent form

minyan
HEBREW for 'number'
the minimum number of people required by Jewish law to be present for a religious service to be held

> the minimum number is ten male adults (usually including boys over the age of thirteen)

plural ***minyanim*** or ***minyans***

mir
RUSSIAN for 'world'
a peasant farming commune in pre-Revolutionary Russia
plural ***mirs*** or ***miri***

mirabile dictu
LATIN
wonderful to tell

mirabile visu
LATIN
wonderful to see

mirliton
FRENCH
1 a toy reed-pipe
2 a small almond tart made with puff pastry

miscellanea
a collection of writings on different subjects or by different authors

mise en place
FRENCH
the preparation carried out in a restaurant before a meal is cooked and served

mise en scène
FRENCH
1 the process of setting a stage, arranging scenery, props, etc
2 the resulting arrangement
3 any setting or background

misère
FRENCH for 'misery, poverty'
(cards) an undertaking to take no tricks

miserere mei
LATIN
have mercy on me

miso
JAPANESE
a paste prepared from soya beans and fermented in brine, used for flavouring
plural ***misos***

missa or ***Missa***
LATIN
the Roman Catholic mass

missa solemnis or ***Missa solemnis***
LATIN
high mass

mistral
FRENCH, from PROVENÇAL
a violent cold dry northerly wind in southern France

mitrailleur
FRENCH
1 a machine-gunner
2 a mitrailleuse

mitrailleuse
FRENCH
a machine-gun that discharges a stream of small missiles

Mitteleuropa or ***Mittel-Europa***
GERMAN
Central Europe

mittimus
LATIN, literally 'we send'
1 *(law)* a warrant for the imprisonment of a person charged with a crime
2 *(law)* a writ by which a record is transferred from one court to another
3 *(informal)* dismissal, discharge
4 a nickname for a magistrate

mitzvah
HEBREW for 'commandment'
a good deed
see also BAR MITZVAH, BATH MITZVAH
plural ***mitzvoth*** or ***mitzvahs***

Mlle
see MADEMOISELLE

MM
see MONSIEUR

Mme
see MADAME

modello
ITALIAN
an artist's detailed sketch or sculptural model for a larger work
plural ***modelli*** or ***modellos***

moderato
ITALIAN
(music)
1 at a moderate speed
2 a movement or passage to be played at this speed

modicum
LATIN
a small quantity

modiste
FRENCH
a fashion designer

modus
LATIN
1 manner, mode
2 the way in which anything works
plural ***modi***

modus operandi
LATIN
method of operation, way of working

modus vivendi
LATIN
1 way of life or living
2 an arrangement or compromise enabling those who differ to get on together for a time

moire
FRENCH
watered silk or other fabric with a watered appearance

> from the English word *mohair*; the term was originally applied to watered mohair

moiré
FRENCH
1 watered
2 describing the optical effect or shifting wavy pattern seen when two surfaces covered with regular lines are superimposed
3 a watered appearance on cloth or metal
4 moire

moiser
YIDDISH
an informer

mole
AMERICAN SPANISH
(in Mexican cookery) a sauce containing chilli and chocolate, served with meat dishes

molto
ITALIAN
(music) very; much

mon
JAPANESE
a Japanese family badge or crest
see also KIKUMON, KIRIMON
plural ***mon***

mondain
FRENCH
1 worldly; fashionable
2 a person who lives in fashionable society
feminine ***mondaine***

monocoque
FRENCH, literally 'single shell'
1 an aircraft fuselage in which all or most of the structural load is carried by the skin
2 a motor-vehicle structure in which the body and chassis are a single unit
3 the hull of a boat made in one piece

monsieur
FRENCH
1 a man, a gentleman
2 (as a form of address) sir
3 (*Monsieur*; prefixed to a name) Mr
abbrev **M** (sense 3)
plural ***messieurs*** or ***Messieurs***

> the French plural abbreviation for sense 3 is *MM*; the abbreviation *Messrs* is used in English as the plural of *Mr*

monstre sacré
FRENCH, literally 'sacred monster'
a famous person, especially a star of stage or screen, whose appeal to the public is increased by their eccentricity

montage
FRENCH
1 a composite picture, photograph, film, etc
2 the act or process of making a montage by piecing together elements from other pictures, photographs, films, etc
3 the editing of a cinema film

mont-de-piété
FRENCH, literally 'mount of piety, bank of pity'
a state pawnshop
plural ***monts-de-piété***

monte di pietà
ITALIAN, literally 'mount of piety, bank of pity'
a state pawnshop
plural ***monti di pietà***

montero
SPANISH
1 a huntsman
2 a huntsman's helmet-like cap with a flap
plural ***monteros***

moquette
FRENCH
a type of carpet or soft-furnishing fabric with a velvety pile

morale
from FRENCH *moral*
the level of confidence, optimism, strength of purpose, etc, of a person or group

> the French noun *morale* is not used in this sense

moratorium
LATIN
1 an emergency measure authorizing the suspension of payment of debts for a given period of time
2 this period of time
3 a temporary ban on or cessation of any activity
plural ***moratoria*** or ***moratoriums***

morbidezza
ITALIAN for 'softness'
the delicate or sensual rendering of flesh-tints in painting

morceau
FRENCH
1 a morsel; a fragment
2 a piece of music
3 a short literary composition
plural ***morceaux***

more
LATIN
in the manner

more majorum
LATIN
after the manner of our or their ancestors

mores
LATIN
customs, manners

more suo
LATIN
in his or her own way, in characteristic fashion

morgue
FRENCH
haughtiness, arrogance

morituri te salutant
LATIN
those who are to die salute thee

said by gladiators to the Roman emperor

moshav
HEBREW for 'dwelling'
1 an agricultural settlement in Israel
2 a co-operative association of privately-owned farms
plural ***moshavim***

mot
FRENCH
1 a word
2 a pithy or witty saying
see also BON MOT

motif
FRENCH
1 a dominant or recurrent theme in a musical or literary work
2 a shape or design repeated in a pattern
3 a single design or ornament added to a garment, such as the symbol or name of the manufacturer or designer

mot juste
from FRENCH *le mot juste* meaning 'the right word'
the word that fits the context exactly; the most appropriate word for the required purpose

moto perpetuo
ITALIAN
1 perpetual motion
2 a piece of music that consists of a rapid unbroken succession of notes

motoscafo
ITALIAN
a motorboat
plural ***motoscafi***

motu
MAORI
a small reef island in the S Pacific
plural ***motu*** or ***motus***

motu proprio
LATIN
of one's own accord, without consultation

mouchard
FRENCH
a police informer

mouchoir
FRENCH
a handkerchief

moue
FRENCH
a grimace of discontent, a pout

moujik
see MUZHIK

moulage
FRENCH
the making of moulds, especially of objects of interest in criminal investigation

moulin
FRENCH
1 a mill
2 a shaft in a glacier worn by water running down a crack

moussaka or ***mousaka***
from MODERN GREEK *mousakâs*
a Greek or Turkish dish consisting of alternate layers of minced lamb, aubergines, and tomatoes, usually covered with béchamel sauce and cheese

mousse
FRENCH for 'moss'
1 a light sweet or savoury dish made with cream, eggs, flavouring, etc, whisked separately and then folded together, usually eaten cold
2 a cosmetic preparation dispensed from an aerosol as a foam, especially one used to style hair

mousseline
FRENCH
1 fine French muslin
2 very thin glassware

mousseux
FRENCH
(said of wine) sparkling

mouvementé
FRENCH
full of movement, lively

mozzetta or ***mozetta***
ITALIAN
a short cape to which a hood may be attached, worn by popes, cardinals, bishops, and abbots

muckluck, mukluk or ***mucluc***
ESKIMO
an Eskimo sealskin boot

mudéjar
SPANISH
a Spanish Moor, especially one permitted to remain in Spain after the Christian reconquest
plural ***mudéjares***

mudra
SANSKRIT for 'sign, token'
1 any of the symbolic hand gestures used in Hindu religious ceremonies and classical Indian dance
2 a posture in which the body is held in yoga, an asana

muesli
SWISS GERMAN
a dish of rolled oats, nuts, fruit, etc, eaten especially as a breakfast cereal

mufti
ARABIC, literally 'an expounder of Muslim law'
1 the civilian dress of one who usually wears a uniform
2 plain clothes
3 a civilian

mujahidin, mujahedin or ***mujaheddin***
ARABIC for 'fighters'
Islamic fundamentalist freedom fighters

mulatto
from SPANISH *mulato* meaning 'little mule'
the offspring of a Black person and a

person of European descent
plural ***mulattos*** or ***mulattoes***
feminine ***mulatta***

multum in parvo
LATIN, literally 'much in little'
a large amount in a small space

multum non multa
LATIN
much, not many things

muscae volitantes
LATIN, literally 'fluttering flies'
floating black specks before the eyes

musique concrète
FRENCH
a kind of music of the mid-20th century, made up of odds and ends of recorded sound

mutatis mutandis
LATIN
with the necessary changes

mutato nomine
LATIN
the name being changed

mutuus consensus
LATIN
mutual consent

muu-muu
from HAWAIIAN *mu'u mu'u*
a simple loose dress worn chiefly in Hawaii

muzhik, moujik or *mujik*
RUSSIAN
a Russian peasant

mystique
FRENCH
1 an incommunicable spirit, gift, or quality
2 a sense or aura of mystery and power surrounding a person, activity, etc

N

nacelle
FRENCH
1 the basket of a hot-air balloon, or the corresponding part of an airship
2 the streamlined outer casing of an aircraft engine

nada
SPANISH
1 nothing
2 nothingness

naevus
LATIN
a birthmark or mole on the skin
plural ***naevi***

nagari
SANSKRIT, literally 'town-script'
1 devanagari, the script in which Sanskrit, Hindi, and other Indian languages are written
2 the group of alphabets to which devanagari belongs
see also DEVANAGARI

naissant
FRENCH for 'being born'
coming into being; in the early stages of development

naïve, naive, naïf or ***naif***
FRENCH
1 with natural or unaffected simplicity
2 artless; ingenuous; credulous

> *naïve* is the feminine form of the French adjective *naïf*; the usual form for both genders in modern English is *naive*

naïveté, naiveté, naïvety or ***naivety***
FRENCH
1 natural simplicity
2 artlessness; credulity

nan or ***naan***
HINDI
a type of slightly leavened bread, as baked in India and Pakistan, similar to pitta bread

nargileh, narghile or ***nargile***
PERSIAN, from *nārgīl* meaning 'coconut' (from which it used to be made)
a hookah

narquois
FRENCH
mocking, malicious
feminine ***narquoise***

nasi goreng
MALAY, literally 'fried rice'
a dish of Malaysian origin, consisting of rice fried with meat or fish and other ingredients

natale solum
LATIN
native soil

natura abhorret vacuum
LATIN
nature abhors a vacuum

natura naturans
LATIN
creative nature

natura naturata
LATIN
created nature

nature morte
FRENCH, literally 'dead nature'
(art) still life

navarin
FRENCH
a stew of mutton or lamb with root vegetables

NB or ***nb***
see NOTA BENE

né
FRENCH for 'born'
used in giving the original name of a titled man
compare NÉE

nebula
LATIN for 'mist'
a faint misty appearance in the night sky produced either by a group of distant stars or by diffused gaseous matter

nec cupias, nec metuas
LATIN
neither desire nor fear

nécessaire
FRENCH for 'necessary'
1 a vanity case
2 a workbox

necessitas non habet legem
LATIN
necessity has no law

née
FRENCH for 'born'
used in giving the maiden name of a married woman
compare NÉ

négligé
FRENCH for 'neglected'
1 casual or informal dress
2 a negligee
3 casually or informally dressed
4 careless

negligee, negligée or ***négligé***
from FRENCH *négligé*
a woman's thin light dressing-gown

négociant
FRENCH
a merchant, especially a wine-merchant

nemesis
GREEK for 'retribution'
1 retributive justice
2 something that cannot be achieved
3 a rival or opponent who cannot be beaten
plural ***nemeses***

nemine contradicente
LATIN, literally 'no one opposing'
without opposition
abbrev **nem. con.**

nemine dissentiente
LATIN, literally 'no one dissenting'
without dissent
abbrev **nem. diss.**

nemo me impune lacessit
LATIN
no one provokes me with impunity

> the motto of the kings of Scotland and of the Order of the Thistle; also inscribed round the milled edge of a Scottish one-pound coin

nemo repente fuit turpissimus
LATIN
no one ever became utterly bad all at once

ne plus ultra
LATIN, literally 'no more beyond'
the uttermost point or extreme, usually of perfection

➪ said to have been inscribed in ancient times on the Pillars of Hercules (the Rock of Gibraltar and the N African promontory on the opposite side), at the entrance to the Mediterranean Sea

n'est-ce pas
FRENCH
is it not so?

netsuke
JAPANESE
a small carved ornament once used to fasten small objects, such as a purse or tobacco-pouch, to a sash

nexus
LATIN
1 a bond
2 a linked group
plural ***nexus***

niaiserie
FRENCH
foolishness

nihil ad rem
LATIN, literally 'nothing to the point'
totally irrelevant

nihil obstat
LATIN, literally 'nothing hinders'
a religious book censor's permission to print

nihonga
JAPANESE, literally 'Japanese painting'
a style of painting characterized by bright colours and traditional images

nil admirari
LATIN
to wonder at nothing

nil desperandum
LATIN
nothing is to be despaired of; never despair

ninja or ***Ninja***
JAPANESE
(in feudal Japan) one of a body of trained assassins and spies skilled in ninjitsu
plural ***ninja*** or ***ninjas***

ninjitsu or ***ninjutsu***
JAPANESE
a Japanese martial art with strong emphasis on stealth and camouflage

niramiai
JAPANESE
(in sumo wrestling) a period at the beginning of a fight in which the opponents attempt to intimidate each other by stamping, thigh-slapping, and glaring

nirvana or ***Nirvana***
SANSKRIT, literally 'a blowing out'
1 (in Buddhism and Hinduism) the ultimate state of spiritual tranquillity attained through release from everyday concerns and extinction of individual passions
2 a place or state of perfect bliss

nisei
JAPANESE, literally 'second generation'
an American or Canadian born of Japanese immigrant parents
see also ISSEI, SANSEI

nisi
LATIN for 'unless'
(law) to take effect on the specified date unless, in the meantime, some reason is given why it should not

nisi prius
LATIN, literally 'unless previously'
(law) (especially in the US) the trial of a civil case before a single judge and jury

> originally from the opening words of a writ directing that a case be tried at Westminster

abbrev **np, n.p.**

nl or ***n.l.***
see NON LICET, NON LIQUET

no, No, noh or ***Noh***
JAPANESE
the traditional Japanese style of drama, which developed out of a religious dance

noblesse
FRENCH for 'nobility'
1 nobleness
2 nobles collectively

noblesse oblige
FRENCH
noble birth or rank imposes obligations

> usually referring to the duty of the privileged to help those less fortunate than themselves

nodus
LATIN for 'knot'
1 a knotty problem, a difficulty or complication
2 a knotlike mass of tissue or cells, a swelling or knoblike protuberance
plural ***nodi***

noisette
FRENCH for 'hazelnut'
1 a small piece of meat, usually lamb, cut off the bone and rolled
2 a sweet containing or flavoured with nuts

nolens volens
LATIN, literally 'unwilling, willing'
willy-nilly

noli-me-tangere or ***noli me tangere***
LATIN, literally 'do not touch me'
1 a warning against touching, interference, meddling, etc
2 a plant that ejects its ripe seeds at a light touch
3 a work of art showing Christ appearing to Mary Magdalene after the Resurrection

nolle prosequi
LATIN
(law)
1 the plaintiff or prosecutor will proceed no further with the suit
2 an entry on a record to this effect

nolo contendere
LATIN, literally 'I do not wish to contend'
(law) a legal plea by which the accused does not admit guilt but accepts conviction, eg when wishing to avoid lengthy legal proceedings

nolo episcopari
LATIN, literally 'I do not wish to be a bishop'
refusal of a position of responsibility

nom
FRENCH
a name

nom de guerre
FRENCH, literally 'war name'
an assumed name; a pseudonym

nom de plume
PSEUDO-FRENCH

pen-name

> not used in French

nom de théâtre
FRENCH
stage-name

nomen
LATIN
a name
plural ***nomina***

nomenklatura
RUSSIAN
office-holders and managers in a communist regime, especially formerly in E Europe

> usually derogatory

non compos mentis
LATIN
not of sound mind
see also COMPOS MENTIS

non est inventus
LATIN
(law) he has not been found

> usually referring to a person against whom a writ has been issued

non licet
LATIN, literally 'it is not allowed'
(law) not permitted, unlawful
abbrev **nl, n.l.**

non liquet
LATIN, literally 'it is not clear'
(law) (said of evidence, etc) unclear
abbrev **nl, n.l.**

non multa, sed multum
LATIN, literally 'not many but much'
not great in number but great in significance

non nobis, Domine
LATIN
not unto us, O Lord

> Psalm 115

non obstante
LATIN, literally 'not hindering'
notwithstanding

non placet
LATIN, literally 'it does not please'
a negative vote

non possumus
LATIN
we cannot

> a form of refusal

non sequitur
LATIN, literally 'it does not follow'
1 a conclusion that does not follow logically from the foregoing premises
2 the drawing of such a conclusion
3 any remark, event, or action that bears no relation to what has gone before
abbrev **non seq.**

nosce teipsum
LATIN
know thyself

> a translation of GNŌTHI SEAUTON

nostalgie de la boue
FRENCH, literally 'nostalgia for mud'
a craving for depravity or degradation, especially sordid sexual experiences, or for a physical life devoid of civilized refinements

nostrum
LATIN, literally 'our own'

1 a patent medicine
2 any favourite remedy or solution

nota bene
LATIN
note or mark well
abbrev **NB, nb**

> the abbreviation is the usual form

notabilia
LATIN
1 things worthy of notice
2 noteworthy sayings

nougat
FRENCH
a hard chewy sweet containing chopped almonds, pistachio nuts, cherries, etc

nous
GREEK
1 intellect
2 talent
3 *(slang)* common sense

nous verrons (ce que nous verrons)
FRENCH
we shall see (what we shall see)

nouveau riche
FRENCH
1 a person with newly-acquired wealth but without good taste, breeding, or manners
2 an upstart

> also used as an adjective

plural ***nouveaux riches***

nouveau roman
FRENCH, literally 'new novel'
the anti-novel, a type of novel of the mid-20th century that largely discards plot, characterization, and other elements of conventional novel-writing

nouvelle
FRENCH
a long short story

nouvelle cuisine
FRENCH
a style of simple French cookery characterized by the use of fresh produce, light sauces, and elegant presentation

Nouvelle Vague
FRENCH for 'New Wave'
a movement in French cinema, beginning in the late 1950s, in which traditional narrative techniques and box-office appeal were abandoned in favour of a freer, simpler, understated style

> also used as an adjective and applied to movements in other arts

nova
from LATIN *nova (stella)* meaning 'new (star)'
a star that suddenly increases in brightness for a number of days or years
plural ***novae*** or ***novas***

novella
ITALIAN
1 a tale or short story
2 a short novel
plural ***novelle*** or ***novellas***

novus homo
LATIN for 'new man'
1 a Roman magistrate whose ancestors had never held office
2 an upstart

noyade
FRENCH
execution by drowning, as carried out at Nantes during the French Revolution

noyau
FRENCH for 'fruit-stone'
a liqueur made from brandy flavoured with bitter almonds or fruit-stones

np or ***n.p.***
see NISI PRIUS

nuance
FRENCH
a delicate or subtle degree or shade of difference

nuée ardente
FRENCH, literally 'burning cloud'
a cloud of hot gas, ash, etc, from a volcano, spreading horizontally

nugae
LATIN
trifles

nulla nuova, buona nuova
ITALIAN
no news is good news

nulli secundus
LATIN
second to none

numero uno
ITALIAN
(informal) number one, the most important person or thing, often oneself

numerus clausus
LATIN, literally 'closed or restricted number'
a quota that limits the number of students, especially those of a particular group, entering an academic institution

nunc dimittis or ***Nunc Dimittis***
LATIN, literally 'now lettest thou depart'
the song of Simeon (Luke 2.29–32) in the Roman Catholic breviary and the Anglican evening service

from the opening words

nunc est bibendum
LATIN
now is the time to drink

nunchaku
JAPANESE
a weapon consisting of two short thick sticks joined by a length of chain, used in some martial arts

nuncio
ITALIAN
1 an ambassador from the pope
2 a messenger

the modern Italian form is *nunzio*

nuoc mam
VIETNAMESE
a spicy sauce made from raw fish

nyet
RUSSIAN
no

O

obbligato
ITALIAN, literally 'bound, obliged'
(music) an accompaniment forming an essential part of a piece of music, especially that played by a single instrument accompanying a voice
plural ***obbligatos*** or ***obbligati***

obi
JAPANESE
a broad sash worn with a kimono

obiit
LATIN
died

obiit sine prole
LATIN
died without issue
abbrev **osp, o.s.p.**

obiter
LATIN
by the way, incidentally

obiter dictum
LATIN
1 something said by the way, an incidental remark
2 *(law)* a comment made by a judge that does not bear directly on the case and therefore need not influence the decision
plural ***obiter dicta***

objet d'art
FRENCH
an object of artistic value
plural ***objets d'art***

objet trouvé
FRENCH, literally 'found object'
a natural or man-made object displayed as a work of art
plural ***objets trouvés***

oblast
RUSSIAN
an administrative district in some republics of the former Soviet Union

obscurum per obscurius
LATIN
the obscure by the still more obscure

> referring to an attempt to explain something obscure by means of something that is even more obscure

octroi
FRENCH
1 a commercial privilege, eg of exclusive trade
2 a tax levied on goods brought into a town or city
3 the place where such a tax is paid

oderint dum metuant
LATIN
let them hate so long as they fear

odi et amo
LATIN
I hate and I love

> referring to the love-hate syndrome

odium
LATIN
1 hatred
2 offensiveness
3 blame

odium theologicum
LATIN
1 the hatred of theologians for each other
2 the acrimony of theological debate or controversy

the word *theologicum* may be replaced by *medicum, musicum, scholasticum,* etc, with reference to doctors, musicians, scholars, etc

oeil-de-boeuf
FRENCH for 'ox-eye'
1 a little round window
2 an octagonal vestibule
plural ***oeils-de-boeuf***

oeuvre
FRENCH
work (of an artist, writer, etc)

okimono
JAPANESE
a Japanese ornament or figurine

olé
SPANISH
an exclamation of approval, support, or encouragement, sometimes used in English as an expression of triumph

from ARABIC *wa-llāh* meaning 'by god'

olla-podrida
SPANISH, literally 'rotten pot'
1 a Spanish mixed stew of meat and vegetables
2 any incongruous mixture or miscellaneous collection

oloroso
SPANISH for 'fragrant'
a golden-coloured medium-sweet sherry
plural ***olorosos***

om or ***Om***
SANSKRIT
in Hinduism, a sacred syllable intoned at the beginning and end of prayers and as a mantra for meditation

omadhaun
from IRISH *amadan*
a fool

ombudsman or ***Ombudsman***
SWEDISH for 'representative'
1 in Sweden and Denmark, an official appointed to investigate complaints against the administration
2 in Britain, a government official who investigates complaints against government departments; the Parliamentary Commissioner for Administration
3 any official with a similar function

omertà
ITALIAN
a conspiracy of silence

omne ignotum pro magnifico
LATIN
everything unknown is taken to be magnificent

omnia vincit amor or ***amor vincit omnia***
LATIN
love overcomes all things

on-dit
FRENCH, literally 'it is said'
rumour; hearsay
plural ***on-dits***

onus
LATIN
1 burden
2 responsibility

onus probandi
LATIN
(law) the burden of proof, the responsibility of proving an allegation, etc

oomiak
see UMIAK

op cit
see OPERE CITATO

opéra bouffe
FRENCH
funny or farcical opera

opera buffa
ITALIAN
comic opera, especially of the 18th century

> as opposed to OPERA SERIA

opéra comique
FRENCH
opera with some spoken dialogue

> in the 19th century the term was applied to any French opera of this type, whether comic or tragic, including the original version of Bizet's *Carmen*

opera seria
ITALIAN
serious opera

> as opposed to OPERA BUFFA

opere citato
LATIN
in the work cited
abbrev **op cit**

> the abbreviation is the usual form

optimates
LATIN
the aristocracy, originally in ancient Rome
singular ***optimate***

optime
LATIN
very well indeed
abbrev **opt**

opus
LATIN
a work, especially a musical composition numbered in order of publication
plural ***opuses*** or ***opera***
abbrev **op**

opus Dei
LATIN
1 the work of God
2 liturgical worship
3 in Benedictine monastic practice, the primary duty of prayer

opus operantis
LATIN
the effect of a sacrament ascribed (as by Protestants) to the spiritual disposition of the recipient

opus operatum
LATIN
due celebration of a sacrament involving grace flowing from the sacramental act (the Roman Catholic view)

ora et labora
LATIN
pray and work

ora pro nobis
LATIN
pray for us

oratorio
ITALIAN
1 a story, usually biblical, set to music and performed by choir and orchestra without scenery, costumes, or acting
2 the form of such a composition
plural ***oratorios***

orbis terrarum
LATIN, literally 'circle of lands'
the whole world

ordre du jour
FRENCH for 'order of the day'
1 an agenda for business at a meeting, in parliament, etc
2 a proclamation by a dictator or military commander

origami
JAPANESE
the Japanese art of folding paper into shapes and figures

O si sic omnia!
LATIN
O that all things were thus!

osp or ***o.s.p.***
see OBIIT SINE PROLE

osso bucco
ITALIAN for 'marrow-bone'
an Italian dish of veal knuckle stewed in wine with tomatoes, herbs, etc

ostinato
ITALIAN for 'obstinate'
(music) a ground-bass, a bass part constantly repeated with varying melody and harmony
plural ***ostinatos*** or ***ostinati***

Ostpolitik
GERMAN
a country's policy with regard to the (formerly Communist) countries of E Europe

O tempora! O mores!
LATIN
O the times! O the manners!

usually lamenting a decline in contemporary standards of behaviour

otium cum dignitate
LATIN
dignified leisure

ottava
ITALIAN
an octave

ottava rima
ITALIAN
a stanza consisting of eight lines, rhyming a b a b a b c c

oubliette
FRENCH, from *oublier* meaning 'to forget'
1 a dungeon with no opening except in the roof
2 a concealed pit in the floor of a dungeon into which a victim could be thrown

outrance
FRENCH
1 the utmost extremity
2 the bitter end
see also À OUTRANCE

outré
FRENCH
1 beyond what is customary or proper
2 extravagant, fantastic
feminine ***outrée***

outremer
FRENCH, literally 'beyond (the) sea'
overseas

ouvrage
FRENCH
work

ouvrier
FRENCH
a worker or operative
feminine ***ouvrière***

ouzo
MODERN GREEK
an aniseed-flavoured liqueur

ovum
LATIN
1 an egg
2 *(biology)* the egg cell, or female gamete
plural ***ova***

Oxoniensis
LATIN
of Oxford
abbrev **Oxon.**

ozeki
JAPANESE
a champion sumo wrestler

P

p
see PIANO

pabulum
LATIN
1 food of any kind, especially that of plants and lower animals
2 fuel
3 nourishment for the mind

pace
LATIN, ablative of *pax* meaning 'peace'
with or by the leave of ...

> used to express disagreement, followed by the name of the person with whom the speaker or writer disagrees

pacha
see PASHA

pactum
LATIN
a pact or agreement

pactum illicitum
LATIN
an illegal agreement

pactum nudum
LATIN, literally 'naked pact'
an informal agreement in which a consideration is not given

padre
PORTUGUESE, SPANISH, and ITALIAN
1 father, a title given to priests
2 an army chaplain
3 a parson

padrone
ITALIAN
1 an innkeeper or owner of a café or restaurant
2 an employer, especially among Italian Americans
plural ***padroni***

paella
SPANISH
a dish containing rice, seafood, chicken, saffron, vegetables, etc

paillette
FRENCH
a spangle

pair
FRENCH
any of the even numbers in roulette
compare IMPAIR

pakka
see PUKKA

pakora
HINDI
an Indian dish consisting of chopped vegetables, etc, formed into balls, coated with batter, and deep-fried

palais
FRENCH
a palace

palais de danse
FRENCH
a dance-hall

palazzo
ITALIAN
1 an Italian palace, often one converted into a museum
2 a house built in this style

palette
FRENCH
1 a small board, usually with a thumb-hole, on which a painter mixes colours
2 the assortment or range of colours used by a particular painter or for a particular picture
3 *(figurative)* a range or selection

palmam qui meruit ferat
LATIN
let him who has won the palm wear it

panache
FRENCH, literally 'plume'
1 knightly splendour
2 grand manner, theatricality, flamboyance, swagger
3 sense of style

> the word originally referred to a plume of feathers on a helmet

panada
SPANISH
a thick binding sauce made with breadcrumbs or flour and seasoning

panem et circenses
LATIN, literally 'bread and circus-games'
food and amusements at public expense

> a formula for keeping the common people happy. The usual translation in English is 'bread and circuses'

panta rhei
GREEK
all things are in a state of flux

Panzer or ***panzer***
GERMAN
1 armour
2 a tank

paparazzo
ITALIAN
a photographer who specializes in spying on or harassing famous people in order to obtain candid photographs of them
plural ***paparazzi***

> from the name of a photographer in the film *La Dolce Vita* (1960)

papier-mâché
PSEUDO-FRENCH
1 a moulding material consisting of paper-pulp or sheets of paper pasted together
2 made of papier-mâché

> coined in English from FRENCH *papier* meaning 'paper' and *mâché* meaning 'chewed'

papillote
FRENCH
(cookery)
1 frilled paper used to decorate the bones of chops, etc
2 oiled or greased paper in which meat is cooked and served
see also EN PAPILLOTE

paprika
HUNGARIAN
a hot spice derived from a species of capsicum

parador
SPANISH
a castle, convent, etc, converted for use as tourist accommodation in Spain
plural ***paradores***

paranoia
GREEK
1 a form of mental disorder characterized by constant delusions, especially of grandeur or persecution

2 intense fear or suspicion, usually irrational or unfounded

paratha
HINDI
a flat round cake of unleavened bread, traditionally eaten with Indian food

par avion
FRENCH
1 by air
2 by airmail
see also AVION

par excellence
FRENCH, literally 'by excellence'
superior to all others; beyond compare; in the highest degree

par exemple
FRENCH
1 for example
2 indeed!

parfait
FRENCH for 'perfect'
a frozen dessert made from whipped cream, fruit, and eggs

pari-mutuel
FRENCH, literally 'mutual bet'
1 a betting-machine which automatically pools stakes and distributes winnings, a totalizator
2 the tote, a system of betting in which the winners receive a proportion of the total money staked

pari passu
LATIN
1 with equal pace, in step
2 together, without priority

parlando
ITALIAN for 'speaking'
(music) in declamatory style; recitative

parole
FRENCH for 'word', from the phrase *parole d'honneur* meaning 'word of honour'
1 the conditional release of a prisoner
2 the promise of good behaviour made by such a prisoner

parquet
FRENCH
a floor covering of wooden blocks fitted together in a pattern

parterre
FRENCH
1 a formal arrangement of flower-beds
2 the pit of a theatre, especially the part below the gallery

parti
FRENCH
1 a group of people
2 a decision
3 a marriageable person

particeps criminis
LATIN
someone who helps with the commission of a crime before or after the event

partie carrée
FRENCH, literally 'square party'
a party consisting of two men and two women

partim
LATIN
in part

parti pris
FRENCH, literally 'side taken'
bias, prejudice

partita
ITALIAN
(music)
1 a suite
2 a set of variations

Partitur
GERMAN
a score in music

partitura
ITALIAN
a score in music

parturiunt montes, nascetur ridiculus mus
LATIN
the mountains are in labour, a ridiculous mouse will be born

> said when a great deal of fuss and effort produces something relatively insignificant

parure
FRENCH
a set of jewels or other ornaments

parvenu
FRENCH
someone who has recently risen to wealth or power, especially undeserved, but lacks the social refinement to go with it; an upstart
feminine ***parvenue***

pas
FRENCH
1 a step or dance, especially in ballet
2 action
3 precedence
plural ***pas***

pas de deux
FRENCH
a ballet sequence involving two dancers

> a *pas de trois* involves three dancers, a *pas de quatre* involves four, etc

pas devant (les enfants/ domestiques)
FRENCH
not in front of the children/servants

> a warning against indiscretion in the presence of children or servants; also used jocularly

pasha or ***pacha***
from TURKISH *paşa*
a Turkish title formerly given to governors and high-ranking military and naval officers

pashm, pashim or ***pashmina***
PERSIAN for 'wool'
the fine underfleece of the goats of northern India, used for making rugs, shawls, etc

paso doble
SPANISH
1 a march usually played at bullfights
2 a two-step
3 the music for this dance

pas redoublé
FRENCH
a quickstep

passé
FRENCH for 'passed'
1 out of date; outmoded; old-fashioned
2 past one's best, faded
feminine ***passée***

passe-partout
FRENCH, literally 'pass everywhere'
1 a master-key
2 a kind of simple picture-frame in which the picture is held by strips pasted over the edges
3 adhesive tape or paper used for this purpose

passepied
FRENCH, literally 'pass foot'
a dance of Breton origin, slightly quicker than a minuet, popular in the 17th and 18th centuries

pas seul
FRENCH
a dance for one person, a solo dance

passim
LATIN
1 everywhere
2 occurring frequently throughout the text referred to
3 here and there
see also SIC PASSIM

pasta
ITALIAN for 'paste'
shapes or strips of flour-and-water dough, usually boiled or baked and served with a sauce
see also CONCHIGLIE, FETTUCCINE, MACARONI, SPAGHETTI, etc

pasticcio
see PASTICHE

pastiche
FRENCH
1 a literary, musical, or artistic composition made up of bits of other works or imitations of another's style
2 a jumble; a pot-pourri

> the Italian equivalent is *pasticcio*

pastille
FRENCH
a small fruit-flavoured sweet, often medicated

pastrami
YIDDISH, from ROMANIAN *pastramă*
strongly spiced smoked beef

pâté
FRENCH
a spreading paste made of meat, fish, etc, blended with herbs and spices

pâté de foie gras
FRENCH
pâté made from fattened goose liver

pater
LATIN
(slang) father

> usually facetious

paterfamilias
LATIN
1 the father or other male head of a family or household
2 any man regarded as exerting a paternal influence on others

> sense 2 is often facetious

plural ***patresfamilias*** or ***paterfamiliases***

paternoster
from LATIN *Pater noster* meaning 'Our Father' (the first words of the Lord's Prayer)
1 (also *Paternoster*) the Lord's Prayer
2 a muttered formula or spell
3 a large bead in a rosary, at which the Lord's Prayer is repeated
4 a rosary
5 a lift for goods or passengers, consisting of a series of compartments moving on a continuous belt

pater patriae
LATIN
the father of his country

pathēmata mathēmata
GREEK
one learns by suffering

patio
SPANISH for 'courtyard'
a paved area adjoining a house, where outdoor meals can be served, etc

pâtisserie or ***patisserie***
FRENCH
1 a shop selling fancy cakes and pastries
2 such cakes and pastries

patois
FRENCH
1 spoken regional dialect
2 jargon

patria potestas
LATIN
the authority of a father over his children, especially in ancient Rome

pavane
FRENCH, from SPANISH or ITALIAN *pavana*
1 a slow formal dance of Spanish origin, popular in Europe in the 16th and 17th centuries
2 the music for such a dance

pavé
FRENCH
1 pavement
2 a setting of jewellery with the stones close together, covering the metal

pax
LATIN
1 peace
2 *(informal)* let's call a truce

pax vobiscum
LATIN
peace be with you

pays
FRENCH
country

paysage
FRENCH
1 a landscape
2 a landscape painting

pc or ***p.c.***
see POST CIBUM

peau de soie
FRENCH, literally 'skin of silk'
a type of smooth silk or rayon fabric

peccadillo
from SPANISH *pecadillo*
a trifling fault, a small misdemeanour
plural ***peccadillos*** or ***peccadilloes***

peccavi
LATIN, literally 'I have sinned'
an admission of guilt or sin

> the word was allegedly used by Sir Charles Napier in a punning announcement of the conquest of Sind in 1843

plural ***peccavis***

peignoir
FRENCH, from *peigner* meaning 'to comb'
a woman's lightweight dressing-gown, originally worn when combing the hair

peine forte et dure
FRENCH, literally 'strong and severe punishment'
a kind of torture or capital punishment that involves pressing with heavy weights

pelota
SPANISH for 'ball'
any of various related games of Basque origin in which two players hurl a ball against a marked wall using a basket-like racket strapped to their wrist

penchant
FRENCH for 'leaning'
1 a taste, liking, or inclination
2 bias

pendente lite
LATIN
during the process of litigation

penetralia
LATIN
1 the innermost parts of a building
2 the most holy place in a temple
3 secret matters or mysteries

pensée
FRENCH
thought

penseroso
see IL PENSEROSO

pensieroso
ITALIAN
1 thoughtful
2 melancholy

pension
FRENCH
1 a boarding-house in France and some other European countries
2 full board
see also DEMI-PENSION

pensionnat
FRENCH
a boarding-school

pentimento
ITALIAN for 'repentance'
(art)
1 the revealing of a painting, or part of a painting, beneath a later work
2 the part or painting revealed

the term also refers to a detail painted over by the original artist

plural ***pentimenti***

per
LATIN
1 through
2 by means of
3 according to

per annum
LATIN
yearly
abbrev **per an.**

per ardua ad astra
LATIN
by steep and difficult ways to the stars

the motto of the Royal Air Force

percale
FRENCH
a closely woven fabric used for sheets, etc

per capita
LATIN, literally 'by heads'
for each person
see also CAPUT

per cent
from LATIN *per centum*
in the hundred; for each hundred

per contra
LATIN
1 on the contrary
2 as a contrast

per diem
LATIN
daily

perdu
FRENCH for 'lost'
1 concealed
2 someone lying in concealment or ambush
see also ENFANTS PERDUS

père
FRENCH
1 father
2 (following a name) senior
compare FILS

perestroika
RUSSIAN
reconstruction or restructuring, specifically that of the political and economic system of the former Soviet Union in the 1980s

per fas et nefas
LATIN
through right and wrong

pergola
ITALIAN
a framework for climbing plants, usually passing overhead to form a covered walk

peri
PERSIAN
1 (in Persian mythology) a beautiful but malevolent being with supernatural powers
2 a fairy

per impossibile
LATIN
1 by an impossibility
2 if it were so, which it is not

per incuriam
LATIN
(law) through lack of care

> designating a court decision that is mistaken and therefore not binding as a precedent

peripeteia or ***peripetia***
GREEK
a sudden change of fortune, especially in drama

per mensem
LATIN
monthly

per mille
LATIN
1 by the thousand
2 in each thousand
abbrev **per mil, per mill**

> the abbreviation *per mil* is the usual form

per minas
LATIN
(law) by means of threats, by menaces

permis de séjour
FRENCH
1 permission to reside in a foreign country
2 the permit issued

perpetuum mobile
LATIN
perpetual motion

per pro
LATIN
1 for and on behalf of
2 short for PER PROCURATIONEM
abbrev **pp, p.p.**

per procurationem
LATIN
by the agency of another, by proxy
abbrev **pp, p.p., per pro**

> the abbreviation *pp* or *p.p.* is the usual form, used when signing a letter or document on behalf of another. The agent's name should follow the abbreviation in the sense of *per procurationem*, but in modern usage often precedes it, in sense 1 of *per pro*

per saltum
LATIN
1 at a single leap
2 all at once

per se
LATIN
by itself; in itself, intrinsically; essentially

persiflage
FRENCH
banter; flippancy

persona
LATIN, literally 'an actor's mask'
1 person
2 the outermost part of the consciousness, the expression of the personality
3 social façade or public image
4 a character in fiction, especially drama
see also DRAMATIS PERSONAE, IN PROPRIA PERSONA
plural ***personae*** or ***personas***

persona grata
LATIN
a person who is acceptable, liked, or favoured, especially one who is diplomatically acceptable to a foreign government

> the opposite, *persona non grata*, is loosely used of anyone who is not wanted or welcome within a particular group. Both phrases are also used adjectivally

persona muta
LATIN
a character in an opera who neither speaks nor sings

persona non grata
see PERSONA GRATA

personnel
FRENCH for 'personal'
1 the people employed in any organization, such as a business or the armed services
2 an office or department that deals with employees' appointments, records, welfare, etc
see also MATÉRIEL

per stirpes
LATIN
(said of an inheritance) bequeathed to families who subdivide it equally among themselves, rather than directly to individuals

pesante
ITALIAN
(music)
1 heavy
2 heavily

pesto
ITALIAN
an Italian sauce made chiefly of basil and cheese, with nuts and olive oil, originating in Liguria

pétillant
FRENCH
(said of wine) slightly sparkling

petit ami
FRENCH, literally 'small friend'
a boyfriend; a lover
feminine ***petite amie***

petit bourgeois
FRENCH
a member of the lower middle class

petite
FRENCH
(said of a woman) small in stature and build

petite bourgeoisie
FRENCH
the lower middle class

petit four
FRENCH, literally 'small oven'
a small sweet biscuit, usually decorated with icing, marzipan, etc

petitio principii
LATIN
(logic) begging the question

petit maître
FRENCH, literally 'small master'
a fop or dandy

petit mal
FRENCH, literally 'small ill'
a mild form of epilepsy without convulsions
compare GRAND MAL

petit pain
FRENCH
a bread-roll

petit point
FRENCH
1 a small diagonal stitch used in embroidery or tapestry
2 work done in this stitch
compare GROS POINT

petits pois
FRENCH
small green peas

petrissage
from FRENCH *pétrissage*
massage by longitudinal rubbing and lateral squeezing

philosophe
FRENCH
a philosopher; a thinker of the type of the 18th-century French Encyclopedists

physique
FRENCH
bodily type, build, or constitution

pia desideria
LATIN
pious regrets

pia fraus or ***fraus pia***
LATIN, literally 'pious fraud'
something deceitful or dishonest done for a religious or moral purpose

pianissimo
ITALIAN
(music)
1 very soft
2 very softly
abbrev **pp**

piano
ITALIAN
(music)
1 soft
2 softly
abbrev **p**

piano nobile
ITALIAN, literally 'noble storey'
the floor of a large house or villa where the main reception rooms are situated, usually the first floor

piazza
ITALIAN
a place or square surrounded by buildings

picador
SPANISH
a mounted bullfighter with a lance

Pickelhaube or ***pickelhaube***
GERMAN
a German spiked helmet

picot
FRENCH for 'point, prick'
1 a loop in a decorative edging
2 a raised knot in embroidery
3 to ornament with picots

pièce de résistance
FRENCH
1 the best, most impressive, or most important item
2 the main course or principal dish of a meal

pièce d'occasion
FRENCH
a literary or musical work composed, prepared, or used for a special occasion

pied-à-terre
FRENCH, literally 'foot on the ground'
a house or flat kept for temporary or occasional lodging
plural ***pieds-à-terre***

pied noir
FRENCH, literally 'black foot'
a N African, especially Algerian, person of French descent
plural ***pieds noirs***

pierrot
FRENCH
a white-faced clown in a loose long-sleeved costume, especially a member of a group of entertainers at seaside resorts, etc
feminine ***pierrette***

pietà
ITALIAN for 'pity'
(art) a representation of the Virgin Mary with the dead Christ across her knees

pietra dura
ITALIAN, literally 'hard stone'
inlaid mosaic work with hard semi-precious stones, such as jasper, agate, etc
plural ***pietre dure***

pilau, pillau, pilaw or ***pilaf***
from PERSIAN *pilāw*
a highly spiced oriental dish of rice with chicken, fish, etc

> also used as an adjective

piña colada or ***pina colada***
SPANISH, literally 'strained pineapple'
a drink made from pineapple juice, rum, and coconut

pince-nez
FRENCH, literally 'pinch nose'
a pair of glasses held on the nose with a spring clip
plural ***pince-nez***

pinxit
LATIN
he or she painted this

> sometimes added to the signature of the artist on a painting

abbrev **pinx., pxt**

piquant
FRENCH for 'stinging'
1 having a pleasantly spicy taste
2 stimulating, provocative

pique
FRENCH
1 a feeling of anger, resentment, or wounded pride
2 animosity
3 to anger, offend, or wound the pride of
4 to arouse, stir, or provoke

piqué
FRENCH for 'pricked'
1 a stiff corded cotton fabric
2 inlaid work of gold or silver in points or strips on tortoiseshell or ivory

pir or ***Pir***
PERSIAN for 'old man, chief'
a Muslim title of honour given to a holy man or religious leader

pirouette
FRENCH
1 (in dancing, etc) a spin performed on the point of the toe or on the ball of the foot
2 to perform such a spin

pirozhki or ***piroshki***
RUSSIAN, literally 'little pies'
small triangular pastries filled with meat, fish, or vegetables

pis aller
FRENCH
a temporary substitute, a stopgap
see also AU PIS ALLER

pissoir
FRENCH
a public urinal

piste
FRENCH
a beaten track, especially a ski run

piton
FRENCH
a metal peg or spike to which a rope may be attached, used in mountaineering

pitta or ***pita***
MODERN GREEK for 'cake, pie'
a type of slightly leavened bread originating in the Middle East, usually baked in flat hollow ovals

più
ITALIAN
(music) more

più mosso
ITALIAN
(music) quicker

pizza
ITALIAN
a flat round piece of dough topped with cheese, tomato, and various other ingredients, then baked

pizzeria
ITALIAN
a restaurant that specializes in pizzas

pizzicato
ITALIAN for 'twitched'
(music)
1 played by plucking the string
2 this manner of playing
3 a passage so played
plural ***pizzicatos***

place
FRENCH
a public square

placebo
LATIN, literally 'I shall please'
1 a substance that is administered as a drug but has no medicinal content, given to humour or reassure a patient
2 a similar substance administered to a control group in drug trials
plural ***placebos***

placet
LATIN, literally 'it pleases'
1 a vote of assent in a governing body
2 permission to publish and carry out an ecclesiastical order, such as a papal bull or edict

plafond
FRENCH
a ceiling, especially decorated

plage
FRENCH
a fashionable beach

planchette
FRENCH, literally 'little plank'
a board mounted on two castors and a pencil point, used as a medium for automatic writing and supposed spirit messages

plat du jour
FRENCH
dish of the day, a dish on a menu that is specially recommended on a particular day

plaudite
LATIN
applaud; clap your hands

plaza
SPANISH
a public square or open paved area in a city or town

pleidiol wyf i'm gwlad
WELSH
loyal am I to my country

> inscribed round the milled edge of a Welsh one-pound coin

pleno jure
LATIN
with full authority

plethora
GREEK for 'fullness'
1 excess
2 a large amount or number

plié
FRENCH for 'bent'
a movement in ballet in which the knees are bent while the body remains upright

plissé
FRENCH
(said of a fabric) chemically treated to produce a shirred or puckered effect

plus ça change, plus c'est la même chose
FRENCH, literally 'the more it changes, the more it is the same thing'
the more things appear to change, the more they remain fundamentally the same

> used by the French writer Alphonse Karr in *Les Guêpes* (1849)

p.m., pm or ***PM***
see POST MERIDIEM, POST MORTEM

pocas palabras
SPANISH
few words

poco
ITALIAN
little

poco a poco
ITALIAN
little by little

pococurante
ITALIAN, literally 'little caring'
1 uninterested
2 indifferent
3 nonchalant

podsol or ***podzol***
RUSSIAN
any of a group of soils characterized by a greyish-white infertile topsoil and a brown subsoil, typical of regions with a subpolar climate

poeta nascitur, non fit
LATIN
a poet is born, not made

pogrom
RUSSIAN for 'destruction, devastation'
an organized massacre, originally applied to massacres of Russian Jews

poi
HAWAIIAN
a Hawaiian dish, a paste of fermented taro root

poilu
FRENCH for 'hairy'
a nickname for a French private soldier

point d'appui
FRENCH
a point of support, a prop or fulcrum

pointe
FRENCH
(ballet) the extreme tip of the toe

pointillisme or ***pointillism***
FRENCH
(in painting) the use of separate dots

of pure colour instead of mixed pigments

poisson
FRENCH
a fish

poisson d'avril
FRENCH
an April fool

polder
DUTCH
1 a piece of low-lying reclaimed land
2 the first stage in its reclamation

polenta
ITALIAN
an Italian dish resembling porridge, usually made from ground maize

Politburo
RUSSIAN
the chief policy-making committee of a Communist country, most notably the former Soviet Union

politesse
FRENCH
superficial politeness

politico
ITALIAN or SPANISH
(informal) a politician, or a person who is interested in politics

usually derogatory

pollice verso
LATIN, literally 'with the thumb turned'
the signal made by the spectators for the death of a Roman gladiator

poltergeist
GERMAN, from *poltern* meaning 'to make a racket' and *Geist* meaning 'ghost'
1 a mysterious invisible force said to throw or move things about
2 a noisy ghost

poncho
SPANISH
1 a S American cloak, a blanket with a hole for the head
2 a cyclist's waterproof cape of similar design
3 any similar garment

pons asinorum
LATIN, literally 'bridge of asses'
1 the fifth proposition in the first book of Euclid's *Elements*, which some students found hard to grasp
2 any severe test of a beginner

pont-levis or ***pontlevis***
FRENCH
a drawbridge

poori
see PURI

populus vult decipi, ergo decipiatur
LATIN
the people wish to be fooled, therefore let them be fooled

portamento
ITALIAN
(music) a continuous glide from one note to another
plural ***portamenti***

porte-bonheur
FRENCH
a good-luck charm

porte-cochère
FRENCH
a covered entrance for vehicles, originally for carriages, leading into a courtyard

porte-monnaie
FRENCH
a purse

portico
ITALIAN
a row of columns along the front or side of a building; a colonnade

portière
FRENCH
a curtain hung over the door or doorway of a room

portmanteau
FRENCH
a large travelling-bag that folds back flat from the middle

posada
SPANISH
a Spanish inn

poseur
FRENCH
a person who adopts poses and affects opinions, etc, in order to impress others

feminine ***poseuse***

posse
LATIN for 'to be able'
1 power
2 possibility
3 a posse comitatus
4 any group temporarily established for some purpose

see also IN POSSE

posse comitatus
LATIN, literally 'force of the county'
a body of men called out by the sheriff to assist in enforcing the law

post cibum
LATIN
after food

used in medical prescriptions

abbrev **pc, p.c.**

poste restante
FRENCH, literally 'post remaining'
a facility at a post office for holding mail until it is collected by the addressee

post factum
LATIN
after the event, retrospective

post hoc, ergo propter hoc
LATIN
after this, therefore because of this

a fallacious line of reasoning

postiche
FRENCH
1 counterfeit or false
2 a superfluous and inappropriate addition
3 a hairpiece, a wig

post meridiem
LATIN
after midday, ie in the afternoon or evening
abbrev **p.m., pm, PM**

the abbreviation is the usual form

post mortem
LATIN
after death
abbrev **PM, pm**

post prandium
LATIN
after a meal

used in medical prescriptions

abbrev **pp, p.p.**

pot-au-feu
FRENCH
1 a large earthenware cooking-pot or casserole
2 a stew, usually of beef and vegetables, traditionally cooked in such a pot in France

pot-pourri or ***potpourri***
FRENCH, literally 'rotten pot'
1 a fragrant mixture of dried petals, leaves, spices, etc, used to scent a room
2 a medley or miscellany

originally applied to a mixed stew

pouf or ***pouffe***
FRENCH
a large firm drum-shaped or cube-shaped cushion for use as a low seat

poule
FRENCH
1 a hen, especially a chicken for boiling
2 a promiscuous young woman

poule de luxe
FRENCH
(slang) a prostitute
plural ***poules de luxe***

pourboire
FRENCH, literally 'for drinking'
a gratuity, a tip

pour encourager les autres
FRENCH
to encourage the others

from Voltaire's *Candide* (1759), on the shooting of Admiral Byng

pourparler
FRENCH, literally 'for speaking'
an informal preliminary conference

pousse-café
FRENCH, literally 'push coffee'
a cordial, a liqueur, or a combination of several in layers, served after coffee

pp or ***p.p.***
see PER PRO, PER PROCURATIONEM, PIANISSIMO, POST PRANDIUM

praeludium
LATIN
a prelude
plural ***praeludia***

Pralltriller
GERMAN
(music) an upper or inverted mordent, a grace note in which the principal note is preceded by itself and the note above

prana
SANSKRIT
1 the breath of life
2 (in yoga) breath as the essential life force

pranayama
SANSKRIT
(in yoga) controlled breathing

précieuse
FRENCH
a woman affecting fastidious over-refinement

from the literary women of 17th-century France who were extremely fastidious in their use of language

précis
FRENCH
1 a summary of a piece of writing
2 to make a précis of
plural ***précis***

preludio
ITALIAN
a prelude
plural ***preludi***

premier danseur
FRENCH
the principal dancer of a ballet company, etc
feminine ***première danseuse***

première or ***premiere***
FRENCH
the first performance of a play or showing of a film

presto
ITALIAN
(music)
1 very quick, quicker than allegro
2 very quickly
3 a presto movement or passage
plural ***prestos***

prêt-à-porter
FRENCH
1 ready-to-wear
2 ready-to-wear garments

pretzel
GERMAN DIALECT
a crisp salted biscuit twisted into the shape of a loose knot

> the standard German form is *Brezel*

preux chevalier
FRENCH
a valiant knight

prie-dieu
FRENCH, literally 'pray God'
a piece of furniture designed for prayer, with a place for kneeling and a support for the arms or for a book

prima ballerina
ITALIAN
the leading ballerina in a ballet company
plural ***prima ballerinas*** or ***prime ballerine***

prima donna
ITALIAN
1 the leading female singer in an opera company
2 a person who is temperamental and hard to please
plural ***prima donnas*** or ***prime donne***

prima facie
LATIN
1 at first sight
2 *(law)* (said of evidence) sufficient to support a charge
3 *(law)* (said of a case) supported by prima facie evidence

primeur
FRENCH
1 novelty
2 early fruit or other produce

primo
ITALIAN
1 first
2 *(music)* the first or principal part in a duet
compare SECONDO
plural ***primos***
feminine ***prima***

primum mobile
LATIN for 'prime mover'
1 in medieval astronomy, the outermost of the revolving spheres of the universe, which was thought to carry the others round every 24 hours
2 any great source of motion or action

primus inter pares
LATIN
first among equals
feminine ***prima inter pares***

> the feminine form is a modern coinage

Privatdozent, privat-dozent or ***privat-docent***
GERMAN, literally 'private lecturer'
in German universities, a teacher who is not a member of the salaried staff

prix fixe
FRENCH
fixed price

prn or ***p.r.n.***
see PRO RE NATA

pro
LATIN
for

pro aris et focis
LATIN, literally 'for altars and firesides'
for the sake of one's religion and one's home

pro bono publico
LATIN
for the public good

procès-verbal
FRENCH
a written statement or report
plural ***procès-verbaux***

procureur
FRENCH
a procurator

procureur général
FRENCH
in France, the public prosecutor-in-chief

pro forma, pro-forma or ***proforma***
LATIN, literally 'for the sake of form'
1 (said of an invoice, etc) issued before the goods are dispatched
2 a pro forma invoice
3 an official form or record for completion

pro hac vice
LATIN
for this occasion

pro indiviso
LATIN, literally 'as undivided'
applied in law to rights which two or more persons hold in common

projet de loi
FRENCH
a legislative bill

pro memoria
LATIN
for a memorial

promenade
FRENCH
1 a broad paved walk, especially along a sea front
2 a place where people walk to and fro
3 a stroll, usually for pleasure or show
4 a processional sequence in a dance

pronto
SPANISH
(slang) promptly, quickly

pronunciamento
SPANISH
1 a manifesto
2 a formal proclamation
plural ***pronunciamentos*** or ***pronunciamentoes***

pro patria
LATIN
for one's country

pro rata
LATIN
in proportion

pro re nata
LATIN, literally 'for a thing born'
1 for a special emergency
2 as the need arises or as circumstances dictate
abbrev **prn, p.r.n.**

prosciutto
ITALIAN, literally 'pre-dried'
finely cured uncooked ham, often smoked
plural ***prosciutti*** or ***prosciuttos***

prosit
LATIN, literally 'may it be of use'
good luck to you

> a drinking toast used in Germany

pro tanto
LATIN
for so much

protégé
FRENCH for 'protected'
someone under the protection or patronage of another
feminine ***protégée***

pro tempore
LATIN
for the time being
abbrev **pro tem**

proviso
from LATIN *prōvisō quod* meaning 'it being provided that'
1 a provision or condition
2 a clause in a document that contains a condition or stipulation
plural ***provisos*** or ***provisoes***

proxime accessit
LATIN, literally 'he or she came closest'
the person next in order of merit to the winner
plural ***proxime accessits***

psyche
GREEK
1 the soul, spirit, or mind
2 the principle of mental and emotional life, conscious and unconscious

pudendum
LATIN, literally 'something to be ashamed of'
the external genital organs, especially the female genitalia
plural ***pudenda***

pueblo
SPANISH
1 (in Spanish-speaking countries) a town or settlement
2 a communal habitation of the Indians of New Mexico, etc
plural ***pueblos***

puissance
FRENCH for 'power'
a showjumping competition with very high jumps

puja
SANSKRIT
(Hinduism)
1 worship, or an act of worship
2 reverential observance
3 a festival

pukka, pucka or ***pakka***
from HINDI *pakkā* meaning 'cooked, ripe'
1 thoroughly good
2 thorough, complete
3 properly done; solidly built
4 straightforward; genuine

pulque
AMERICAN SPANISH
a fermented drink made in Mexico from agave sap

pundonor
SPANISH, from *punto de honor*
a point of honour
plural ***pundonores***

Punica fides
LATIN
Punic faith, ie treachery

purdah
▮ from URDU and PERSIAN *pardah* meaning 'curtain'
1 in Hindu and Muslim communities, the concealment of women from the sight of strangers, by means of a screen or curtain in the home or a veil worn in public
2 the screen, curtain, or veil used for this
3 *(figurative)* seclusion

purée
▮ FRENCH
1 food reduced to pulp, eg by processing in a liquidizer or rubbing through a sieve
2 to make a purée of

puri or ***poori***
▮ HINDI
a small cake of unleavened bread, deep-fried and served hot

pur sang
▮ FRENCH, literally 'pure blood'
1 thoroughbred
2 total

putsch
▮ SWISS GERMAN DIALECT
1 a sudden revolutionary outbreak
2 a coup d'état

putto
▮ ITALIAN
a plump naked young boy, often winged, in Renaissance or baroque art
plural ***putti***

pxt
see PINXIT

Q

qasida
ARABIC
a formal Arabic poem of praise or mourning

QED or ***q.e.d.***
see QUOD ERAT DEMONSTRANDUM

QEF
see QUOD ERAT FACIENDUM

QEI
see QUOD ERAT INVENIENDUM

qi, chi or ***ch'i***
from CHINESE *qì* meaning 'breath, energy'
(in Chinese medicine) an individual person's life force, the free flow of which within the body is believed to ensure physical and spiritual health

qigong or ***qi gong***
CHINESE
a system of meditational exercises for promoting physical and spiritual health by deep breathing

ql or ***q.l.***
see QUANTUM LIBET

qqv or ***qq.v.***
see QUOD VIDE

qs or ***q.s.***
see QUANTUM SUFFICIT

qua
LATIN
in the capacity of

quadratura
ITALIAN
(art) a work having a trompe l'oeil effect, eg a wall or ceiling painted with arches, colonnades, etc, in strong perspective
plural ***quadrature***

quadrille
FRENCH
1 a square dance for four couples or more, in five movements
2 music for such a dance

quaere
LATIN
1 inquire!; used to introduce a question or raise a query
2 a query or question

quae vide
see QUOD VIDE

qualis ab incepto
LATIN
as from the beginning

quand même
FRENCH
nevertheless, all the same

quantum
LATIN
1 quantity, amount
2 *(physics)* a minimum amount of some entity which is such that all other amounts are integral multiples of it
plural ***quanta***

quantum libet
LATIN
(in prescriptions) as much as you please
abbrev **ql, q.l.**

quantum meruit
LATIN, literally 'as much as he or she has earned'
(law) a fair reward for services rendered where there is no agreed rate of payment

quantum sufficit
LATIN
(in prescriptions) a sufficient quantity
abbrev **qs, q.s.**

quantum vis
LATIN
as much as you wish
abbrev **qv, q.v.**

quartier
FRENCH
a district of a French town or city

quartier latin
FRENCH for 'Latin quarter'
a district of Paris, on the left bank of the Seine, originally inhabited by writers, artists, and students

quasi
LATIN
as if, as it were

quattrocento
ITALIAN, literally 'four hundred'
the 15th century in reference to Italian art and literature

> the Italian word refers to the 1400s, *mille* meaning 'one thousand' being understood

quelque chose
FRENCH
1 something unspecified
2 an unimportant thing

quenelle
FRENCH
a poached dumpling of minced chicken, veal, or fish

quesadilla
MEXICAN SPANISH
(in Mexican cookery) a tortilla filled with cheese, chillis, etc, folded and fried or grilled

que sais-je?
FRENCH
what do I know?

> the motto of the French writer Michel de Montaigne (1533-92)

questionnaire
FRENCH
a set of printed questions distributed to a number of people, used to collect statistical information, survey opinions, etc

quia timet
LATIN, literally 'because he or she fears'
(law) of or relating to an injunction to prevent a possible future harmful act

quiche
FRENCH
a savoury flan of eggs, milk, cheese, ham, etc, baked in a pastry case

quid pro quo
LATIN, literally 'something for something'
something given or taken in recompense or retaliation

quieta non movere
LATIN, literally 'not to move things that are at rest'
to let sleeping dogs lie

quinta
SPANISH and PORTUGUESE
a country house in Spain or Portugal

quis custodiet ipsos custodes?
LATIN
who will guard the guards themselves?

qui s'excuse s'accuse
FRENCH
those who excuse themselves accuse themselves

qui tam
LATIN, literally 'who as much'
a legal action by an informer partly on their own behalf and partly on behalf of the state

qui va là?
FRENCH
who goes there?

qui vive?
FRENCH, literally '(long) live who?' (ie whom do you support?)
who goes there?

> chiefly used in English in the phrase *on the qui vive* meaning 'on the alert' or 'lively and ready for action'

quoad hoc
LATIN, literally 'as far as this'
in respect of this

quod erat demonstrandum
LATIN
which was to be proved or demonstrated
abbrev **QED, q.e.d.**

> the abbreviation is the usual form; used at the end of a proof or demonstration

quod erat faciendum
LATIN
which was to be done
abbrev **QEF**

quod erat inveniendum
LATIN
which was to be found
abbrev **QEI**

quod vide
LATIN
which see
abbrev **qv, q.v.**

> the abbreviation is the usual form; used in cross-references

plural ***quae vide,*** *abbrev* **qqv, qq.v.**

quo jure?
LATIN
by what right?

quondam
LATIN for 'formerly'
former

quorum
LATIN, literally 'of whom'
the minimum number of people who must be present at a meeting, etc

quot homines, tot sententiae
LATIN
as many men, so many opinions

quo vadis?
LATIN
where are you going?

> the words used by Peter to Christ (John 16.5 in the Vulgate) and, according to tradition, by Christ to Peter as he fled from Rome

quo warranto
LATIN
(law) a writ requiring a person to show by what warrant they hold or claim a franchise or office

qv or ***q.v.***
see QUANTUM VIS, QUOD VIDE

R

R
see REGINA, REX

racloir
FRENCH
a scraper

raconteur
FRENCH
a teller of anecdotes
feminine ***raconteuse***

raga
SANSKRIT for 'colour, tone (in music)'
1 in traditional Hindu music, a rhythmic or melodic pattern used as the basis for improvisation
2 a piece composed around such a pattern

ragoût or ***ragout***
FRENCH
1 a highly seasoned stew of meat and vegetables
2 a mixture

raison d'état
FRENCH, literally 'reason of state'
the principle that national interests take precedence over individual rights, morality, etc

raison d'être
FRENCH
reason for existence; purpose or cause

raisonné
FRENCH
logically set out, systematically arranged, and usually provided with notes

raisonneur
FRENCH for 'arguer'
(in a play or novel) a character who embodies the author's point of view or expresses the author's opinions

raj
HINDI
1 rule, sovereignty
2 government, especially the British government of India, 1858–1947

raja or ***rajah***
HINDI
1 an Indian prince or king
2 a Malay chief

raki or ***rakee***
from TURKISH *rāqī*
an aniseed-flavoured spirit of Turkey and the E Mediterranean

raku
JAPANESE for 'pleasure, enjoyment'
a type of coarse-grained lead-glazed pottery fired at a low temperature, used especially to produce Japanese tea bowls

râle or ***rale***
FRENCH
a sound from a diseased lung

rallentando
ITALIAN
(music) becoming slower
abbrev **rall.**

Ramadan
ARABIC
1 the ninth month of the Muslim calendar, during which fasting is

observed between dawn and dusk
2 the fast observed at this time

ramen
JAPANESE
a Japanese dish of clear broth containing vegetables, noodles, and often pieces of meat

rangatira
MAORI
a Maori leader or chief

rani or ***ranee***
HINDI
an Indian princess or queen

rappel
FRENCH
1 *(military)* call to arms by the beating of a drum
2 abseiling

rapport
FRENCH
1 relation; connection
2 a feeling of sympathy and understanding; a close emotional bond
see also EN RAPPORT

rapporteur
FRENCH
a person who carries out an investigation and draws up a report for a committee, etc

rapprochement
FRENCH
the establishment or renewal of a close, friendly relationship, especially between states

rara avis
LATIN, literally 'rare bird'
a rare person or thing

Rathaus
GERMAN
town hall

ratio decidendi
LATIN
(law) the reason or principle on which a decision is based

ravioli
ITALIAN
small square pasta cases with a savoury filling of meat, cheese, etc

re
LATIN, ablative of *rēs* meaning 'thing'
with reference to
see also IN RE

> chiefly used in business or official correspondence

Realpolitik or ***realpolitik***
GERMAN
practical politics based on the realities and necessities of life, rather than on moral or ethical ideas

réchauffé
FRENCH
1 a reheated dish
2 a reworking of old material

recherché
FRENCH
1 carefully chosen
2 particularly choice
3 far-fetched or tenuous
4 rare or exotic

récit
FRENCH
1 narrative, especially as opposed to dialogue in a book
2 a book consisting largely of narrative

recitativo
ITALIAN
1 a style of singing resembling speech
2 a passage to be sung in this manner, especially in the narrative part of an opera

➪ despite its pronunciation, the variant *recitative* (the usual form in English) is not of French origin

plural ***recitativos*** or ***recitativi***

réclame
FRENCH for 'advertisement'
1 publicity
2 the seeking or securing of publicity or notoriety

recto
from LATIN *rēctō (foliō)* meaning 'on the right (leaf)'
1 the right-hand page of an open book
2 the front page of a leaf
compare VERSO
plural ***rectos***

reculer pour mieux sauter
FRENCH, literally 'to draw back to take a better leap'
to make a strategic retreat in preparation for a more effective attack

reductio ad absurdum
LATIN, literally 'reduction to the absurd'
1 a way of disproving a proposition by showing that its logical consequence is absurd
2 a way of proving a proposition by showing that the contrary is absurd
3 the application of a principle to an absurd extreme

referendum
LATIN, literally 'something to be carried back'
the principle or practice of submitting a question of national importance to the vote of the entire electorate
plural ***referenda*** or ***referendums***

reflet
FRENCH
an iridescent or metallic lustre

regalia
LATIN, literally 'royal things'
1 royal privileges or powers
2 the emblems of royalty, ie the crown, sceptre, etc
3 the emblems, ceremonial clothing, etc, of any position of authority

régie
FRENCH
1 a system of government monopoly, especially in tobacco
2 the government department concerned
3 the tobacco sold

régime or ***regime***
FRENCH
1 government
2 a system of government
3 a particular government
4 a regimen

regimen
LATIN
a course of treatment, especially diet and exercise, which is necessary for good health

Regina
from LATIN *regina* meaning 'queen'
the title used by a reigning queen
abbrev **R**

régisseur
FRENCH
1 manager
2 stage manager
3 (in a ballet company) director

regius
LATIN for 'royal'
designating a professor whose chair was founded by Henry VIII or, in Scotland, by the Crown

Reich
GERMAN
1 the German state
2 Germany as an empire

re infecta
LATIN
without finishing the business

reistafel
see RIJSTTAFEL

relâche
FRENCH
1 relaxation; rest
2 no performance

religieuse
FRENCH
a nun

religieux
FRENCH
a monk or friar

religioso
ITALIAN
(music) in a devotional manner

reliquiae
LATIN
remains, especially fossil remains

remanet
LATIN, literally 'it remains'
1 a remainder
2 a postponed case or parliamentary bill

remuage
FRENCH
the process of turning wine bottles so that the sediment collects at the cork end for removal

> a process used in the production of champagne and similar wines

renaissance
FRENCH
1 a new birth
2 rebirth, revival
3 (*Renaissance*) the revival of arts, literature, etc, in Europe in the 14th–16th centuries, marking the transition from the Middle Ages to the modern world

rencontre
FRENCH
1 a chance meeting or encounter
2 a clash or skirmish between armies, adversaries, etc

rendezvous
from FRENCH *rendez-vous* meaning 'present yourselves'
1 an appointed meeting-place
2 a meeting by appointment
3 to meet or assemble at an appointed place

rentier
FRENCH
a person who lives on income from rents or investments

repêchage or ***repechage***
FRENCH, literally 'a fishing out again'
a supplementary heat or competition that gives competitors eliminated in earlier heats or competitions a second chance to go on to the final

repertoire
from FRENCH *répertoire*
a stock of pieces, songs, plays, etc, that a person or company is prepared to perform

répétiteur
FRENCH
1 a coach, a tutor
2 a person who rehearses opera singers, etc

répondez s'il vous plaît
FRENCH
(on an invitation, etc) please reply
abbrev **RSVP**

the abbreviation is the usual form

reportage
FRENCH
1 journalistic reporting or style
2 gossip
3 a documentary film or article presented without spoken or written commentary

repoussé
FRENCH for 'pushed back'
1 (said of metal) raised in relief by hammering from behind or inside; embossed
2 repoussé work

reprise
FRENCH
1 *(music)* resumption of an earlier theme
2 to renew or repeat

requiem
LATIN for 'rest' (the first word of the introit)
1 a mass for the rest of the soul of the dead
2 music for such a mass
3 any music of similar character

requiescat in pace
LATIN
may he or she rest in peace
abbrev **RIP**

the abbreviation is the usual form, inscribed on gravestones, etc

res extincta
LATIN
(law) the thing does not exist, ie the subject matter of a contract no longer exists or did not exist when it was drawn up

res gestae
LATIN
1 exploits
2 *(law)* facts relevant to the case and admissible in evidence

residuum
LATIN
a residue
plural ***residua***

res ipsa loquitur
LATIN
(law) the thing speaks for itself, ie the fact that an accident has happened is deemed to be evidence of negligence unless the defendant proves otherwise

res judicata
LATIN
a case or suit already decided

respice finem
LATIN, literally 'look to the end'
consider the result or consequences

restaurateur
FRENCH
the keeper of a restaurant

sometimes misspelt with the *-n-* of *restaurant*

restitutio in integram
LATIN
(law) the restoration of the parties to a contract to the relative positions occupied by them before the contract was made

résumé
FRENCH
1 a summary
2 (especially in the US) a curriculum vitae

resurgam
LATIN
I shall rise again

retroussé
FRENCH
(said especially of the nose) turned up at the end

retsina
GREEK
a Greek resin-flavoured wine

revanche
FRENCH
1 revenge
2 the recovery of territory lost to an enemy

revenant
FRENCH, literally 'coming back'
1 a person who returns after a long absence, especially from the dead
2 a ghost

revenons à nos moutons
FRENCH, literally 'let us return to our sheep'
let's get back to the subject

rêverie, reverie or ***revery***
FRENCH
1 an undirected train of thought; a daydream
2 mental abstraction

rêveur
FRENCH
a daydreamer
feminine ***rêveuse***

revue
FRENCH for 'review'
a show made up of musical items and sketches, usually humorous or satirical

Rex
from LATIN *rex* meaning 'king'
the title used by a reigning king
abbrev **R**

rhumba
see RUMBA

riant
FRENCH
1 laughing
2 merry

ricksha, rickshaw, jinricksha or ***jinrickshaw***
from JAPANESE *jinrikisha* meaning 'man-power carriage'
a small two-wheeled hooded carriage drawn by a person or attached to a bicycle or motorcycle

ricochet
FRENCH
1 the rebound of a bullet or other projectile hitting a hard surface
2 to rebound in this way

rictus
LATIN
an unnatural gape or grin

rien ne va plus
FRENCH, literally 'nothing goes any more'
a term used by croupiers to indicate that no more bets may be placed
see also LES JEUX SONT FAITS

rifacimento
ITALIAN
a reworking of a literary or musical composition
plural ***rifacimenti***

rigor mortis
LATIN
stiffening of the body after death

rijsttafel, rijstafel or ***reistafel***
DUTCH, literally 'rice table'
a selection of Indonesian rice dishes served with a variety of other foods

rikishi
JAPANESE

a sumo wrestler
plural ***rikishi***

rinforzando
ITALIAN for 'reinforcing'
(music) with sudden accent

RIP
see REQUIESCAT IN PACE

ripieno
ITALIAN for 'full'
(music)
1 supplementary, reinforcing
2 for all or nearly all the orchestra or choir
3 a supplementary instrument or performer
plural ***ripienos*** or ***ripieni***

riposte
FRENCH
1 *(fencing)* a quick return thrust after a parry
2 a ready and witty retort

rishi
SANSKRIT
a sage or poet

Risorgimento
from ITALIAN *risorgimento* meaning 'revival, rebirth'
1 the Renaissance
2 the liberation and unification of Italy in the 19th century

risotto
ITALIAN
an Italian dish of rice cooked in a meat or seafood stock with onions, tomatoes, cheese, etc
plural ***risottos***

risqué
FRENCH for 'risky'
bordering on the rude or indecent

risus
LATIN
1 a laugh
2 a grin

risus sardonicus
LATIN, literally 'sardonic grin'
(medicine) a drawing back of the corners of the mouth by muscular spasm, as in tetanus

ritardando
ITALIAN
(music) with diminishing speed
abbrev **rit.**

rite de passage
FRENCH
any of the rituals or ceremonies, such as those associated with birth, puberty, marriage, or death, that mark a person's transition from one period of life to another

> first used by the French anthropologist Arnold van Gennep (1873-1957)

plural ***rites de passage***

ritenuto
ITALIAN for 'restrained'
(music) slowing down
abbrev **rit.**

ritornello
ITALIAN
(music)
1 a short instrumental passage in a vocal work, eg a prelude or refrain
2 a passage for the whole orchestra in a concerto
plural ***ritornelli*** or ***ritornellos***

rive gauche
FRENCH for 'left bank'
the artistic quarter of Paris on the south bank of the Seine

rivière
FRENCH for 'river'
a necklace of diamonds or other precious stones, usually in several strings

robe de chambre or ***robe-de-chambre***
FRENCH
a dressing-gown
plural ***robes de chambre*** or ***robes-de-chambre***

rocaille
FRENCH
artificial rockwork or similar decoration

rodeo
SPANISH
1 a place where cattle are assembled
2 a round-up of cattle
3 an exhibition of cowboy skills
plural ***rodeos***

roi fainéant
FRENCH
a king without royal power
see also FAINÉANT

> applied to the later Merovingian kings of France, whose 'mayors of the palace' governed the country

roji
JAPANESE
a form of Japanese garden design incorporating a path of stepping stones that are sprinkled with water to concentrate the eye and mind on objects in the immediate field of vision

role or ***rôle***
from FRENCH *rôle*
1 a part played by an actor
2 a person's function in life, business, etc

romal
see RUMAL

Roma locuta, causa finita
LATIN
Rome has spoken, there is nothing more to be said

> said eg when someone makes a dogmatic remark or speech that puts an end to a discussion

roman à clef or ***roman à clé***
FRENCH, literally 'novel with a key'
a novel with characters based on real people under fictitious names

roman à thèse
FRENCH
a novel that sets out to demonstrate a thesis or proposition

roman à tiroirs
FRENCH, literally 'novel with drawers'
a novel with an episodic structure

roman fleuve
FRENCH, literally 'river novel'
a novel written as a series of self-contained narratives telling the story of a family, etc, over successive generations; a saga novel

rondeau
FRENCH
1 a form of poem characterized by closely-knit rhymes and a refrain
2 *(music)* a rondo
plural ***rondeaux***

rondo
ITALIAN
a musical composition, often the last movement of a sonata, in which the principal subject recurs in alternation with other subjects
plural ***rondos***

rooinek
AFRIKAANS, literally 'red neck'
an Afrikaans nickname for a British or English-speaking person

rosé
FRENCH for 'pinkish'

a pinkish table wine produced by removing red grape skins at an early stage of the fermentation process, or by mixing red and white wines

Rosh Hashanah
HEBREW, literally 'head of the year'
the Jewish festival of New Year

roti
HINDI for 'bread'
(in Indian and Caribbean cookery)
1 a cake of unleavened bread
2 a kind of sandwich made of this wrapped around curried vegetables, seafood, or chicken

rôti
FRENCH
roast, roast meat, joint

rôtisserie or ***rotisserie***
FRENCH
1 a cooking apparatus with a spit on which meat, poultry, etc, may be cooked by direct heat
2 a shop or restaurant selling or serving meat cooked in this way

roturier
FRENCH
a plebeian
feminine **roturière**

roué
FRENCH, literally 'broken on the wheel'
a debauched or disreputable man; a rake

> a name given by the Duke of Orléans, regent of France from 1715 to 1723, to his dissolute companions. The implication was that such men deserved to be broken on the wheel, a form of torture or punishment in which the victims were stretched out on a wheel and had their limbs broken with iron bars

rouge
FRENCH for 'red'
1 a cosmetic powder used to redden the cheeks
2 to colour with rouge

rouge-et-noir
FRENCH, literally 'red and black'
a gambling card-game played on a table with two red and two black marks on which stakes are laid

> the game is also called *trente-et-quarante* meaning 'thirty and forty', 30 being a winning number and 40 a losing number

roulade
FRENCH
1 *(music)* a melodic embellishment; a vocal or instrumental flourish, such as a run or turn
2 *(cookery)* a rolled-up slice of meat, cake, etc, usually with a filling

rouleau
FRENCH
1 a roll or coil, often of ribbon
2 a cylindrical pile of coins, counters, or other disc-shaped objects
plural **rouleaus** or **rouleaux**

roulette
FRENCH, literally 'little roller or wheel'
1 a gambling game in which a ball is dropped onto a spinning wheel and rolls into one of a set of numbered and coloured compartments
2 a tool with a toothed disc for engraving rows of dots, for perforating paper, etc

roux
from FRENCH *(beurre) roux* meaning 'brown (butter)'
(cookery) a mixture of butter and

flour cooked together and used to thicken sauces, etc
plural ***roux***

RSVP
see RÉPONDEZ S'IL VOUS PLAÎT

ruat caelum
LATIN
though the heavens fall
see also FIAT JUSTITIA, RUAT CAELUM

rubato
ITALIAN for 'stolen or robbed'
(music)
1 in a rhythm or tempo modified or distorted for the sake of expression
2 such a rhythm or tempo

> from the phrase *tempo rubato*, referring to time 'stolen' from one note to lengthen another

plural ***rubati*** or ***rubatos***

ruche
FRENCH
1 a frill of lace or other material, especially pleated
2 to trim with a ruche

rumal or *romal*
PERSIAN
1 a handkerchief
2 a headcloth

rumba or *rhumba*
SPANISH
1 a lively Afro-Cuban dance, or a ballroom dance based on a modification of it
2 a piece of music for this dance
3 to dance the rumba

rum baba
see BABA AU RHUM

rusé
FRENCH
artful, cunning
feminine ***rusée***

ruse contre ruse
FRENCH
cunning against cunning

ruse de guerre
FRENCH
a stratagem of war

rus in urbe
LATIN
the country in town

> referring to a rural atmosphere, area, etc, within a town or city

rya
SWEDISH
1 a type of Scandinavian rug with a knotted pile and a distinctive colourful pattern
2 the weave, pattern, or style typical of such a rug

ryokan
JAPANESE
a traditional Japanese inn

S

SA
see SOCIÉTÉ ANONYME

sa or ***s.a.***
see SECUNDUM ARTEM, SINE ANNO

sabot
FRENCH
a wooden shoe or clog, as formerly worn by the French peasantry

sabotage
FRENCH
1 deliberate destruction or damage carried out by discontented workers, rebels, enemies, rivals, etc
2 action taken to prevent the fulfilment of any plan, aim, etc

> also used as a verb

saboteur
FRENCH
a person who carries out sabotage

sachet
FRENCH
1 a small sealed packet containing a liquid, cream, etc, such as shampoo
2 a small bag containing a scented substance
3 a bag for holding handkerchiefs, etc

sadhu or ***saddhu***
SANSKRIT
a wandering Hindu holy man, living on charity

saeter
NORWEGIAN
(in Norway)
1 an upland meadow providing summer pasture for cattle, where butter and cheese are made
2 a hut on a saeter providing shelter for those looking after the animals

saeva indignatio
LATIN
fierce indignation

safari
SWAHILI, from ARABIC *safarīya* meaning 'a journey'
an expedition, especially one for hunting or observing animals in Africa

sahib
ARABIC
a form of address used in India to people of rank and formerly to Europeans; sir; Mr

> the Arabic term originally meant 'friend'

saikei
JAPANESE, literally 'cultivation scenery'
1 a Japanese miniature landscape of bonsai trees, etc, growing on rocks or stones
2 the art of cultivating such landscapes

sake, saké or ***saki***
JAPANESE
an alcoholic drink made from fermented rice

salaam
from ARABIC *salām* meaning 'peace'
1 a word and gesture of salutation in the East, chiefly among Muslims

2 obeisance

3 to perform a salaam, a low bow with the palm of the right hand on the forehead

salami

ITALIAN, plural of *salame*
a highly seasoned Italian sausage, usually served thinly sliced

sal Atticum

LATIN, literally 'Attic salt'
wit of a dry, delicate, and refined nature

salle

FRENCH
hall; room

salon

FRENCH
1 a reception room

2 a social gathering of distinguished people at the house of a fashionable hostess

3 a shop or business establishment providing beauty treatments, hairdressing, or similar services

4 a room or hall where paintings, sculptures, etc, are exhibited

salsa

SPANISH and ITALIAN for 'sauce'
1 (in Mexican cookery) a spicy sauce made with tomatoes, onions, chillies, and oil

2 a type of rhythmic Latin-American big-band music, with elements of jazz and rock

3 a dance performed to this music

4 to dance the salsa

salus populi suprema lex esto

LATIN
let the welfare of the people be the final law

salut

FRENCH
an informal greeting or farewell

salve

LATIN, literally 'be well'
hail! (addressed to one person)
plural ***salvete*** (addressed to more than one person)

salvo jure

LATIN, literally 'the right being saved'
(law) without prejudice

sal volatile

LATIN, literally 'volatile salt'
ammonium carbonate, or a solution of it; smelling-salts

samadhi

HINDI
(in yoga) a state of super-awareness brought about by profound meditation, in which the yogi becomes one with the object of meditation

samba

PORTUGUESE
1 a lively Brazilian dance, or a ballroom dance developed from it
2 music for this dance
3 to dance the samba

sambuca

LATIN
1 an ancient musical instrument like a harp
2 an Indian liquorice-flavoured liqueur made from aniseed

samisen or ***shamisen***

JAPANESE
a Japanese guitar-like instrument with three strings

samiti

HINDI
(in India) an organization or

committee of workers, usually involved in political activity

samizdat

from RUSSIAN *sam* meaning 'self' and *izdatelstvo* meaning 'publishing'
in the former Soviet Union, the clandestine or illegal printing and distribution of banned or dissident writings

samosa

HINDI
a small triangular pasty stuffed with spiced vegetables or meat and deep-fried
plural ***samosas*** or ***samosa***

samovar

RUSSIAN, literally 'self-boiler'
a metal urn for boiling water to make tea, etc, often elaborately decorated, traditionally heated by a central charcoal-filled pipe

sampan or ***sanpan***

from CHINESE *san* meaning 'three' and *pan* meaning 'board'
a small flat-bottomed oriental boat, usually propelled by oars

samsara

from SANSKRIT *saṁsāra* meaning 'passing through'
1 *(Hinduism)* the never-ending cycle of birth, death, and rebirth
2 *(Buddhism)* the passage of a person's soul into another body or state

samurai

JAPANESE, from *samurau* meaning 'to attend (one's lord)'
1 a member of an aristocratic class of Japanese warriors between the 11th and 19th centuries
2 this class collectively
plural ***samurai***

san

JAPANESE
a Japanese title or form of address equivalent to 'Mr' or 'Mrs', placed after the name

sanctum

LATIN, from *sanctus* meaning 'holy'
1 a sacred place
2 a private room

> chiefly used in the phrase *inner sanctum*

sanctum sanctorum

LATIN
1 the holy of holies; the inner chamber of the Jewish tabernacle
2 *(informal)* any particularly private place

sang-de-boeuf

FRENCH, literally 'ox-blood'
a deep red colour, as found on old Chinese porcelain

sangfroid

from FRENCH *sang froid* meaning 'cold blood'
coolness, composure, self-possession

sangria

from SPANISH *sangría* meaning 'bleeding'
a Spanish drink made with red wine, fruit juice, sugar, and soda water

sannyasi or ***sannyasin***

HINDI
a Hindu ascetic or hermit who lives by begging

sanpan

see SAMPAN

sans

FRENCH
without

sans-appel
FRENCH, literally 'without appeal'
a person against whose decision there is no appeal

sans cérémonie
FRENCH
without ceremony, informally

sansculotte
FRENCH, literally 'without breeches'
1 (in the French Revolution) a nickname for an extreme republican, probably because they wore pantaloons instead of knee-breeches
2 any violent revolutionary
see also CULOTTES

sansei
JAPANESE, literally 'third generation'
a resident of the US or Canada born of the offspring of Japanese immigrant parents
see also ISSEI, NISEI

sans gêne
FRENCH
at ease, unconstrained, unceremonious

sans peur et sans reproche
FRENCH
without fear and without reproach

sans phrase
FRENCH
without circumlocution

sans souci
FRENCH
without care or worry

sarafan
RUSSIAN
a Russian peasant woman's cloak

sarape or ***serape***
MEXICAN SPANISH
a woollen riding-blanket, usually brightly coloured, worn around the shoulders by Mexican men

sardana
CATALAN
1 a Catalan dance in a ring formation
2 the music for this, usually played on the flute and drum

sari or ***saree***
HINDI
a traditional garment of Hindu women, a long cloth wrapped round the body and draped over one shoulder and sometimes the head

sarong
from MALAY *sārung*
a skirt-like garment worn by Malaysian men and women, a cloth wrapped round the waist or chest

sashimi
JAPANESE, literally 'pierce flesh'
a Japanese dish of thinly-sliced raw fish served with soy sauce, grated radish, etc

sastruga
from RUSSIAN *zastruga*
one of the long parallel ridges of snow and ice that form on open windswept plains in snowy regions
plural ***sastrugi***

sati
see SUTTEE

satis verborum
LATIN, literally 'enough of words'
enough said

satori
JAPANESE
a state of sudden enlightenment, sought in Zen Buddhism

satyagraha
▮ SANSKRIT, literally 'reliance on truth'
1 Mahatma Gandhi's policy of passive resistance to British rule in India
2 any non-violent campaign for reform

Sauerbraten or ***sauerbraten***
▮ GERMAN, literally 'sour roast'
a German dish of beef marinated in vinegar and braised

Sauerkraut or ***sauerkraut***
▮ GERMAN, literally 'sour cabbage'
a German dish of shredded cabbage pickled in salt water

sauna
▮ FINNISH
1 a Finnish form of steam bath, in which the steam is created by pouring water on hot coals
2 a building or room equipped for it

sauté
▮ FRENCH, from *sauter* meaning 'to jump'
(cookery)
1 fried lightly and quickly
2 to fry lightly and quickly
3 a dish of food that has been sautéed
plural ***sautés*** or ***sautées***

sautoir
▮ FRENCH
a long necklace, or a pendant on a long chain or ribbon

sauve qui peut or ***sauve-qui-peut***
▮ FRENCH, literally 'save who can'
a state of panic; a stampede

savant
▮ FRENCH
1 a learned person, a scholar
2 learned, accomplished
see also IDIOT SAVANT
feminine ***savante***

savoir-faire
▮ FRENCH, literally 'to know how to do'
1 expertise
2 tact
3 savoir-vivre

savoir-vivre
▮ FRENCH, literally 'to know how to live'
good breeding; familiarity with the usages and conventions of polite society

sayonara
▮ JAPANESE
goodbye

saz
▮ PERSIAN
a stringed instrument of Turkey, N Africa, and the Middle East

sbirro
▮ ITALIAN
an Italian police officer
plural ***sbirri***

sc.
see SCILICET, SCULPSIT

scagliola
▮ ITALIAN, literally 'little chip of marble'
a polished imitation marble consisting of ground gypsum bound with glue

scampi
▮ ITALIAN for 'shrimps'
a dish of large prawns coated in breadcrumbs and deep-fried

scena
▮ ITALIAN
an operatic scene; an elaborate

dramatic recitative followed by an aria
plural ***scene***

scenario
ITALIAN
1 an outline of a play, film, etc, scene by scene
2 any imagined, suggested, or projected sequence of events, plan of action, situation, etc
plural ***scenarios***

scène à faire
FRENCH
the climactic scene in a play, opera, etc

Schadenfreude or ***schadenfreude***
GERMAN, from *Schaden* meaning 'harm' and *Freude* meaning 'joy'
malicious pleasure in the misfortunes of others

schechita, shechita or ***shehitah***
from HEBREW *shehitah* meaning 'slaughter'
(Judaism) the slaughtering of animals in accordance with rabbinical law

schema
GREEK
1 a scheme or plan
2 a diagrammatic outline or synopsis
plural ***schemata***

schemozzle
see SHEMOZZLE

scherzando
ITALIAN for 'joking'
(music)
1 in a playful manner
2 a scherzando passage or movement
plural ***scherzandos*** or ***scherzandi***

scherzo
ITALIAN for 'joke'
(music) a lively piece of music, especially a vigorous or light-hearted movement in a symphony or sonata
plural ***scherzos*** or ***scherzi***

Schläger or ***schläger***
GERMAN
the sword used by students in German universities where the duelling tradition has been preserved

schlemiel, schlemihl or ***shlemiel***
YIDDISH
(slang) a pitifully clumsy or unfortunate person

from Peter *Schlemihl*, a character created by the German writer Adelbert von Chamisso in 1814, or *Shelumiel*, a biblical general notorious for losing battles

schlep, schlepp or ***shlep***
YIDDISH
(slang)
1 to carry or pull with effort; to drag
2 a clumsy, stupid, or incompetent person
3 a person of no importance

schlimazel
see SHEMOZZLE

schlock or ***shlock***
YIDDISH
(slang)
1 of inferior quality
2 something of inferior quality, especially shoddy merchandise

Schloss or ***schloss***
GERMAN
a castle, palace, or manor house

schmaltz or ***shmaltz***
YIDDISH, from GERMAN *Schmalz* meaning 'cooking fat, grease'
sickly or excessive sentimentality, especially in music or art

schmelz
from GERMAN *Schmelz* meaning 'enamel'
glass used in decorative work

schmooze or ***shmooze***
YIDDISH
(slang)
1 to chat or gossip
2 such a chat, especially at a social gathering

schmuck or ***shmuck***
YIDDISH, from GERMAN *Schmuck* meaning 'ornament'
(slang) a pitiful, stupid, or obnoxious person

> originally a euphemism for 'penis'

Schnapps, schnapps or ***schnaps***
GERMAN for 'dram'
any of various strong alcoholic drinks, especially Dutch gin distilled from potatoes

schnell
GERMAN
1 quick
2 quickly

schnitzel
from GERMAN *Schnitzel*
a veal cutlet
see also WIENER SCHNITZEL

schnorrer
YIDDISH
(slang) a beggar

schnozzle
YIDDISH
(slang) the nose

schola cantorum
LATIN, literally 'school of singers'
1 a choir or choir school attached to a church, cathedral, etc
2 the part of a church or cathedral occupied by the choir

Schrecklichkeit
GERMAN
frightfulness

schtik or ***schtick***
see SHTIK

schuit or ***schuyt***
DUTCH
a Dutch flat-bottomed boat, used on canals and along the coast

schuss
from GERMAN *Schuss* meaning 'shot'
(skiing)
1 a straight slope
2 a fast run on such a slope
3 to make a fast run

Schutzstaffel
GERMAN, literally 'protection squad'
Hitler's personal bodyguard, later expanded into an élite military force in Nazi Germany
abbrev **SS**

> the abbreviation is the most familiar form

Schwärmerei
GERMAN
sentimental enthusiasm, wild devotion, fanaticism

scienter
LATIN
(law) having knowledge, being aware; knowingly, wilfully

scilicet
LATIN, from *scire licet* meaning 'it is permitted to know'
to wit, namely
abbrev **scil., sc.**

scintilla
LATIN for 'spark'
a hint or trace

sciolto
ITALIAN
(music) in a free manner

scire facias
LATIN, literally 'make it known'
(law) a writ requiring a person to appear and show cause why a record, such as a judgement or patent, should not be enforced or annulled
abbrev **sci. fa.**

scirocco
see SIROCCO

scordato
ITALIAN
(music) put out of tune

scordatura
ITALIAN
a temporary departure from the normal tuning of a stringed instrument

scrutin de liste
FRENCH, literally 'list ballot'
a method of voting for the French Chamber of Deputies, in which the voter may choose any combination from the full list of candidates for the department

sculpsit
LATIN
he or she sculpted this

> sometimes added to the signature of the sculptor

abbrev **sc., sculp.**

sd or ***s.d.***
see SINE DIE

séance or ***seance***
FRENCH for 'sitting, session, meeting'
a gathering at which a medium attempts to contact the spirits of the dead, usually on behalf of other people present

sec
FRENCH
(said of wine) dry

secateurs
from FRENCH *sécateur*
small sharp shears for pruning

secco
ITALIAN
1 (said of wine) dry
2 *(music)* unaccompanied
3 *(art)* painting on dry plaster
plural ***seccos***

seco
SPANISH
(said of wine) dry

secondo
ITALIAN for 'second'
(music) the secondary part in a duet
plural ***secondi***
compare PRIMO

secretaire
from FRENCH *secrétaire* meaning 'secretary'
a cabinet that folds out to form a writing-desk

secundum
LATIN
following, according to

secundum artem
LATIN, literally 'according to art'
1 scientifically
2 professionally
abbrev **sa, s.a.**

secundum naturam
LATIN
according to nature
abbrev **sn, s.n.**

secundum ordinem
LATIN
in order

secundum quid
LATIN
in some respects only

secundum regulam
LATIN
according to rule
abbrev **sec. reg.**

se defendendo
LATIN
in self-defence

segno
ITALIAN
(music) a sign to mark the beginning or end of a repeated passage
see also DAL SEGNO
plural **segnos**

seguidilla
SPANISH, literally 'little series'
1 a Spanish verse form of seven lines
2 a Spanish dance
3 a tune for this dance

seicento
ITALIAN, literally 'six hundred'
the 17th century in reference to Italian art, literature, etc

> the Italian word refers to the 1600s, *mille* meaning 'one thousand' being understood

seiche
SWISS FRENCH
a periodic fluctuation from side to side of the surface of a body of water, such as a lake or harbour, caused by changes in barometric pressure, etc

seigneur
FRENCH
a feudal lord or lord of a manor, especially in France or French Canada
see also DROIT DU SEIGNEUR, GRAND SEIGNEUR

semper
LATIN
always

semper fidelis
LATIN
always faithful

semper idem
LATIN
always the same
feminine **semper eadem**

semper paratus
LATIN
always ready

semplice
ITALIAN
(music) simply, without embellishments

> also used as an adjective

sempre
ITALIAN for 'always'
(music) in the same manner throughout

senatus populusque Romanus
LATIN
the Roman senate and people
abbrev **SPQR**

senhor
PORTUGUESE
1 a man, a gentleman
2 (as a form of address) sir
3 (*Senhor*; prefixed to a name) Mr

senhora
PORTUGUESE
1 a married woman, a lady
2 (as a form of address) madam
3 (*Senhora*; prefixed to a name) Mrs

senhorita
PORTUGUESE
1 an unmarried woman, a young lady
2 (as a form of address) miss
3 (*Senhorita*; prefixed to a name) Miss

se non è vero, è (molto) ben trovato
ITALIAN
if it is not true, it is (very) well invented
see also BEN TROVATO

señor
SPANISH
1 a man, a gentleman
2 (as a form of address) sir
3 (*Señor*; prefixed to a name) Mr

señora
SPANISH
1 a married woman, a lady
2 (as a form of address) madam
3 (*Señora*; prefixed to a name) Mrs

señorita
SPANISH
1 an unmarried woman, a young lady
2 (as a form of address) miss
3 (*Señorita*; prefixed to a name) Miss

senza
ITALIAN
(music) without
abbrev **sen.**

senza sordino
ITALIAN
(music) played without a mute

seppuku
see HARA-KIRI

seraglio
from ITALIAN *serraglio*
1 the women's quarters in a Muslim house or palace
2 a harem
3 a Turkish palace, especially that of the sultans at Constantinople

serape
see SARAPE

seriatim
LATIN
in succession, one after another, one by one

serra
PORTUGUESE, from LATIN, literally 'saw'
a mountain range

servus servorum Dei
LATIN
a servant of the servants of God

> a title of the pope

sesquipedalia verba
LATIN, literally 'words a foot and a half long'
very long words

> coined by Horace in *Ars Poetica*, giving rise to the English adjective *sequipedalian* meaning 'long, cumbersome, polysyllabic'

se tenant or ***se-tenant***
FRENCH, literally 'holding together'
denoting two or more stamps joined

together in a row or block, at least one of which differs from the other(s)

sforzando or ***sforzato***
ITALIAN, from *sforzare* meaning 'to force'
(music) with sudden emphasis
abbrev **sf, sfz**

sfumato
ITALIAN, literally 'shaded off'
(in painting and drawing) a misty, indistinct effect achieved by gradually blending together areas of different colour or tone
plural ***sfumatos***

sgian-dubh, skean-dhu or ***skene-dhu***
GAELIC, literally 'black knife'
a dirk, a dagger stuck in the stocking in full Highland dress

sgraffito
ITALIAN
1 decorative work in which different colours are revealed by partial removal of outer layers of material
2 pottery with such decoration
plural ***sgraffiti***

shah
PERSIAN
the king of Persia (now Iran)

shalom (aleichem)
HEBREW
peace (be with you), a greeting or farewell used especially by Jewish people

shaman
RUSSIAN
a priest who uses magic to cure illness, commune with gods and spirits, prophesy, influence the weather, etc

shamisen
see SAMISEN

shashlik or ***shashlick***
from RUSSIAN *shashlyk*
a type of lamb kebab

shaster or ***shastra***
from SANSKRIT *śāstra*
(Hinduism) a holy writing

shechita or ***shehitah***
see SCHECHITA

sheikh or ***sheik***
from ARABIC *shaikh*
1 an Arab chief
2 a Hindu convert to Islam

shemozzle, schemozzle or ***shlemozzle***
YIDDISH
(slang)
1 a mess
2 a quarrel or rumpus

from GERMAN *schlimm* meaning 'bad' and HEBREW *mazzāl* meaning 'luck', which also combine to form the Yiddish noun *schlimazel* meaning 'a persistently unlucky person', used in US slang

sherbet
TURKISH and PERSIAN, from ARABIC *sharāb* meaning 'drink'
1 an effervescent drink
2 powder for making such a drink
3 a kind of water-ice
4 a fruit-juice drink
see also SORBET

sherwani
HINDI
(in India) a man's knee-length coat buttoning up to the chin
plural ***sherwanis***

shiatsu or ***shiatzu***
JAPANESE, literally 'finger pressure'
a Japanese massage technique that aims to heal and promote health by the application of pressure, especially with the fingers and palms of the hands, to parts of the body away from the affected regions

shibboleth
HEBREW, probably meaning 'ear of corn' or 'flooded stream'
1 the catchword or catchphrase of a group, party, etc, by which members may be identified
2 a slogan
3 a peculiarity of speech

from the Bible (Judges 12.5–6): the test-word used by the Gileadites to identify the Ephraimites, who could not pronounce the sound *sh*

shikar
URDU
1 hunting, especially of big game
2 game
3 booty

shikari or ***shikaree***
URDU
1 a hunter, especially of big game
2 a sportsman

shiksa or ***shikse***
YIDDISH
a non-Jewish girl or woman

shippo
from JAPANESE *shippô* meaning 'seven precious things, something beautiful'
Japanese cloisonné ware

shlemiel
see SCHLEMIEL

shlemozzle
see SHEMOZZLE

shlep
see SCHLEP

shlock
see SCHLOCK

shmaltz
see SCHMALTZ

shmooze
see SCHMOOZE

shmuck
see SCHMUCK

shogi
JAPANESE
a Japanese form of chess

shogun
JAPANESE, from *sho* meaning 'to lead', and *gun* meaning 'army'
any of the hereditary military governors who were the effective rulers of Japan from the 12th century until the 1860s

shoyu
JAPANESE
a rich soy sauce made from soya beans naturally fermented with wheat or barley, used as a flavouring in oriental, especially Japanese, cookery

shraddha
see SRADDHA

shtik, shtick, schtik or ***schtick***
YIDDISH for 'piece, part, slice'
a familiar routine or line of chat associated with a particular comedian, etc

shufti or ***shufty***
ARABIC, literally 'have you seen?'
(informal) a look, glance

> the Arabic word is also informal

sic
LATIN
so, thus

> printed in brackets after a quoted word or phrase to show that the original has been faithfully reproduced even though apparently incorrect

sicilienne
FRENCH, feminine of *sicilien* meaning 'Sicilian'
a ribbed silk fabric

sic passim
LATIN, literally 'so throughout'
a phrase used to indicate that a word, spelling, etc, has been printed in the same form throughout a book, article, etc

sic transit gloria mundi
LATIN, literally 'thus passes the glory of the world'
a comment on the transitory nature of worldly fame or success

siddha yoga
see MAHA YOGA

siddhi
SANSKRIT for 'fulfilment'
(in Hinduism, Buddhism, and Jainism) the supernatural powers that come with the spiritual perfection attained by meditation, etc

Sieg heil
GERMAN, literally 'victory hail!'
a Nazi salute

sierra
SPANISH, from LATIN *serra* meaning 'saw'
a mountain range, especially in Spanish-speaking countries and the US

siesta
SPANISH, from LATIN *sexta (hōra)* meaning 'sixth (hour)'
a midday or afternoon nap

signor or ***signore***
ITALIAN
1 a man, a gentleman
2 (as a form of address) sir
3 (*Signor* or *Signore*; prefixed to a name) Mr
plural ***signors*** or ***signori***

signora
ITALIAN
1 a married woman, a lady
2 (as a form of address) madam
3 (*Signora*; prefixed to a name) Mrs
plural ***signore***

signorina
ITALIAN
1 an unmarried woman, a young lady
2 (as a form of address) miss
3 (*Signorina*; prefixed to a name) Miss
plural ***signorine***

si jeunesse savait, si vieillesse pouvait
FRENCH
if youth but knew, if age but could

s'il vous plaît
FRENCH
if you please

si monumentum requiris, circumspice
LATIN
if you seek his monument, look around you

➪ inscribed on the tomb of the architect Sir Christopher Wren in St Paul's Cathedral

simpatico
ITALIAN and SPANISH
(informal) congenial, pleasant

simpliciter
LATIN
1 simply, naturally
2 unconditionally, absolutely

simpliste
FRENCH
simplistic, naive

simulacrum
LATIN
1 an image
2 a semblance or superficial likeness
plural ***simulacra*** or ***simulacrums***

sine
LATIN
without

sine anno
LATIN, literally 'without year'
without date
abbrev **sa, s.a.**

sine die
LATIN, literally 'without a day'
1 without a fixed date
2 (said of a meeting or other business) indefinitely adjourned
abbrev **sd, s.d.**

sine dubio
LATIN
without doubt

sine prole
LATIN
without issue, without children
see also DECESSIT SINE PROLE, OBIIT SINE PROLE
abbrev **sp, s.p.**

sine qua non
LATIN, literally 'without which not'
an indispensable condition
see also CAUSA SINE QUA NON

sinfonia
ITALIAN
1 a symphony
2 a symphony orchestra

sinfonia concertante
ITALIAN
an orchestral work with parts for more than one solo instrument

Singspiel or ***singspiel***
GERMAN, literally 'singing play'
a type of German comic opera with spoken dialogue, popular in the 18th and early 19th centuries

➪ the term was later applied in Germany to musical comedy

si quis
LATIN, literally 'if anybody (wants, knows, has found, etc)'
a public notice, especially one announcing the impending ordination of a parish priest, allowing for objections to be raised

sirocco or ***scirocco***
ITALIAN
a hot, dry, dusty wind blowing from N Africa into S Europe
plural ***siroccos*** or ***sciroccos***

Sittlichkeit
GERMAN
1 morals, morality
2 that which is becoming or suitable

sitzkrieg
from GERMAN *sitzen* meaning 'to sit' and *Krieg* meaning 'war'
1 the period of comparatively little military action at the beginning of World War II, from September

1939 to May 1940
2 any similar period in any war

si vis pacem, para bellum
LATIN
if you want peace, prepare for war

skean-dhu or ***skene-dhu***
see SGIAN-DUBH

slàinte
GAELIC
good health!

slalom
NORWEGIAN, literally 'sloping path'
1 a downhill ski race on a winding course between posts or trees
2 a similar canoe race between hanging poles

smörgåsbord
SWEDISH, literally 'sandwich table'
an assortment of hot and cold savoury dishes served as a buffet

smørrebrød
DANISH, literally 'bread and butter'
hors d'oeuvres served on slices of buttered bread

smorzando or ***smorzato***
ITALIAN, from *smorzare* meaning 'to tone down, to extinguish'
(music) gradually fading away; growing slower and softer

sn or ***s.n.***
see SECUNDUM NATURAM

sobriquet or ***soubriquet***
FRENCH
1 a nickname
2 an assumed name

société anonyme
FRENCH, literally 'anonymous society'
a limited company
abbrev **SA**

softa
TURKISH
a Muslim theological student, attached to a mosque

soi-disant
FRENCH
self-styled, pretended, would-be

soigné
FRENCH
1 well-groomed
2 elegantly simple
3 carefully done
feminine ***soignée***

soirée
FRENCH
an evening party, social meeting, entertainment, etc

soixante-neuf
FRENCH, literally 'sixty-nine' (from the position adopted)
a sexual position in which both partners simultaneously orally stimulate each other's genitalia

solarium
LATIN for 'sundial'
a place for sunbathing or equipped with sunlamps, sunbeds, etc

solitaire
FRENCH for 'solitary'
1 a recluse
2 a game for one person in which pegs or marbles are removed from a board until only one remains
3 (especially in the US) the card game patience
4 a gemstone, especially a diamond, set by itself

solus
LATIN
alone

> originally used in stage directions

feminine **sola**

solvitur ambulando
LATIN, literally 'it is solved by walking'
the problem can be solved by practical experiment, by actual performance

soma or ***Soma***
SANSKRIT
a plant, or its intoxicating juice, used in ancient Indian religious ceremonies and personified as a god

sombrero
SPANISH, from *sombra* meaning 'shade'
a broad-brimmed hat worn in Mexico and elsewhere
plural ***sombreros***

sommelier
FRENCH
a wine waiter or steward in a restaurant or hotel

sonata
ITALIAN
(music) a composition, usually in three or more movements, for a solo instrument

sonatina
ITALIAN
a short sonata

son et lumière
FRENCH, literally 'sound and light'
a dramatic spectacle presented after dark at a site of interest, especially a famous building, involving lighting effects, spoken words, and music on an appropriate theme

sopra
ITALIAN
(music) above

soprano
ITALIAN
(music)
1 the highest singing voice
2 a singer with such a voice
3 a part for such a voice
4 of or possessing such a voice
5 denoting an instrument of corresponding range
plural ***sopranos*** or ***soprani***

sorbet
FRENCH
a kind of water-ice, especially one made from fruit juice, sugar, egg whites, etc

> from ITALIAN *sorbetto*, ultimately from the same Arabic source as SHERBET

sordino
ITALIAN
(music) a mute or damper to soften or deaden the sound of an instrument
see also CON SORDINO, SENZA SORDINO
plural ***sordini***

sortes Biblicae
LATIN
divination by selecting a passage at random from the Bible

> Virgil or Homer may be used instead, in which case *Biblicae* is replaced by *Virgilianae* or *Homericae*

sortie
FRENCH for 'exit, going out, outing'
1 a sudden attack by besieged troops
2 an operational flight by a military aircraft

sostenuto
ITALIAN
(music)
1 sustained
2 with full time allowed for each note

sotto voce
ITALIAN, literally 'below the voice'
in an undertone or aside

soubrette
FRENCH
(theatre) the part of a pert, coquettish maid in comedy

soubriquet
see SOBRIQUET

soufflé
FRENCH, literally 'blown'
a light sweet or savoury dish made with whisked egg whites and other ingredients

soupçon
FRENCH for 'suspicion'
a hardly perceptible quantity, a dash

sourdine
FRENCH
(music) a mute

sous-chef
FRENCH
a chef next in rank to the head chef in a hotel, restaurant, etc

soutache
FRENCH
a narrow braid used for trimming

soutane
FRENCH
a cassock

souteneur
FRENCH, literally 'supporter'
a prostitute's pimp

souvenir
FRENCH for 'memory'
a memento; an item kept as a reminder of a place, occasion, etc

soviet
from RUSSIAN *sovet*
a council, especially one of those that made up the local and national government of the former Soviet Union

sp or ***s.p.***
see SINE PROLE

spaghetti
ITALIAN, literally 'little cords'
pasta in the form of long cordlike strands, thicker than vermicelli

Spätlese or ***spätlese***
GERMAN, literally 'late harvest'
a sweet white wine made from grapes harvested after the main vintage

spécialité de la maison
FRENCH, literally 'speciality of the house'
the dish regarded by a restaurant as its best and most characteristic or exclusive

spiccato
ITALIAN
(music) half staccato, with the bow bouncing lightly off the strings

spiel
from GERMAN *Spiel* meaning 'play, game'
1 a story or line of talk, especially one that is plausible and persuasive
2 to talk glibly

spina bifida
LATIN, literally 'split spine'
a congenital defect in which one or more vertebrae fail to unite during the development of the embryo, often resulting in paralysis

spiritoso
ITALIAN
(music) with spirit

splendide mendax
LATIN, literally 'nobly lying'
untruthful for a good reason

spolia opima
LATIN, literally 'the richest spoils'
1 the arms taken in single combat by a leader from a leader
2 any supreme achievement

sponte sua
LATIN
of one's own accord, voluntarily

SPQR
see SENATUS POPULUSQUE ROMANUS

Sprachgefühl or ***sprachgefühl***
GERMAN
an instinctive feeling and aptitude for a language, its word patterns, idiom, usage, etc

Sprechgesang or ***sprechgesang***
GERMAN, literally 'speaking-song'
(music) a style of vocalization between singing and speaking, originated by Arnold Schoenberg

spritzer
from GERMAN *Spritzer* meaning 'splash'
a drink of white wine and soda water

spritzig
GERMAN
1 (said especially of wine) sparkling
2 a slightly sparkling white wine
3 the tangy quality of such a wine

sputnik
RUSSIAN, literally 'travelling companion'
any of a series of man-made earth satellites launched by the former Soviet Union

from the name of the first such satellite, launched in 1957

sraddha or ***shraddha***
from SANSKRIT *śraddha*
(in Hinduism and Buddhism) an offering to the spirit of a dead ancestor

SS
see SCHUTZSTAFFEL

Stabat Mater
LATIN, literally 'the mother stood'
1 a Latin hymn commemorating the sorrows of the Virgin Mary
2 a musical setting of this

from the opening words of the hymn

staccato
ITALIAN
(music)
1 with each note detached or disconnected
2 a staccato passage or manner
plural ***staccatos***

stalag
from GERMAN *Stamm* meaning 'base' and *Lager* meaning 'camp'
a German prisoner-of-war camp in World War II

stanza
ITALIAN
a group of lines of verse arranged in a definite pattern, forming a unit of a poem

starets or ***staretz***
RUSSIAN
(in Russia) a holy man, a religious teacher or spiritual adviser

statim
LATIN
immediately, at once
abbrev **stat.**

status quo
LATIN, literally 'the state in which'
1 the existing condition, an unchanged situation
2 (also *status quo ante*) the condition or situation existing before a particular change
see also IN STATU QUO

stein or ***Stein***
from GERMAN *Stein* meaning 'stone'
a large metal or earthenware beer mug, often with a hinged lid

steppe
from RUSSIAN *step*
a dry, grassy, and generally treeless plain, as in SE Europe and Asia

stet
LATIN, literally 'let it stand'
1 (in proofreading, etc) an instruction to ignore a correction or restore a deletion
2 to restore after marking for deletion

stet fortuna domus
LATIN
may the fortune of the house last long

stiletto
ITALIAN, literally 'little dagger'
1 a dagger with a narrow blade
2 a pointed instrument for making eyelets
3 a high thin heel on a woman's shoe
plural ***stilettos***

stimulus
LATIN for 'goad'
1 something that produces a response in a living organism
2 anything that rouses someone to action or increased activity; a spur or incentive
plural ***stimuli***

strapontin
FRENCH
a folding seat, as in a taxi, theatre, etc

stretto
ITALIAN for 'contracted'
(music)
1 part of a fugue in which the subject and answer are brought closely together
2 a passage, especially a coda, in quicker time
plural ***stretti***

stria
LATIN
1 a fine streak, furrow, or threadlike line, usually parallel to others
2 *(architecture)* one of the fillets between the flutes of columns, etc
plural ***striae***

stringendo
ITALIAN, literally 'pressing'
(music) with increasing speed

stucco
ITALIAN
1 any kind of plaster or cement used to coat exterior walls or make architectural mouldings
2 a decorative work on a building done in stucco
3 to face or decorate with stucco
plural ***stuccos***

stupa
SANSKRIT
a dome-shaped Buddhist memorial shrine

Sturm und Drang
GERMAN, literally 'storm and stress'
1 a German literary movement of the latter half of the 18th century, characterized by realism, extravagant passion, and rousing action
2 turmoil

> the title of a play by the German dramatist F. M. von Klinger (1752–1831)

stylus
from LATIN *stilus* meaning 'writing instrument'
a needle-like device that transmits sound vibrations from the grooves of a record as it is played

suave
FRENCH
1 (said of a person, especially a man) polite, sophisticated, and smoothly affable, especially superficially so
2 smooth, bland

suaviter in modo, fortiter in re
LATIN
gentle in manner, resolute in deed

sub divo
LATIN, literally 'under the sky'
in the open air

subito
ITALIAN
(music)
1 suddenly
2 immediately

sub Jove
LATIN, literally 'under Jupiter (the god of the sky)'
in the open air

sub judice
LATIN
(law) under consideration by a judge or court and therefore not able to be publicly discussed or reported

subpoena
LATIN, literally 'under a penalty'
1 a writ commanding that a person, such as a witness or defendant, attend a court of law at a specified time
2 to serve someone with such a writ

sub rosa
LATIN, literally 'under the rose (a traditional symbol of secrecy)'
privately, confidentially

sub specie
LATIN
under the appearance or aspect (of)

sub verbo
LATIN
under the word

> used as a reference in dictionaries, etc

abbrev **sv, s.v.**

sub voce
LATIN
under that heading

> used as a reference in dictionaries, etc

abbrev **sv, s.v.**

succah
see SUKKAH

succès de scandale
FRENCH
success of a book, play, film, etc, due to the scandal created by or connected with it

succès d'estime
FRENCH, literally 'success of esteem or approval'
success with more honour than profit

succès fou
FRENCH
extraordinary success

succubus
from LATIN *succuba* meaning 'whore'
a devil supposed to assume a female body and have sexual intercourse with men in their sleep
compare INCUBUS
plural ***succubuses*** or ***succubi***

suede or ***suède***
from FRENCH *(gants de) Suède* meaning '(gloves of) Sweden'
leather with a soft velvety finish, used for gloves, shoes, etc

also used as an adjective

suggestio falsi
LATIN
misrepresentation
see also SUPPRESSIO VERI (SUGGESTIO FALSI)

sui generis
LATIN, literally 'of its own kind'
the only one of its kind

sui juris
LATIN, literally 'of one's own right'
having full legal capacity to act

suite
FRENCH
1 a train of followers or attendants
2 a set, as of furniture or rooms
3 a sequence of instrumental movements, usually dance tunes, in related keys
4 a sequel
see also EN SUITE

suivante
FRENCH
a lady's maid

sukiyaki
JAPANESE
a Japanese dish of thinly-sliced beef, vegetables, soy sauce, etc, cooked quickly together, often at the table

sukkah or ***succah***
HEBREW for 'hut, tabernacle'
a hut or shelter roofed with branches, used by orthodox Jews as temporary living accommodation during the festival of Sukkoth (the Feast of Tabernacles)

summa cum laude or ***maxima cum laude***
LATIN
with greatest distinction
see also CUM LAUDE, MAGNA CUM LAUDE

summum bonum
LATIN
the chief good, especially as the ultimate ethical objective

sumo
JAPANESE
a traditional Japanese form of wrestling between contestants of great bulk, won by forcing one's opponent out of the ring or causing them to touch the ground with any part of the body other than the soles of the feet
plural ***sumos***

sumotori
JAPANESE
a sumo wrestler
plural ***sumotori*** or ***sumotoris***

suo jure
LATIN
in one's own right

suo loco
LATIN
in one's (or its) rightful place

supercherie
FRENCH
deception; hoax; fraud

suppressio veri (suggestio falsi)
LATIN
suppression of truth (is suggestion of the false)

> in law, *suppressio veri* is passive misrepresentation and *suggestio falsi* active misrepresentation

supra
LATIN
above
abbrev **sup.**

supremo
SPANISH
a supreme head; a leader with unlimited powers
plural ***supremos***

Sûreté
FRENCH
the French criminal investigation department

sur le tapis
FRENCH, literally 'on the carpet (as a table cover)'
under discussion

sur place
FRENCH
on the spot

sursum corda
LATIN
lift up your hearts

surveillance
FRENCH
1 a watch kept over someone or something, especially over criminals (and their activities) by the police
2 vigilant supervision
3 superintendence

sushi
JAPANESE
a Japanese dish comprising small cakes of cold rice topped with raw fish, vegetables, etc

sutra
SANSKRIT for 'thread'
1 (in Sanskrit literature) an aphoristic rule or a book of aphorisms on ritual, grammar, metre, philosophy, etc
2 (in Buddhist sacred literature) any of a group of writings including the sermons of Buddha and other doctrinal works
see also KAMA SUTRA

suttee or ***sati***
from SANSKRIT *satī* meaning 'true wife'
1 a former Hindu custom in which a widow burned herself on her husband's funeral pyre
2 a woman who sacrificed her life in this way

suum cuique
LATIN
to each his own

sv or ***s.v.***
see SUB VERBO, SUB VOCE

svelte
FRENCH
attractively slim; graceful, lissom, lithe

swami
from HINDI *svāmī* meaning 'lord, master'
1 a Hindu idol
2 a Hindu religious instructor
3 a mystic

swaraj
from SANSKRIT *svarājya* meaning 'own rule'
(in Indian history) self-government, independence, home rule

swastika or ***svastika***
from SANSKRIT *svastika*, from *svasti* meaning 'wellbeing'
1 an ancient symbol, a cross with arms bent at right angles, emblematic of the sun, good luck, etc
2 this symbol adopted as the emblem of the Nazi Party

sympathique
FRENCH
congenial, evoking a sense of affinity or harmony

T

tabi

JAPANESE

a sock with a thick sole and a division for the big toe, worn with Japanese sandals

tabla

HINDI

an Indian percussion instrument, a pair of small drums played with the hands

tableau (vivant)

FRENCH, literally '(living) picture'

a motionless representation, often of some famous scene from history, by living people in costume

plural ***tableaux (vivants)***

table d'hôte

FRENCH, literally 'host's table'

a meal at a fixed price in a hotel or restaurant

plural ***tables d'hôte***

taboo or ***tabu***

from TONGAN *tabu* meaning 'holy, unclean'

1 any social or ritual prohibition, restraint, ban, exclusion, etc

2 subject to taboo; forbidden

tabula rasa

LATIN, literally 'scraped tablet'

1 a clean slate (literally and figuratively)

2 a mind ready to receive information, having no previous knowledge or experience

plural ***tabulae rasae***

tac-au-tac

FRENCH

(fencing) a series of close attacks and parries between fencers of equal skill

tace

LATIN

be silent!

tacet

LATIN

(music) it is silent

> marked on a score to indicate a passage or movement in which a particular instrument or voice does not take part

taco

MEXICAN SPANISH

in Mexican cooking, a very thin rolled pancake with a meat filling, usually fried

plural ***tacos***

taedium vitae

LATIN

weariness of life

tae kwon do or ***taekwondo***

KOREAN, literally 'kick-fist method'

a Korean martial art similar to karate

Tag

see DER TAG

tagliatelle

ITALIAN

pasta cut into long ribbons

tahina or ***tahini***
ARABIC
an oily paste made of crushed sesame seeds

tahsil
HINDI
in India, a division of a district for revenue and certain other purposes

taiaha
MAORI
a Maori weapon in the form of a carved staff, now held during ceremonial public speaking

t'ai chi (chu'an)
CHINESE, literally 'great art of boxing'
a Chinese system of exercise and self-defence in which co-ordination and balance keep effort to a minimum

taiga
from RUSSIAN *taigá*
marshy pine forest spreading across much of subarctic N America and Eurasia, with tundra to the north and steppe to the south

tailleur
FRENCH
a woman's tailored suit

taipan
CHINESE
a foreigner living in China and head of a foreign business there

tala
SANSKRIT for 'hand-clapping'
a traditional rhythmic pattern in Indian music

tales
LATIN
(law)
1 the filling of vacancies on a jury from among those present in court
2 the people summoned in this way

from the phrase *tales de circumstantibus* meaning 'such of the bystanders'

tamale or ***tamal***
from SPANISH *tamal*
a highly seasoned Mexican dish of meat, chilli sauce, and maize dough usually wrapped in a corn husk and steamed or baked

tamari
JAPANESE
a concentrated sauce made of soya beans and salt

tamasha
ARABIC and PERSIAN
1 an entertainment, a show
2 a fuss or commotion

tambour
FRENCH
1 a drum
2 a circular embroidery frame for keeping the fabric taut
3 embroidery done on a tambour

Tannenbaum
GERMAN
1 a fir tree
2 a Christmas tree

tant mieux
FRENCH
so much the better

tanto
ITALIAN
(music) so much; too much

tanto uberior
LATIN
so much the richer

tant pis
FRENCH
so much the worse

tantra or ***Tantra***
SANSKRIT for 'thread, fundamental doctrine'
any of a number of Hindu and Buddhist writings giving religious teaching and ritual instructions, including the use of incantations, diagrams, etc

tao or ***Tao***
CHINESE for 'way, path'
1 (in Taoism) the absolute entity that is the source of all existence and change
2 (in Confucianism and some other philosophies) the way to be followed, right or proper conduct

taoiseach
IRISH for 'chief, leader'
the prime minister of the Republic of Ireland

tapa
SPANISH
a light savoury snack or appetizer, especially one using Spanish ingredients and cooking methods
plural ***tapas***

> the plural form is the more frequent, as in *tapas bar*

tapadera or ***tapadero***
SPANISH for 'lid, cover'
the leather guard in front of a Mexican stirrup
plural ***tapaderas*** or ***tapaderos***

tapotement
FRENCH
the use of light taps in massage

taramasalata
MODERN GREEK
a Greek dish, a pink creamy paste made from the smoked roe of cod or other fish mixed with olive oil and garlic

tarantas or ***tarantass***
RUSSIAN
a four-wheeled horse-drawn Russian vehicle mounted on poles

tartine
FRENCH
a slice of bread with butter or jam

tazza
ITALIAN for 'cup'
1 a shallow cup mounted on a circular foot
2 a saucer-shaped bowl
plural ***tazze*** or ***tazzas***

Te Deum
LATIN
1 a Latin hymn expressing praise and thanksgiving
2 a musical setting of this

> from its opening words, *Te Deum laudamus* meaning 'Thee, God, we praise'

te igitur
LATIN, literally 'thee therefore'
1 the opening words of the canon of the mass
2 a service-book on which oaths were taken

téléférique
FRENCH
a light cable car, especially one that is electrically propelled

telega
RUSSIAN
a four-wheeled Russian cart

témoignage
FRENCH
a factual unprejudiced account or testimony

tempera
ITALIAN
(art)

1 an emulsion, especially one made with egg yolk, used as a medium for powdered pigments
2 the paint so produced
3 the technique of painting with this
4 a painting so produced

> ➪ from LATIN *temperāre* meaning 'to mix proportionately'

tempo
🔊 ITALIAN
(music) time; speed and rhythm
plural ***tempos*** or ***tempi***

tempora mutantur, nos et mutamur in illis
🔊 LATIN
the times change, and we with them

tempore
🔊 LATIN
in the time of
abbrev **temp.**

tempura
🔊 JAPANESE
a Japanese dish of seafood or vegetables deep-fried in batter

tempus edax rerum
🔊 LATIN
time, consumer of things

tempus fugit
🔊 LATIN
time flies

tendre
🔊 FRENCH for 'tender'
tenderness, fondness

tenet
🔊 LATIN, literally 'he or she holds'
any opinion, principle, belief, or doctrine held by a person or group

tenuto
🔊 ITALIAN, literally 'held'
(music)
1 sustained
2 a sustained note or chord
plural ***tenutos***

teocalli
🔊 NAHUATL, from *teotl* meaning 'god' and *calli* meaning 'house'
a Mexican pyramid temple

ter in die
🔊 LATIN
three times a day

> ➪ used in medical prescriptions

abbrev **tid, t.i.d.**

terminus ad quem
🔊 LATIN, literally 'the end or limit to which'
a finishing point

terminus ante quem
🔊 LATIN, literally 'the end or limit before which'
the time or date before which the event in question must have occurred

terminus a quo
🔊 LATIN, literally 'the end or limit from which'
a starting point

terminus post quem
🔊 LATIN, literally 'the end or limit after which'
the time or date after which the event in question must have occurred

terra alba
🔊 LATIN, literally 'white earth'
any of various white earthlike substances such as gypsum, kaolin, pipeclay, etc

terracotta
🔊 ITALIAN, literally 'baked earth'
1 an unglazed earthenware made from a mixture of clay and sand, used for statues, pottery, etc

2 a work of art or other object made of this
3 its deep reddish-brown colour

> also used as an adjective

terrae filius
LATIN
a son of the soil; a person of humble birth

terra firma
LATIN
solid ground, dry land

> often as opposed to sea or air, said on return from a journey by boat, plane, etc

terra incognita
LATIN
an unexplored or unknown country or region

terra nullius
LATIN, literally 'nobody's land'
land that is not part of the sovereign territory of any country

terre verte
FRENCH
green earth; any green earthy mineral used as a pigment, usually a silicate of iron

terrine
FRENCH
1 a dish or casserole, originally of earthenware, in which food may be cooked and served
2 food cooked or served in such a dish, especially pâté

tertium quid
LATIN, literally 'some third thing'
1 a third unknown thing related to two known things
2 something intermediate between opposites
3 the third person in an eternal triangle

tertius gaudens
LATIN, literally 'third (person) rejoicing'
a third person who gains from or takes advantage of a dispute between others

> the word *gaudens* is sometimes replaced by *gaudat* meaning 'rejoices'

terza rima
ITALIAN, literally 'third rhyme'
an Italian verse-form in triplets, in which the middle line of each triplet rhymes with the first and third lines of the next
plural ***terze rime***

tessera
LATIN for 'dice, small cube'
a small piece of stone, glass, etc, used in mosaics
plural ***tesserae***

tessitura
ITALIAN for 'texture'
the natural range of a voice or of a vocal part in a piece of music

testamur
LATIN, literally 'we testify'
a certificate of having passed an examination

teste
LATIN, ablative of *testis* meaning 'witness'
on the testimony of ...

> followed by the name of a person

testudo
LATIN for 'tortoise'
1 a wheeled shelter used by Roman soldiers under attack from above

2 a similar shelter made by joining shields
3 a vaulted roof
plural ***testudos*** or ***testudines***

tête
FRENCH
a head

tête-à-tête
FRENCH, literally 'head to head'
1 a private confidential interview
2 an S-shaped sofa on which two people may sit face to face
3 confidential, secret
4 in private conversation
5 face to face
plural ***tête-à-têtes*** or ***têtes-à-têtes***

tête-bêche
FRENCH for 'head-to-tail'
(said of a postage stamp) printed in an inverted position in relation to the one beside it

tête-de-pont
FRENCH
a bridgehead

tête folle
FRENCH, literally 'mad head'
a scatterbrained person

textus receptus
LATIN
the received text of the Greek New Testament

TGV
see TRAIN À GRANDE VITESSE

thalassa, thalassa!
GREEK
the sea, the sea!

> the exultant cry of Xenophon's men when they first caught sight of the Black Sea on their retreat from Asia

thé dansant
FRENCH, literally 'dancing tea'
a dance held in the afternoon, at which tea is served
plural ***thés dansants***

thesaurus
LATIN for 'treasure, treasury', from GREEK
1 a book with systematically arranged lists of words and their synonyms, antonyms, etc
2 any book regarded as a 'treasury' of knowledge, words, quotations, etc

thesis
GREEK, literally 'putting'
1 a long dissertation, especially one based on original research and presented for a doctorate
2 a subject dealt with in this way
3 a proposition or unproved statement put forward as a basis for argument or discussion
plural ***theses***

tiara
GREEK
1 a jewelled semicircular head-ornament worn by women
2 the Jewish high-priest's mitre
3 the pope's triple crown

tic douloureux
FRENCH, literally 'painful tic'
a disorder of the fifth cranial nerve causing paroxysms of pain in face and forehead

tid or ***t.i.d.***
see TER IN DIE

tiers état
FRENCH
(in pre-Revolutionary France) the third estate, the commons

> the first 'estate' was the nobility, the second the clergy

tifosi
ITALIAN, from *tifo* meaning 'typhus'
fans or devotees, especially of a sport
singular ***tifoso***

tika
HINDI
a red mark or pendant on the forehead of Hindu women, formerly of religious significance but now worn for ornament

timbale
FRENCH
a dish of meat, fish, etc, cooked in a cup-shaped mould or shell

timbre
FRENCH
the tone of a voice, musical instrument, etc, as opposed to pitch and loudness

timeo Danaos et dona ferentes
LATIN
I fear the Greeks, even when they bring gifts

expressing distrust of any show of generosity by the enemy

timpani or ***tympani***
ITALIAN
a set of orchestral kettledrums
abbrev (informal) **timps**
singular ***timpano*** or ***tympano***

tinaja
SPANISH
a very large full-bellied earthenware jar, used especially for storing and maturing wine

tirage à part
FRENCH
an offprint or article reprinted separately from a periodical

tirailleur
FRENCH
a skirmisher, a sharpshooter

tiramisu
ITALIAN
a dessert made from pieces of sponge soaked in coffee and Marsala layered with mascarpone and chocolate

tisane
FRENCH
a medicinal drink, an infusion of herbs, flowers, etc

toccata
ITALIAN, from *toccare* meaning 'to touch'
(music) a composition intended to display the performer's technique or touch in a series of runs and chords before breaking into a fugue

toga
LATIN
the outer garment of a citizen of ancient Rome, a long piece of cloth wound round and draped over the body

toga praetexta
LATIN, literally 'bordered toga'
a toga with a deep border of purple, worn by boys, magistrates, etc

toga virilis
LATIN, literally 'manly toga'
1 a toga worn from the age of 14, as a sign of manhood
2 any symbol of maturity

toile
FRENCH
1 a thin cotton or linen dress material
2 a sample of a garment made in cheap material so that alterations may be made

toilette
FRENCH
the act of washing and dressing oneself

toison d'or
FRENCH
the golden fleece

tomus
LATIN
tome or volume
abbrev **tom.**

tondo
ITALIAN, short for *rotondo* meaning 'round'
a circular painting or carving
plural ***tondi*** or ***tondos***

tonneau
FRENCH for 'cask, tun'
1 the rear part of an open car in which passengers sit
2 a detachable cover to protect the rear passenger seats in an open car when not in use
plural ***tonneaus*** or ***tonneaux***

topi or *topee*
HINDI
a hat, especially a pith helmet worn in India as protection against sunstroke

> a *sola topi* is made from the pithy stems of the sola plant; through association with the sun the word *solar* is sometimes wrongly used in place of *sola*

toque
FRENCH
a woman's close-fitting brimless hat

torchère
FRENCH
a tall ornamental candlestick or lampstand

torchon
FRENCH
1 a duster or dishcloth
2 bobbin lace of loose texture and geometrical design, or a machine-made imitation
3 rough paper for watercolour painting

toreador
SPANISH
a bullfighter, especially on horseback

torero
SPANISH
a bullfighter on foot
plural ***toreros***

torso
ITALIAN
1 the trunk of a statue or human body, without head or limbs
2 anything incomplete or unfinished
plural ***torsos*** or ***torsi***

tortilla
SPANISH, literally 'little cake'
1 a Mexican round flat cake made from maize or wheat flour cooked on a griddle, usually eaten hot with a filling
2 a thick Spanish omelette made mainly of potato and egg

totidem verbis
LATIN
in so many words, in just these words

toties quoties
LATIN
as often as; on each occasion

toto caelo
LATIN, literally 'by the whole heavens'
diametrically opposed

touché
FRENCH for 'touched'
an exclamation claiming or acknowledging a hit in fencing, a point scored in argument, etc

toujours
FRENCH
always, ever, for ever

toujours perdrix
FRENCH, literally 'always partridge'
too much of a good thing

toupee or ***toupet***
from FRENCH *toupet*
a wig or hairpiece worn to disguise baldness

tour de force
FRENCH
a feat of strength or skill; an outstanding effort or performance
plural ***tours de force***

tour d'horizon
FRENCH
a general survey, a review

tournedos
FRENCH
a small round thick beef fillet

tourniquet
FRENCH
a bandage or other device used to stop bleeding by compressing an artery

tout à fait
FRENCH
entirely; wholly

tout au contraire
FRENCH
on the contrary

tout à vous
FRENCH, literally 'wholly yours'
yours truly

tout comprendre c'est tout pardonner
FRENCH
to understand everything is to pardon everything

tout court
FRENCH
briefly, without preface, simply

tout de même
FRENCH
all the same; nevertheless

tout de suite
FRENCH
at once, immediately

tout ensemble
FRENCH
general appearance or effect
see also ENSEMBLE

tout le monde
FRENCH, literally 'all the world'
everybody

tovarish, tovarisch or ***tovarich***
from RUSSIAN *tovarishch*
comrade

tracasserie
FRENCH
turmoil

traduttori traditori
ITALIAN
translators are traitors, ie a translation can never be completely true to the original

tragédienne or ***tragedienne***
FRENCH
an actress who specializes in tragic roles

trahison
FRENCH
treason; treachery

trahison des clercs
FRENCH
the treason of intellectuals, the entry of academics into politics

Train à Grande Vitesse
FRENCH
a high-speed French passenger train
abbrev **TGV**

trait
FRENCH for 'line, stroke'
a characteristic or distinguishing feature

tranche
FRENCH for 'slice'
a block or portion, eg of money, taxation, an issue of shares, etc

trattoria
ITALIAN
an Italian restaurant
plural ***trattorias*** or ***trattorie***

trauma
GREEK for 'wound'
1 an injury
2 an emotional shock that may be the origin of a neurosis
3 the state or condition caused by a physical or emotional shock
plural ***traumas*** or ***traumata***

trecento
ITALIAN, literally 'three hundred'
the 14th century in reference to Italian art, etc

> the Italian word refers to the 1300s, *mille* meaning 'one thousand' being understood

tre corde
ITALIAN, literally 'three strings'
(music) a direction to pianists to release the soft pedal
compare UNA CORDA

tremolo
ITALIAN
(music) a tremulous effect achieved by rapidly repeating the same note, eg on a stringed or keyboard instrument, or by fluctuating the pitch of a sung note

> also used as an adjective

plural ***tremolos***

trente-et-quarante
see ROUGE-ET-NOIR

triage
FRENCH for 'sorting'
1 in war, etc, the selection for treatment of those casualties most likely to survive
2 allocation of resources to where they will have the most effect, rather than to where the need is most urgent or severe

tricot
FRENCH for 'knitting'
a hand-knitted woollen fabric, or a machine-made imitation of this

tricoteuse
FRENCH
in the French Revolution, any of the women who attended public executions, knitting as they watched

Trinkgeld
GERMAN, literally 'drink money'
a tip or gratuity

triptyque
FRENCH for 'triptych'
an international pass for a car

> so called because it is divided in three sections, like a triptych

tristesse
FRENCH
sorrow, grief, melancholy

trivia
from LATIN *trivium*, literally 'a place where three ways meet'
trifles, trivialities; unimportant details, facts, writings, etc

trocken
GERMAN
(said of wine) dry

troika
RUSSIAN
1 a Russian vehicle drawn by three horses abreast
2 a team of three horses abreast
3 a team of three people, etc, acting equally as leaders, a triumvirate

trompe l'oeil
FRENCH, literally 'deceives the eye'
an effect in painting or architecture that uses minute detail, perspective, etc, to create the illusion of reality

tronc
FRENCH for 'trunk'
1 a collection of tips to be divided out later, eg among waiters
2 the system by which this is done

troppo
ITALIAN
(music) too much; excessively
see also MA NON TROPPO

trottoir
FRENCH
a pavement

troupe
FRENCH
a company, especially of theatrical performers

trousseau
FRENCH, literally 'little bundle'
the clothes, household linen, etc, collected by a bride for her wedding and married life
plural ***trousseaux*** or ***trousseaus***

trouvaille
FRENCH
a lucky find

trucage or ***truquage***
FRENCH
the faking of works of art

truqueur
FRENCH
a faker of works of art

tsar or ***czar***
RUSSIAN, from LATIN *Caesar*
1 the title of the emperors of Russia and the kings of Bulgaria
2 a great potentate or despot

tsarevich, tsarevitch, czarevich or ***czarevitch***
RUSSIAN
a son of a tsar

tsarevna or ***czarevna***
RUSSIAN
1 a daughter of a tsar
2 the wife of a tsarevich

tsarina, czarina, tsaritza or ***czaritsa***
RUSSIAN
a Russian empress

tsunami
JAPANESE, literally 'harbour wave'
a wave that travels very swiftly and reaches a great height, caused by an earthquake or similar disturbance under the sea

> sometimes loosely referred to as a tidal wave, but not associated with the tide

tuan
MALAY
sir, lord, master; a title of respect in the Malay Archipelago and Indonesia

tumulus
LATIN
a burial mound
plural ***tumuli***

tundra
LAPP
an Arctic plain with permanently frozen subsoil and stunted vegetation

tu quoque
LATIN
you too, you're another

> returning an accusation, insult, etc

tutti
ITALIAN for 'all, everyone'
(music)
1 to be performed by the whole orchestra or choir
2 a passage for the whole orchestra or choir

tutti-frutti
ITALIAN, literally 'all fruits'
1 ice-cream containing small pieces of mixed fruits, often candied
2 a sweet or preserve containing or flavoured with mixed fruits

tutu
FRENCH
a ballerina's very short skirt, spreading outwards in layers of stiffened material

tuyère
FRENCH
a nozzle for a blast of air, eg in a furnace or jet engine

tympani
see TIMPANI

tzatziki
MODERN GREEK
a Greek dish made of yoghurt and finely sliced or chopped cucumber, flavoured with garlic, mint, etc, eaten as a dip

U

Übermensch
GERMAN
a superman

uberrima fides
LATIN
complete faith

ubi bene, ibi patria
LATIN
where it goes well with me, there is my homeland

ubique
LATIN
everywhere

ubi sunt (qui ante nos fuerunt)?
LATIN
where are those (who lived before us)?

> referring to the transitory nature of human existence

ubi supra
LATIN
where mentioned above

uhuru
SWAHILI
1 freedom, eg from slavery
2 national independence

uitlander
AFRIKAANS
(in S Africa) a foreigner, originally a British person in the Transvaal or Orange Free State

ukase
from RUSSIAN *ukaz*
1 (in pre-Revolutionary Russia) an edict with force of law
2 any arbitrary decree from any source

ukulele or ***ukelele***
HAWAIIAN, literally 'jumping flea'
a small guitar, usually with four strings

> popularized in Hawaii, but originally Portuguese

ultima ratio
LATIN
the last argument, ie the use of force

ultima ratio regum
LATIN
the last argument of kings, ie war

ultima Thule
LATIN, literally 'farthest Thule'
1 the extreme limit
2 the northernmost land

> Thule, an island discovered by the Greek navigator Pytheas in the 4th century BC, has been variously identified as Shetland, Iceland, Norway, or Jutland

ultimatum
LATIN
1 final terms
2 a final offer or demand
3 a last word
plural ***ultimata***

ultimus haeres
LATIN, literally 'last heir'
(law) the crown or the state, which inherits the property of those who die intestate or without next of kin

ultra
LATIN for 'beyond'
1 extreme, eg in fashion, religion, politics, etc
2 an extremist

ultra vires
LATIN
beyond one's powers or authority

umiak or ***oomiak***
ESKIMO
an open boat, made of wood and stretched skins, usually crewed by women

Umlaut or ***umlaut***
GERMAN, from *um* meaning 'around' and *Laut* meaning 'sound'
1 a vowel change in Germanic languages
2 the diacritical sign (two dots placed over the vowel) indicating such a change

una corda
ITALIAN, literally 'one string'
(music) a direction to pianists to use the soft pedal
compare TRE CORDE

una voce
LATIN
with one voice, by general consent

unberufen
GERMAN
not called for

> said to avert the ill luck that may follow an overconfident or boastful statement

und so weiter
GERMAN
and so forth, et cetera
abbrev **usw, u.s.w.**

> the abbreviation is the usual form

uno animo
LATIN
with one mind, with one accord

uno ictu
LATIN
at one blow

uno saltu
LATIN
in one leap

Unterseeboot
GERMAN, literally 'undersea boat'
a submarine

> hence the English term *U-boat*

urbi et orbi
LATIN
(said of a papal blessing) to the city and to the world

usus est tyrannus
LATIN
custom is a tyrant

usus loquendi
LATIN
current spoken usage

usw or ***u.s.w.***
see UND SO WEITER

ut dictum
LATIN
as said
abbrev **ut dict.**

ut infra
LATIN
as below

uti possidetis
LATIN, literally 'as you possess'
(in international law) the principle under which warring nations, etc, keep the territory or property they hold at the close of hostilities unless otherwise agreed

ut supra
LATIN
as above
abbrev **us, u.s., ut sup.**

V

v
see VERSUS, VIDE

vade in pace
LATIN
go in peace

vade mecum or ***vade-mecum***
LATIN, literally 'go with me'
a useful handbook carried for frequent reference, a pocket-companion

vade retro me, Satana
LATIN
get thee behind me, Satan; stop trying to tempt me

vae victis
LATIN
woe to the conquered

vakil or ***vakeel***
HINDI
an Indian agent or representative

vale
LATIN
farewell! (addressed to one person)
plural ***valete*** (addressed to more than one person)

valet
FRENCH
a male servant who atends to a gentleman's clothes, dressing, grooming, etc

valet de chambre
FRENCH
1 an attendant
2 a footman

valet de place
FRENCH
a person who serves as a guide, messenger, etc, especially for strangers

valise
FRENCH for 'suitcase'
an overnight travelling bag

vaporetto
ITALIAN
a motorboat that serves as a waterbus in Venice
plural ***vaporettos*** or ***vaporetti***

varia lectio
LATIN
a variant reading
abbrev **var. lect., vl, v.l.**
plural ***variae lectiones,*** *abbrev* **vvll, vv.ll.**

variorum
see CUM NOTIS VARIORUM

varium et mutabile semper femina
LATIN
woman is ever a fickle and changeable thing

varna
SANSKRIT for 'class'
any of the four great Hindu castes

vaurien
FRENCH
a good-for-nothing

vedette
FRENCH
1 a mounted sentry stationed to watch an enemy

2 a small boat used for a similar purpose

3 a star of stage or screen

veilleuse
FRENCH
a shaded night-lamp

veld or ***veldt***
DUTCH
(in S Africa) open unforested or thinly-forested grassland

veloce
ITALIAN
(music) with great rapidity

velours or ***velour***
FRENCH
a fabric with velvet-like pile

velouté
FRENCH for 'velvety'
a smooth white sauce made with stock

vendetta
ITALIAN
1 a blood-feud

2 any similarly long-standing, bitter, or violent feud or quarrel

venire (facias)
LATIN, literally '(make) to come'
1 a writ requiring a sheriff to summon a certain number of people to court at a specified time so that jurors may be chosen from them

2 the people so summoned

veni, vidi, vici
LATIN
I came, I saw, I conquered

> attributed to Caesar on his victory over Pharnaces, king of Pontus, in 47BC

ventre à terre
FRENCH, literally 'belly to the ground'
at high speed

verbatim
LATIN
word for word, using exactly the same words

verbatim et literatim
LATIN
word for word and letter for letter

verboten
GERMAN
forbidden

verbum sapienti sat est or ***dictum sapienti sat est***
LATIN
a word is enough to the wise

> the phrase (usually in one of its abbreviated forms) often follows a strong hint

abbrev **verb. sap., verb. sat., verbum sap., verbum sat.**

Verein
GERMAN
union, association

Verlag
GERMAN
a publishing house

vermicelli
ITALIAN, literally 'little worms'
1 very slender strands of pasta

2 small thin pieces of chocolate used for decorating cakes, sweets, etc

vernissage
FRENCH for 'varnishing'
a day before the opening of an exhibition when exhibitors may varnish or retouch their pictures

vers de société
FRENCH, literally 'society verse'
light witty verse

vers d'occasion
FRENCH
occasional verse, produced for a particular event

vers libre
FRENCH
free verse

verso
from LATIN *versō (foliō)* meaning 'on the turned (leaf)'
1 the left-hand page of an open book
2 the back of a leaf of printed or manuscript material
3 the reverse of a coin or medal
compare RECTO
plural ***versos***

versus
LATIN
(in law, sport, etc) against
abbrev **v, vs**

vertigo
LATIN
dizziness, giddiness; a whirling sensation experienced when the sense of balance is disturbed
plural ***vertigos, vertigoes*** or ***vertigines***

veto
LATIN, literally 'I forbid'
1 any authoritative prohibition
2 the power of rejecting or forbidding, or the right to reject or forbid
3 to reject or forbid by a veto
plural ***vetoes***

vexata quaestio
LATIN
a vexed question, a greatly debated matter

via
LATIN
1 a way, a road
2 by way of

via crucis
LATIN
the way of the Cross, the stations of the Cross

via dolorosa
LATIN, literally 'mournful way'
1 the road to Calvary
2 an upsetting or daunting course of action

Via Lactea
LATIN
the Milky Way

via media
LATIN
a middle course

viaticum
LATIN
1 money, provisions, etc, for a journey
2 (in the Roman Catholic Church) the Eucharist given to people in danger of dying
plural ***viaticums*** or ***viatica***

via trita, via tuta
LATIN
a beaten path is a safe path

vibrato
ITALIAN
(music) a throbbing effect, with barely perceptible change of pitch, in singing or the playing of stringed and wind instruments, achieved by vibrating the throat muscles, varying breath pressure, rocking or shaking the finger stopping a string, etc
plural ***vibratos***

vice anglais
from FRENCH *le vice anglais* meaning 'the English vice'
1 flagellation
2 homosexuality

vice versa
LATIN, literally 'the position having been turned'
the other way round

victor ludorum
LATIN, literally 'winner of the games'
the most outstanding athlete, etc

vide
LATIN
see, refer to
abbrev **v**

vide infra
LATIN
see below

videlicet
LATIN
to wit, namely
abbrev **viz**

> the abbreviation is the usual form

vide supra
LATIN
see above

vidimus
LATIN, literally 'we have seen'
1 an attested copy
2 an inspection, eg of accounts

vi et armis
LATIN, literally 'by force and arms'
forcibly

vieux jeu
FRENCH, literally 'old game'
old-fashioned, old-hat

vigilante
SPANISH for 'guard'
a self-appointed and unofficial enforcer of law and order

vignette
FRENCH, literally 'little vine'
1 a short literary essay, especially a character sketch
2 a small decorative design, originally of vine leaves, on the title page of a book
3 a photographic portrait shading off at the edges

vihara
SANSKRIT
a Buddhist or Jain precinct, temple, or monastery

vilayet
TURKISH
a Turkish province

vimana
SANSKRIT, literally 'a marking out'
1 the central shrine of an Indian temple with a pyramidal roof
2 a temple gate
3 a heavenly chariot, a chariot of the gods

vin
FRENCH
wine

vinaigrette
FRENCH
a mixture of oil, vinegar, seasoning, and herbs, used as a salad dressing

vin blanc
FRENCH
white wine

vin de table
FRENCH
undistinguished table wine

vin du pays or ***vin de pays***
FRENCH
country or local wine

vingt-et-un or ***vingt-un***
FRENCH for 'twenty-one'
a card game with the aim of acquiring cards to the value of 21, pontoon

vinho verde
PORTUGUESE, literally 'green wine'
a light, sharp, immature Portuguese wine

vin ordinaire
FRENCH
ordinary or inexpensive table wine

vin rouge
FRENCH
red wine

viola da braccio
ITALIAN, literally 'viol for the arm'
a tenor viol, held along the arm

viola da gamba
ITALIAN, literally 'viol for the leg'
a bass viol, resembling the cello

viola d'amore
ITALIAN, literally 'viol of love'
a viol with sympathetic strings under the fingerboard

virago
LATIN
1 a violent or bad-tempered woman
2 a heroic or manlike woman
3 a strong or aggressive woman
plural ***viragoes*** or ***viragos***

virgo intacta
LATIN, literally 'untouched virgin'
a woman who has not had sexual intercourse and whose hymen is unbroken

virtu
from ITALIAN *virtù*
1 a love of the fine arts
2 a taste for curiosities
3 objects of art or antiquity collectively

virtuoso
ITALIAN
1 a person with remarkable artistic or technical skill, especially a brilliant musician
2 a person with considerable knowledge of or interest in art, antiquities, curiosities, etc

> the feminine form *virtuosa* is not used in modern English, the masculine form being applied to either sex

plural ***virtuosos*** or ***virtuosi***

virtute officii
LATIN
by virtue of office

vis
LATIN
force, power
plural ***vires***

visagiste
FRENCH
an expert in facial make-up

vis a tergo
LATIN
force from behind

> referring to a force that compels or propels

vis-à-vis
FRENCH
1 face-to-face (with)
2 in relation to, with regard to

3 a person who faces, or is opposite to, another

vis inertiae
LATIN
the power of inertia; passive resistance

vis major
LATIN
superior force

vis mortua
LATIN
dead force

> a term used in mechanics

vista
ITALIAN
1 a view into the distance, especially as seen through a long narrow opening, such as an avenue of trees
2 a mental view extending far into the past or future

vis viva
LATIN
living force, equal to the mass of a moving body multiplied by the square of its velocity

vitrage
FRENCH for 'windows, glazing, glass'
a kind of thin curtain for windows or glazed doors

viva
ITALIAN and SPANISH
long live ...!

> followed by the name of a person, institution, etc

see also VIVA VOCE

vivace
ITALIAN
(music)
1 lively
2 in a lively manner

vivarium
LATIN
an artificial enclosure for keeping or raising living animals, usually for study or research
plural ***vivaria*** or ***vivariums***

vivat
LATIN
1 long live ...!
2 an expression of enthusiastic approval; hurrah!

> in sense 1 *vivat* is followed by the name of a person, institution, etc

viva voce
LATIN, literally 'by living voice'
1 orally
2 an oral examination, usually for an academic qualification

> sense 2 is usually shortened to *viva*, which may also be used as a verb meaning 'to examine orally'

vive
FRENCH
long live ...!

> followed by the name of a person, institution, etc

see also QUI VIVE?

vive la différence
FRENCH
long live the difference!

> usually referring to the difference between the sexes, but also applied to national, political, racial, or religious diversity

vivo
ITALIAN
(music) lively

viz
see VIDELICET

vl or ***v.l.***
see VARIA LECTIO

vodka
RUSSIAN, diminutive of *voda* meaning 'water'
a clear alcoholic spirit of Russian origin, traditionally distilled from rye but sometimes made from potatoes, etc

vogue
FRENCH
the mode or fashion at any particular time

from FRENCH *voguer* meaning 'to row': the noun originally referred to the trim of a rowing boat

vogue la galère
FRENCH, literally 'row the boat'
carry on, come what may!

voilà
FRENCH
1 look!, see!
2 there!, there you are!

voilà tout
FRENCH
that's all

voix céleste
FRENCH, literally 'heavenly voice'
an organ stop producing a soft, tremulous sound

vol-au-vent
FRENCH, literally 'flight in the wind'
a small round puff-pastry case with a savoury filling

volens
LATIN, literally 'being willing'
(law) consenting to a course of action that involves a risk of some sort, therefore unable to sue if injury occurs

also used as a noun

volente Deo
LATIN
God willing

volenti non fit injuria
LATIN
no injury is done to a consenting party

volk
DUTCH for 'people, nation'
(in S Africa) the Afrikaner people

Völkerwanderung
GERMAN
the migration of Germanic and other peoples, chiefly in the 4th to 6th centuries

Volkslied
GERMAN
a German folk-song
plural ***Volkslieder***

volksraad or ***Volksraad***
from DUTCH *volk* meaning 'people' and *raad* meaning 'council'
a legislative assembly, especially that of the Transvaal or the Orange Free State before 1900

volte-face
FRENCH, literally 'a turning round'
a sudden and complete reversal of opinion, policy, etc; a U-turn

voulu
FRENCH for 'wanted'
deliberate, studied

vox
LATIN
voice
plural **voces**

vox angelica
LATIN, literally 'angelic voice'
an organ stop producing a soft, tremulous sound

vox audita perit, littera scripta manet
LATIN
the spoken word is lost, the written letter remains
see also LITTERA SCRIPTA MANET

> the literal translation is 'the heard word ...'

vox humana
LATIN
an organ stop producing tones resembling those of the human voice

vox populi
LATIN, literally 'the voice of the people'
public or popular opinion
abbrev **vox pop**

> the abbreviation is especially applied to brief street interviews with members of the public on radio or TV

vox populi vox Dei
LATIN
the voice of the people is the voice of God

voyeur
FRENCH, literally 'one who sees'
a person who derives gratification from surreptitiously watching the sexual activities, etc, of others; a peeping Tom

vozhd
RUSSIAN for 'chief'
a supreme leader in Russia

> often applied to Stalin

vraisemblance
FRENCH, literally 'true appearance'
verisimilitude, an appearance of truth or reality

vs
see VERSUS

vulgo
LATIN
commonly, popularly

vvll or ***vv.ll.***
see VARIA LECTIO

W

wadi or ***wady***
ARABIC
1 the dry bed of a river or stream
2 a river valley

wagon-lit
FRENCH
a sleeping-car on a continental train

wallah or ***walla***
from the HINDI suffix *-wālā*
1 someone employed in, or concerned with, the type of work indicated by the preceding noun
2 someone who occupies an important position in an organization, etc

> in sense 1 the term corresponds to the English suffix *-man*

Wanderjahr
GERMAN, literally 'wander year'
a year of travel or wandering in order to gain experience, especially by a workman who has just completed his apprenticeship
plural **Wanderjahre**

wanderlust
from GERMAN *Wanderlust*, literally 'wander longing'
an urge to travel or move from place to place

Wehrmacht
GERMAN
the armed services of the German Third Reich from 1935–1945

Weinstube
GERMAN
a wine bar

Weltanschauung
GERMAN
outlook on the world, philosophy of life

Weltgeist
GERMAN
the spirit of the world, the spiritual quality of things

Weltpolitik
GERMAN
1 world politics
2 the policy of taking a forceful part in international affairs

Weltschmerz
GERMAN, literally 'world pain'
1 sympathy with universal misery; sorrow for the human lot
2 world-weariness; thoroughgoing pessimism

Weltstadt
GERMAN
a cosmopolitan city

Wiener Schnitzel
GERMAN, literally 'veal cutlet of Vienna'
a veal cutlet coated with beaten egg and breadcrumbs

Wigorniensis
LATIN
of Worcester
abbrev **Wigorn.**

Wintoniensis
LATIN
of Winchester
abbrev **Winton.**

Wirtschaftswunder
GERMAN
an economic miracle, specifically that of Germany's speedy recovery after World War II

wok
CHINESE
a hemispherical pan used in Chinese cookery

won ton
from CANTONESE CHINESE *wan tan* meaning 'pastry'
(in Chinese cookery) a spicy dumpling containing minced pork, usually served in soup

wunderbar
GERMAN
wonderful

wunderkind
from GERMAN *Wunderkind* meaning 'wonder-child'
1 a child prodigy
2 someone who achieves remarkable success early in life
plural ***wunderkinder***

Wurst or ***wurst***
GERMAN, literally 'something rolled'
a large German sausage

wu shu or ***wushu***
CHINESE
the Chinese martial arts

Y

yakimono
◀ JAPANESE, literally 'grill thing' (in Japanese cookery) grilled food, a grilled dish

yakitori
◀ JAPANESE, literally 'grill bird'
a Japanese dish of boneless pieces of chicken grilled on skewers and basted with a thick, sweet sauce

yakuza
◀ JAPANESE, literally 'eight-nine-three' (the worst hand of cards in gambling)
a Japanese gangster, typically involved in drug-dealing, gambling, extortion, gun-running, or prostitution
plural ***yakuza***

yamen
◀ CHINESE
the offices and residence of a mandarin

yang or ***Yang***
◀ CHINESE for 'bright'
one of the two opposing and complementary principles of Chinese philosophy, religion, medicine, etc, influencing destiny and governing nature, seen as the positive, masculine, light, warm, active element
compare YIN

yardang
◀ TURKISH
a ridge formed by wind erosion from sand, silt, etc, usually lying parallel to the prevailing wind direction

yarmulka or ***yarmulke***
◀ YIDDISH
the skullcap worn by Jewish males, especially during prayers or ceremonial occasions

yashmak
◀ from ARABIC *yashmaq*
the double veil worn by Muslim women in public, which leaves only the eyes uncovered

yataghan or ***yatagan***
◀ TURKISH
a long Turkish dagger, usually curved

yeti
◀ from TIBETAN *yeh-teh*
the abominable snowman

yin or ***Yin***
◀ CHINESE for 'dark'
one of the two opposing and complementary principles of Chinese philosophy, religion, medicine, etc, influencing destiny and governing nature, seen as the negative, feminine, dark, cold, passive element
compare YANG

yoga
◀ SANSKRIT for 'union'
1 a system of Hindu philosophy showing how to free the soul from further reincarnations and unite it with the supreme being
2 any of several physical and mental disciplines based on this, or the system of exercises they prescribe
see also HATHA YOGA, MAHA YOGA

yoghurt, yoghourt or ***yogurt***
TURKISH
a semi-liquid food made from fermented milk, often flavoured with fruit

yogi or ***yogin***
from SANSKRIT *yogin*
a person who practises yoga
feminine ***yogini***

Yom Kippur
HEBREW
the Day of Atonement, a Jewish fast day

yoni
SANSKRIT
a representation of the female genitals, the symbol of the Hindu goddess Sakti

yuga or ***yug***
SANSKRIT
any of the four Hindu ages of the world

yukata
JAPANESE
a light kimono, usually of printed cotton, worn as a bathrobe or housecoat

yuko
JAPANESE
an award of five points in judo

yurt
from RUSSIAN *yurta*
a light tent of skins, etc, used by nomads in Siberia

Z

zabaglione
ITALIAN
a frothy dessert made from egg yolks, Marsala, and sugar

zakuska
RUSSIAN
an hors d'oeuvre; a snack
plural ***zakuski***

zapateado
SPANISH, from *zapatear* meaning 'to tap-dance'
a lively Spanish dance for a solo performer, characterized by stamping and clicking of the heels
plural ***zapateados***

zB or ***z.B.***
see ZUM BEISPIEL

Zeitgeist or ***zeitgeist***
GERMAN
the spirit of the age

Zeitvertreib
GERMAN
a pastime

zemstvo
RUSSIAN
(in pre-Revolutionary Russia) a district and provincial assembly
plural ***zemstvos*** or ***zemstva***

Zen
JAPANESE
a branch of Buddhism that stresses the personal experience of enlightenment based on a simple life and uncomplicated methods of meditation

➪ also used as an adjective

zenana
from PERSIAN *zanāna*
in India, Iran, etc, a part of a house in which women and girls are secluded, corresponding to the harem in Arabic-speaking Muslim countries

zingaro or ***zingano***
ITALIAN
a gypsy
plural ***zingari*** or ***zingani***
feminine ***zingara*** or ***zingana,***
plural ***zingare*** or ***zingane***

Zollverein
GERMAN
a customs union, a group of states having free trade among themselves and a common tariff policy towards non-member states

zoon politikon
GREEK
(said of a human being) a political animal

Zugzwang or ***zugzwang***
GERMAN
(chess) a blockade position in which any move is disadvantageous to the blockaded player

zum Beispiel
GERMAN
for example
abbrev **zB, z.B.**

➪ the abbreviation is the usual form

Zwieback
GERMAN
a type of rusk

Appendix

Some foreign place-names with their English equivalents

EUROPEAN

Antwerpen	Antwerp
Athínai	Athens
Basel	Basle
Beograd	Belgrade
Braunschweig	Brunswick
Brugge	Bruges
Bruxelles	Brussels
Bucureşti	Bucharest
Den Haag	The Hague
Firenze	Florence
Fribourg	Freiburg
Genève	Geneva
Genova	Genoa
Gent	Ghent
Göteborg	Gothenburg
Hoek van Holland	Hook of Holland
Kiyev	Kiev
København	Copenhagen
Köln	Cologne
Kórinthos	Corinth
Kraków	Cracow
Lisboa	Lisbon
Livorno	Leghorn
Luzern	Lucerne
Lyon	Lyons
Mantova	Mantua
Marseille	Marseilles
Milano	Milan
Moskva	Moscow
München	Munich
Napoli	Naples
Nürnberg	Nuremberg
Oostende	Ostend
Padova	Padua
Plzeň	Pilsen
Porto	Oporto
Praha	Prague
Roma	Rome
Sevilla	Seville
Sofiya	Sofia
Szczecin	Stettin
Thessaloníki	Salonica
Torino	Turin
Venezia	Venice
Vlissingen	Flushing
Warszawa	Warsaw
Wien	Vienna
Wrocław	Breslau
Zaragoza	Saragossa

OTHERS

Abū Zaby	Abu Dhabi
Adis Abeba	Addis Ababa
Al'Adan	Aden
Alger	Algiers
Al Kuwayt	Kuwait
Al Lādhiqiyah	Latakia
Al Madinah	Medina
Al Mawşil	Mosul
Ar Riyāḍ	Riyadh
Banghāzi	Benghazi
Beyrouth	Beirut
Bizerte	Binzert
Bûr Saîd	Port Said
Dhaka	Dacca
Dimashq	Damascus
Dubayy	Dubai
El Iskandarîya	Alexandria
El Khartûm	Khartoum
El Qâ'hira	Cairo
El Uqsur	Luxor
Guangzhou	Canton
Habana	Havana
Ḥalab	Aleppo
Ḫefa	Haifa
Himş	Homs
Krung Thep	Bangkok
Makkah	Mecca
Muqdisho	Mogadishu
Masqaţ	Muscat
Naẕerat	Nazareth
Sayda	Sidon
Shenyang	Mukden
Sŏul	Seoul
Tanger	Tangier
Tarābulus	Tripoli
Tiranë	Tirana
Yerushalayim (Al Quds)	Jerusalem

LANGUAGE INDEX

DANISH

aquavit
smørrebrød

DUTCH

kraal
maelstrom
polder
rijsttafel
schuit
veld
volk
volksraad

EGYPTIAN

ankh

ESKIMO

igloo
kayak
muckluck
umiak

FINNISH

sauna

FRENCH

à bas
abat-jour
abattoir
abattu
abat-voix
abbé
à bientôt
à bon droit
abonnement
à bras ouverts
abrégé
accablé
accouchement
accoucheur
acharné
à cheval
à compte
à contrecoeur
à corps perdu
à coup sûr
à couvert
acte gratuit
actualités
à demi
à dessein
à deux
à deux mains
adieu
à droite
affaire d'amour
affaire de coeur
affaire d'honneur
affiche
à fond
agaçant
agacerie
à gauche
agent provocateur
à gogo
à grands frais
agrégation
agrégé
agréments
à haute voix
à huis clos
aide
aide-de-camp
aide-mémoire
aigre-doux
aigrette
aiguille
aileron
aîné
à jamais
à la
à l'abandon
à la belle étoile
à la bonne heure
à l'abri
à la campagne
à la carte
à la dérobée
à la guerre comme à la guerre
à la hauteur de
à la lanterne
à la main
à la maître d'hôtel
à la mode
à la page
à l'envi
à l'époque
à l'improviste
allée
allemande
allez-vous-en
allonge
allons
allumeuse
alternat
à main armée
ambiance
âme damnée
âme de boue
amende
amende honorable
âme perdue
à merveille
ami
ami de cour
ami du peuple
amie
à moitié
à mon avis
amour
amour courtois
amour de voyage
amourette
amour-propre
amuse-gueule
ancienne noblesse
ancien régime
andouillette
anomie
à outrance
à pas de géant

spiritoso
staccato
stanza
stiletto
stretto
stringendo
stucco
subito
tagliatelle
tanto
tazza
tempera
tempo
tenuto
terracotta
terza rima
tessitura
tifosi
timpani
tiramisu
toccata
tondo
torso
traduttori traditori
trattoria
trecento
tre corde
tremolo
troppo
tutti
tutti-frutti
una corda
vaporetto
veloce
vendetta
vermicelli
vibrato
viola da braccio
viola da gamba
viola d'amore
virtu
virtuoso
vista
viva
vivace
vivo
zabaglione
zingaro

JAPANESE

aikido
arame
banzai
basho
bonsai
budo
bunraku
bushido
chanoyu
chiyogami
daimio
dan
dojo
futon
gagaku
geisha
geta
go
haiku
hara-kiri
hibachi
ikebana
inro
ippon
issei
judo
judogi
judoka
ju-jitsu
kabuki
kago
kakemono
kami
kamikaze
kana
kanji
karaoke
karate
karateka
kata
katana
kendo
kikumon
kimono
kirimon
koan
koto
kyogen
kyu
maiko
makimono
manga
matsuri
maurikigusari
meishi
mikado
minshuku
miso
mon
netsuke
nihonga
ninja
ninjitsu
niramiai
nisei
no
nunchaku
obi
okimono
origami
ozeki
raku
ramen
ricksha
rikishi
roji
ryokan
saikei
sake
samisen
samurai
san
sansei
sashimi
satori

SPANISH

URDU

VIETNAMESE

WELSH

YIDDISH